Fulbe Voices

Marriage, Islam, and
Medicine in Northern Cameroon

HELEN A. REGIS
Louisiana State University

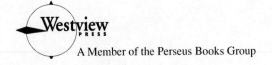
A Member of the Perseus Books Group

Westview Press books are available at special discounts for bulk purchases in the United States by corporations, institutions, and other organizations. For more information, please contact the Special Markets Department at the Perseus Books Group, 11 Cambridge Center, Cambridge MA 02142, or call (617) 252-5298.

Published in 2003 in the United States of America by Westview Press, 5500 Central Avenue, Boulder, Colorado 80301-2877, and in the United Kingdom by Westview Press, 12 Hid's Copse Road, Cumnor Hill, Oxford OX2 9JJ

Find us on the World Wide Web at www.westviewpress.com

A Cataloging-in-Publication data record for this book is available from the Library of Congress.
ISBN 0-8133-4035-7(HC) ISBN 0-8133-3816-6(Pbk.)

The paper used in this publication meets the requirements of the American National Standard for Permanence of Paper for Printed Library Materials Z39.48-1984.

10   9   8   7   6   5   4   3

Fulbe Voices

WESTVIEW CASE STUDIES IN ANTHROPOLOGY SERIES
Series Editor: Edward F. Fischer,
Vanderbilt University

Fulbe Voices: Marriage, Islam, and Medicine in Northern Cameroon,
Helen A. Regis (Louisiana State University)

Daughters of Tunis: Women, Family, and Networks in a Muslim City,
Paula Holmes-Eber (University of Washington)

Tecpán Guatemala: A Modern Maya Town in Global and Local Context,
Edward F. Fischer (Vanderbilt University) and
Carol Hendrickson (Marlboro College)

Forthcoming:

The Lao: Gender, Power, and Livelihood,
Carol Ireson-Doolittle (Willamette University) and
Geraldine Moreno-Black (University of Oregon)

For James Charbonnet
1940–2002

Contents

Series Editor
Preface

In many ways, what makes anthropology unique among the social sciences is a focus on ethnographic fieldwork. We go *there* (be it the remote reaches of Africa or just down the block) to study *them* (who are variably conceived as either more or less like us). It is from the personal, dialectic encounters of fieldwork that we build up our perspectives and produce anthropological understanding. Dealing with real people and the intimacies of their lives makes this a difficult project, but it provides the best way to comprehend the world around us in terms of both the sensual practice of quotidian reality and the abstractions of high theory.

A great deal of what anthropologists learn in the field comes from conversations, sometimes extraordinary but most often mundane. We place high value on what the people we study ("collaborators" more than mere "informants") have to say. Through such dialogues we float ideas, testing the waters of cultural understanding and moving toward an inter-subjective sense of mutual comprehension.

Helen Regis focuses on *Fulbe Voices* in this engaging account of life in a small town in Northern Cameroon. We benefit from Regis's sensitive ear as she relates how Fulbe individuals talk about their lives; we hear in their own words about their regrets and hopes, fears and desires, and struggles with the world in which they live. In writing this book, Regis builds upon recent discourse-centered approaches to culture in the most productive way. She does not hit us over the head with rigid theoretical models, rather she interrogates theory with field data, using it to elucidate the patterns and contradictions of Fulbe life that emerge from lived experience and daily conversations. The result is an artful ethnography, equally illuminating both in terms of its specific descriptions and its critical application of theory.

The significance of this work rests with its ability to convey the vast complexity and fluidity of the rhythms of daily life in Domaayo. Regis has a sharp ethnographic eye, and her narrative transports us to the local Koranic school, allows us to witness the preparations for a boy's circumcision, and makes us privy to women's hushed conversations in the kitchen. We discover that the Fulbe are not the homogeneous, insulated sort of culture group anthropologists of an earlier era sought out. Local patterns of life are ever changing constructions marked by contradiction as much as conformity.

The Fulbe of Domaayo are overwhelmingly farmers and yet their self-perception is built around an image of themselves as noble pastoralists (as opposed to the "pagan" farmers of the countryside). This is a decidedly Muslim society, and yet one that practices its own hybrid form of the Islamic faith. It would be easy to write off these seemingly logical inconsistencies as merely the irrationality of culture, but Regis shows that the Fulbe with whom she converses are not plagued by cognitive dissonance. They are too busy living their lives, hemmed in by structural constraints and yet fully possessing the agency and intentionality to adapt to new circumstances and engage larger systems in a manner consistent with (although not determined by) their own cultural logics.

The Fulbe have a code of behavior known as *pulaaku* that governs the expression of emotions. *Pulaaku* reflects a highly stoic sensibility that to outsiders may seem like a rigid and constraining code of behavior. But this is not some rigid, hidden hegemonic structure. Regis shows that people frequently discuss *pulaaku*, debating its virtues and finer points. More important, it is a code that is worked out through practice, open to variable interpretations, contestation, and change. Even the most institutionalized rituals, such as male circumcision, are not without local controversy. Thus, Regis shows that the Fulbe are not merely enacting age-old cultural paradigms, but they are actively constructing an ever emergent future.

In a similar fashion, Regis contextualizes Fulbe structures of kinship and medical practices. In anthropological classifications, the Fulbe are a polygynous culture, meaning that a man may have more than one wife. Regis takes us beyond this structural fact to show how polygyny plays out on the ground. She shows, for example, the subtle political means through which wives vie for status. She also demonstrates how the Fulbe deal with pain and sickness in idiosyncratic and yet conventionalized ways that link them (through the local health center) to the larger milieu of World Bank politics and neoliberal economic reforms.

Fulbe Voices makes an important contribution to the Westview Case Studies in Anthropology series and to the discipline as a whole. This series presents works that recognize the peoples we study as active agents enmeshed in global as well as local systems of politics, economics, and cultural flows. There is a focus on contemporary ways of life, forces of social change, and creative responses to novel situations as well as the more traditional concerns of classic ethnography. In presenting rich humanistic and social scientific data borne of the dialectic engagement of fieldwork, the books in this series move toward realizing the full pedagogical potential of anthropology: imparting to the reader an empathetic understanding of alternative ways of viewing and acting in the world as well as a solid basis for critical thought regarding the historically contingent nature of ethnic boundaries and cultural knowledge.

Fulbe Voices addresses current theoretical issues in anthropology in a lively and accessible style. It advances our understanding of cultural diversity while uncovering the often hidden webs of global relations that affect us all. And, most important, it coveys the rich texture of Fulbe life in Domaayo at the turn of the twenty-first century.

Edward F. Fischer
Nashville, Tennessee

Acknowledgments

Numerous persons and institutions contributed to making this book possible. I would like to thank Adeline Masquelier, who challenged me to flesh out my narratives and read multiple drafts of early versions of the book. One could not ask for a better critic, ally, and teacher. William Jankowiak inspired me to do ethnography. Barry Hewlett brought me to Africa. Ted Fischer suggested this project to me in 1999, and his close readings greatly improved it. At Tulane University, Carol Trosset, Victoria Bricker, and Judie Maxwell supported my research endeavors materially and intellectually. My cousins Pam Bunte and Rob Franklin warmly welcomed me into the field of anthropology and encouraged my work early on. At Mississippi State, Homes Hogue, Martin Levin, and John Bartkowski believed in me and extended offers of friendship that made the *ville austere* a place of intellectual adventure and spiritual warfare. Jean Rahier, Felipe Smith, Peter Sutherland, Nina Asher, John White, and Shana Walton have been intellectual companions and friends.

In New Orleans and Derby, James Charbonnet, Rick Fifield, Peter Trosclair, Ken Devine, Amasa Miller, Bart Ramsey, Greg Stafford, Neti Vaandrager, Angie Mason, and L. J. Goldstein all supported this project through many years in more ways than I could recount. Much Love.

Cameroon is blessed with a network of scholars, crossing disciplines of history, political science, economics, sociology, and anthropology. I have greatly benefited from many conversations with members of this intellectual fellowship and the numerous provocative and congenial sessions organized at the African Studies meetings and elsewhere. In Cameroon, the Ministry of Public Health, the Ministry of Scientific Research, the University of Yaounde Medical School, and the Institute of Research on Medicinal Plants and the Cameroonian staff at the United States Agency for International Development in Yaounde supported the project in numerous ways. Phoebe Godfrey, M. H. Newberger, and Catherine Till generously offered their friendship and hospitality. Tulane University School of Public Health and Tropical Medicine, the Department of Anthropology and the Graduate School at Tulane , the Mississippi State University Office of Research, and Louisiana State University Department of Geography and Anthropology have all provided support for various stages of this project. I particularly want to thank my colleagues at LSU's Geography and Anthropology Department for providing a congenial atmosphere in which this project could finally come to fruition. Bill Davidson, Joyce Jackson, Miles Richardson, Jill Brody, and Dydia DeLyser especially made me feel welcome and shared with me their intelligence, their wit, and their great humanity.

To the people in Domaayo who took me into their homes and shared with me their struggles and aspirations, I shall always be grateful. Everything that is right about this book is owed to you. All errors and omissions are of course my own. Yaafu!

Domaayo means "on or near the river." There are many small towns in northern Cameroon called Domaayo. This is not one of them.

Finally, I owe the greatest debt of all to my parents, Helen Bunte Regis and Claude François Regis, who gave me the patience, curiosity, and strength to be in the world.

H.A.R.

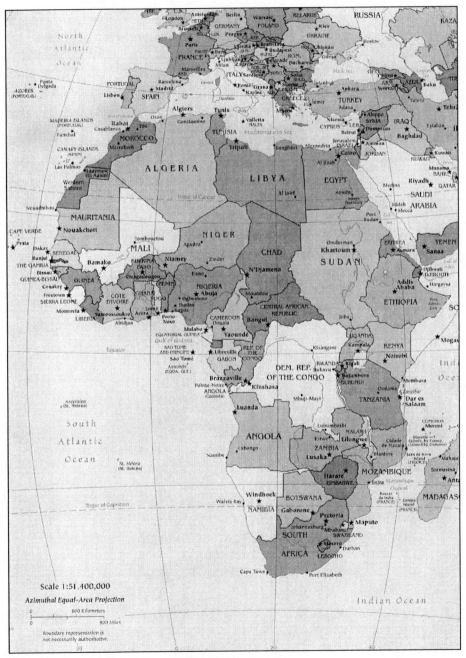

Africa. Cameroon lies just north of the equator on Africa's west coast.

Introduction

THE PEUGEOT AND THE MOTORCYCLE

I arrived in Domaayo in a white Peugeot and left on a red motorcycle. Actually the red motorcycle arrived with me in the back of the Peugeot station wagon. I had come to the field with my professor, Barry Hewlett, to begin work for a public health project on schistosomiasis (bilharzia), a tropical disease caused by a parasite and acquired through contact with infected water. As in many ethnographic research projects, my first task was to obtain permission from the Cameroonian government to carry out my research. Because my work was part of a public health project, I had no difficulty getting a research permit and extended visa in the capital city, Yaounde. But I had yet to negotiate such permission at the village level. My professor and I had visited the chief at his work in a nearby town and arranged to meet with him and the village elders in Domaayo the following day.

We arrived full of anticipation of this initial view of the village where I was to spend twelve months initially doing intensive research. I was accompanied by my professor and the driver of our rental car, whom I shall call Ji'birilla. As is often the case in development projects, the driver was doubling as guide, translator, and culture broker. He drove the two-hour journey over asphalt from Maroua, and then on red dirt roads, until we drove down into a green valley and up to the entrance of a picturesque village, where the chief and the elders were gathered.

We walked up to the assembly and found two chairs that were positioned in front of the chiefs. The other men were seated on the sand under the canopy of a large shade tree. The two chairs had seemingly been hastily arranged, as they faced away from the chief. My professor and I shook the chief's hand as he welcomed us warmly but formally. We simply turned the chairs around to face the chief and sat down before him. It wasn't until many months later that I realized that I had just violated a primary rule of Fulbe social etiquette. I had assumed the chairs were meant to face the chief, and that looking someone in the eye when he speaks to you is a sign of paying attention and of honesty. But as someone kindly explained to me some time later, "the chief looks at you. You do not look at the chief." The chairs had been intended to face away from the chief. And of course, all of the elders (as I remarked at subsequent gatherings) face away from the chief when he speaks. They look down at the ground, occasionally looking quickly at him over their shoulders. Averting one's gaze is a sign of respect. Fulbe culture acknowledges the power of the gaze.

He asked us to explain the purpose of our project, the kinds of things we hoped to learn, and the methods to be used.

My professor did most of the talking. The driver translated, while the chief and the village elders nodded. There was some discussion, of which only some was translated for our benefit. Finally the chief leaned forward and asked pointedly. How does the village benefit from this project? We explained that the project would provide treatment for all residents of the village who tested positive for schistosomiasis at the end of the research period. The elders seemed satisfied at this response, and the chief then called forward a veiled person, a woman, who knelt near the chief. She had been sitting at a distance until now. And the chief was speaking to her at length in Fulfulde (the Fulbe language). She answered softly, her head bowed, and her gaze averted, speaking in monosyllables. "Na'am." (Yes sir.) Her face was deeply incised with scars that run from her forehead and temples down to the corners of her mouth looking almost like whiskers, sculpted into her rich brown skin. The chief turned to me: "You will stay with me as soon as I have built a house for you. Until then, Dija has agreed that you will stay with her family." Thus my fate was decided.

When I returned the next day with my suitcase, she not only provided me with food and shelter, but she also began socializing me into this Fulbe community. Dija became my primary teacher for those first weeks, teaching me basic manners, such as eating with my right hand, and rudimentary vocabulary, as well as more complex rules of social etiquette. I sat with her for hours in her square, adobe-walled kitchen, sipping tea, eating beignets (doughnuts), watching her cook, observing her commerce in basic commodities (sugar, vinegar, oil, coffee), and watching her raise her two adopted children, learning as they did from her scolding and encouragement. Like them, I was in awe of her power and authority. And for the rest of my stay in Domaayo, I remained in fear of hurting her feelings or violating her sense of right and wrong. The other neighborhood women came to jokingly call her Daada Elen, in acknowledgment of her maternal investment in me. I went to weddings with her, and I accompanied her to funerals and baby-naming ceremonies. I sought her advice about appropriate wedding gifts, and she taught me how to deliver condolences. And whenever I went out to social events without her, she quizzed me at length upon my return about who and what I had seen, scolding me when I had failed to notice what she wanted to know (such as the quality of a length of cloth), and thus teaching me about what was important to notice in these events and about my role as conveyor of that important information.

Through Dija, I was plunged into a world of women. But I also enjoyed conversing with men; they often stopped me during my daily round of visits. Some saw me as an opportunity to practice their French, to satisfy their curiosity about the world beyond Domaayo and the well-traveled roads to regional markets. We spoke about politics, geography, religion, and marriage practices. As a foreigner, a student, and a traveler, I was in their minds not quite female. And, at times, they included me in their fellowship as an honorary male. Through these contrasting experiences I became fascinated with understanding the highly segregated and gendered worlds of Fulbe men and women.

The red motorcycle had arrived with me in the back of the Peugeot wagon, but I had not yet learned how to ride. Perhaps this motorcycle is an apt metaphor for the ethnographer's tool kit. We study research methods in our classes and write elaborate research proposals before embarking for the field, but we often find out later that we did not fully comprehend our methods until we began employing them in a new cultural environment. I arrived in the village not knowing how to ride, and my new, red motorcycle staying parked in my host's compound for nearly two weeks as I mustered up the courage to wheel it out onto the sandy road and give it a spin. A gathering of young men quickly grew under the neem tree as villagers realized they were about to see a *nasaara* (European) woman on a motorcycle. I managed to turn the key in the ignition and give it several ineffectual kick starts before Saali, the chief's younger brother, came forward, laughing, to show me what to do. I will always be grateful to him for his generosity and compassion. In the same way, I can never repay the debt I owe to those who taught me about their lives by teaching me their language. The most sophisticated research methods are useless without the gift of friendship.

Though the names of people and places have been changed to protect the privacy of my friends, it is my hope that they will recognize themselves in these pages in their complexity.

FULBE VOICES

Domaayo, a pseudonym, is a small village in Cameroon's Extrême Nord (Far North) province, near the Chad border and only a few hours' drive from Nigeria. Its residents, numbering less than 1,000, are primarily ethnic Fulbe, and are over-

Looking over a compound wall at an approaching storm.

whelmingly practicing Muslims. As I lived and worked in this community of under a thousand people over a period of twenty months, I came to experience a variety of Islam rarely represented in the Western media. The way in which Fulbe
people live as Muslims is one of the central themes of this book. Villagers vary
widely in their level of French (secular) education, literacy in Arabic, the language of the Koran, and their interest in theological issues. But all Domaayo residents engage in moral and political debates in a language shaped by their distinctive understanding of Islam. They argue about the merits of Fulbe marriage
traditions and debate the promise of specific betrothals. They discuss the merits
of "pagan" aspects of their cultural heritage, such as the prominent role of griots
(musicians, genealogists, and men of words) at weddings, and the costly practice
of exchanging gifts and countergifts at baby-naming ceremonies, circumcisions,
and weddings. They agree about the merits of Koranic medicine, herbal remedies, and Western pharmaceuticals, but disagree about which to use in particular
cases. Belief in mischievous, benevolent, or malevolent spirits is generally shared
but bargaining with such spirits is considered un-Islamic, though it is a practice
commonly attributed to one's neighbors. Traditionalists and reformers on each
issue can be found in any village gathering. Yet there is a surprising degree of tolerance for divergent opinions in the civil society of Domaayo.

In this polygynous, patrilineal, and patrilocal family system, men are more
likely than women to be Islamic scholars and teachers, but there are several
women teachers, and others who, having made the pilgrimage to Mecca, are hon-

ored with the title "Hajja." Though the culture sanctions polygyny (men may marry more than one wife), there are men, as well as women, who argue for the merits of monogamous marriage. The divorce rate is high, though lifelong partnerships are praised and admired. In a society where the patrilineal family groups define the social world and all women of childbearing age are meant to be married into a lineage, some women are nonetheless remarked for their freedom and autonomy. Divorced women and those who claim to be "too old for marriage" far before their time are the subject of gossip laced with sharp tones of reproof and, occasionally, admiration.

This book is called *Fulbe Voices* because it centers on everyday conversations between the men and women of Domaayo as they work out the contradictions that run through their culture and the social tensions which often turn on contrasting social positions of men and women, schoolboys and elders, married and free women, as well as rulers and the ruled. In Fulbe talk, social worlds are articulated and transformed. Domaayo Fulbe understandings of gender, kinship, politics, embodiment, sickness, medicine, Islam, and spirit-work are conveyed in their own words, as well as through a close examination of embodied practices. The arguments about tradition and reform, local ways and global flows, structural adjustment and a benevolent state, and democratic aspirations and domination are specifically Fulbe, yet they share many common features with debates going on elsewhere in West Africa, indeed in much of the continent. Domaayo is indeed an "out of the way place" (Tsing 1993), yet it is dramatically enmeshed in national, and transnational processes affecting communities all over the globe.

Fulbe Voices opens with a discussion of Fulbe identity, which is rooted in a history of nomadic pastoralism, migration, and religio-military jihads and vexed by their situation today as postcolonial subjects. Racial, political, and religious identities come together in a complex discourse of superiority and self-deprecation. In chapter two, everyday practices of *pulaaku*, or Fulbeness, are viewed through the prism of Fulbe talk about emotions. Public restraint and the denial of physical needs shape how Fulbe men and women approach everyday life and how they face major life events, such as marriage, death, birth, and sickness. Chapter three centers on Fulbe conversation about the topic of marriage, one that holds considerable interest and distress for many Fulbe men and women who consider that their fortunes are largely determined by whom they marry. Though young women marry into patrilineages where they must struggle to find allies and supporters, young men rely on the solidarity created through communal prayer and the experience of circumcision (the focus of chapter four). I explore the conflicting structures of egalitarianism, which men find in the brotherhood of Islam and in the hierarchies based on differences in age, education, and wealth. The circumcision school, through which all boys must pass, introduces them to these contradictions, as they forge bonds with their peers through their shared suffering and as they learn to fear and respect their elders.

The visceral experience of giving birth is the basis for all womanly authority in Fulbe society. Chapter five examines the many dangers that confront young mothers and their infants and the varied medicinal practices that are employed by mothers to heal and to prevent sickness. Mothers employ multiple healing techniques, combining Koranic medicine, herbal, and pharmaceutical remedies with "women's medicines," which sometimes conflict with Islamic orthodoxy in Domaayo. The Fulbe landscape is inhabited by a parallel world of spirits who make themselves known through their mischievous dealings with humans. In chapter six, Fulbe talk about spirits raises many issues about collective memories of conquest, colonialism, and the uneven workings of power in Fulbe society. Though Islamic scholars recognize the existence of spirits, they also disapprove of the discourse about *mistiraaku,* or witchcraft, which primarily afflicts women and children. Men often claim not to believe in *mistiraaku,* but many women who consider themselves to be devout Muslims seek to protect their children from these predatory forces.

In chapter seven, I examine the major changes in Cameroon's public medicine that reveal close linkages between global institutions, national policies, and seemingly remote places like Domaayo. The World Bank and the International Monetary Fund (IMF) created structural adjustment policies that impacted most of Africa in the 1980s and 90s, and affected many areas of life, from the market place to the medical clinic. Through interviews with public health officials and Domaayo residents, I show how dramatic public-policy changes are produced and experienced in a local community. Fulbe talk about public medicine is a window into how globalization is unfolding in this part of Africa.

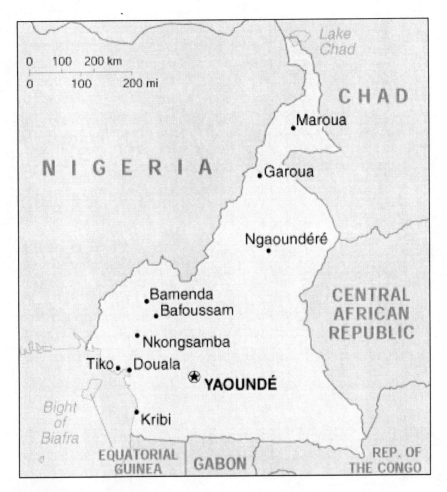

Cameroon

I

Fulbeness, History, and Cultural Pluralism

ROSALINE

A few weeks after my arrival in the village of Domaayo, I was befriended by a fourteen year old Mundang girl named Rosaline. She was bright, strong-willed, and ambitious. Her father had been a Lutheran catechist and a strong believer in the value of Western education. She and her father lived across the river in a small settlement, a cluster of family compounds, near Domaayo proper but not contained by it. She had acquired from her father a strong aversion to Muslim advances, both ideological and social. The latter had become more and more frequent of late, in the concrete form of marriage proposals, which she received from Fulbe men and tenaciously refused. For Rosaline, marriage to a Muslim meant submission to his will and conversion, two unappealing prospects for a defiant Christian girl.

She first approached me when she heard I was looking for a translator and language teacher. She spoke French well, and though I didn't want a Mundang assistant (I worried it would complicate my work in a Fulbe community), I looked forward to her visits and the possibility of communicating easily with another girl. My host family made fun of her obstinacy in her girlhood and paganism. Her refusal to marry was widely discussed in the village. She had strong feelings about my Fulbe friends too. Eventually, we grew apart, but not before I had spent many hours walking with her, picking mangoes from her family orchard, and keeping her company while she sold vegetables at the roadside market. One afternoon, as we walked together through the village, she pointed to a

1

respected *mallum* and *notable,* a scholar and courtier/attendant of the chief, Mal Suudi: "Look! Do you see this man? He is Mundang. He makes himself out to be Fulbe, but he is 100-percent Mundang." She made it clear that she saw him as an impostor, or worse—a traitor.

Her revelation was shocking, but I could not doubt her words. She knew him, and she knew his family. Yet my view of the taken-for-granted character of Fulbe ethnicity in this community was irrevocably shattered. This Islamic scholar in elegant white robes, who often affected the Arab turban and served as a close adviser to the chief—was a Mundang who had converted to Fulbeness? Perhaps a native-born Fulbe person would have immediately found a flaw in what I perceived as his seamless performance of Fulbeness. Upon reflection, I came to admire the enthusiasm with which he had embraced his chosen destiny in Islam and Fulbeness. Rosaline, as was clear from her tone, certainly did not. Later, the same *mallum* himself told me the story of his conversion, and he explained his devotion to spiritual things and his transformation from Mundang to Fulbe . Listening to Mal Suudi, and discussing his story with others, I began to see that the process of ethnic identification and the performance of ethnicity were central issues in this "Fulbe" village. I will return to Mal Suudi and his personal journey of conversion and transformation after first situating the Fulbe spatially and temporally in West Africa.

THE FULBE IN WEST AFRICA

The Fulbe live in every West African country from Senegal to Nigeria and are found as far East as Chad, the Central African Republic, and the Sudan (Boutrais 1994; Riesman 1992). In every one of those states, they are a minority, but their total numbers (estimated between eight and ten million) make them one of the numerically most significant West African ethnic groups. Although the most well-known Fulbe people are nomads, less than half of contemporary Fulbe still raise cattle (Riesman 1992:11). The Fulbe are variously known as Fulani (in Anglophone Africa), Peul (in Francophone Africa), Woodaabe, Mbororo, Fula, Toucouleur, and Halpulaaren. They all speak varieties of Fulfulde, which are mutually comprehensible (between good-willed speakers). Their contemporary distribution in West Africa is due not only to their nomadism, but also to their military and religious activism and leadership. In Cameroon, Guinea, Burkina Faso, Niger and Nigeria, they headed religio-military jihads in the eighteenth and nineteenth centuries and established tributary states, some of which still stood at the time of European colonial expansion into the Sahelian zones (notably in northern Nigeria and Mali) in the late nineteenth and early twentieth centuries.

Most of Domaayo's residents believe that their identity as Fulbe distinguishes them from their "pagan" neighbors known as *haabe.* Yet, when I asked villagers

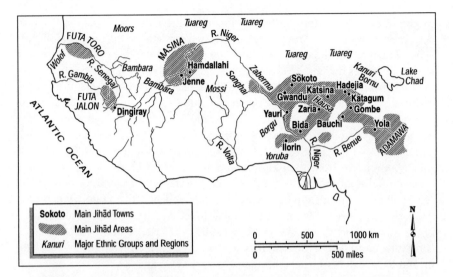

Four Fulbe Jihads. Contemporary Fulbe settlements reflect the histories of pastoralism, migration, and jihads. Drawing by Clifford Duplechin. Adapted from David Robinson's The Holy War of Umar Tal. *Oxford: Clarendon, 1985.*

about their history, ancestry and origins, my questions were often met with puzzled shrugs, suppressed giggles, and embarrassed laughter. Usually the person I was talking to would refer me to someone else, who would in turn tell me to talk to some other "expert" about local history. No one, it seems, wanted to speak (or at least not in public) about their communal ancestry. Eventually, I learned that some of the ancestors of this community were Muslim men who had participated in Shekh Usumaanu's famous nineteenth century jihads, while other ancestors were non-Muslim farmers of non-Fulbe parentage (and therefore "pagan"). Some ancestors were nomadic pastoralists, while others were traders and Islamic clerics. The complexity of actual Fulbe ancestry appeared to contradict their claims to cultural superiority over their non-Fulbe neighbors. Privately, many men admitted that they are not "really Fulbe." However, in their relation to non-Muslim neighbors, they emphatically placed themselves in the Fulbe camp. Somehow, they were both proud of their collective claims to a distinctive Fulbe culture and heritage and worried that their personal claims to membership in that group might be undermined by too much probing.

DOMAAYO

In many parts of West Africa, Fulbe identity is linked with cattle. Most Fulbe people in Domaayo, however, are farmers and traders. Domaayo residents grow millet, sorghum, peanuts, cotton, onions, garlic and some vegetables (such as cucumbers, melons, lettuce, and tomatoes) in irrigated gardens. In the rainy season gardens, okra, mallow, and other vegetables are grown. They will be dried and stored for use in sauces during the dry season, when fresh vegetables are hard to come by. Aside from cotton, the onions they sell are perhaps their greatest agricultural contribution to the Cameroonian economy. Only a few villagers owned cattle in significant numbers, and for most Fulbe people in Domaayo, cattle ownership was a nostalgic icon of their past wealth and glory. They enjoyed yogurt, butter and milk-based porridge (*gaari*) during the rainy season, but these items were usually purchased from the pastoral Fulbe who camped near Domaayo during their annual migration. Villagers admired the freedom and mobility of these "cow Fulbe" who seemed to have retained a greater degree of autonomy than they themselves had been able to since colonial times. For the sedentary Fulbe, many of the things which "make life sweet" must be purchased, and they are therefore constantly reminded of their entanglements in the monied economy and of their incomplete mastery of its operating forces.

The recent dramatic losses of political and economic power have created a tremendous feeling of uncertainty and alienation from state institutions among Fulbe people. The following section provides a brief overview of the Fulbe in West African history and in Cameroon. There follows an exploration of the often contradictory notions of Fulbeness, which coexist in the contemporary Fulbe community in which I did my field work. Identity in Domaayo is variously said to rest on ancestry, a "racial" notion of physical attributes, religion, or the performance of Fulbeness.

FULBE HISTORY

In northern Cameroon, most of the contemporary Fulbe trace their arrival in the region to the 1804 jihad led by Shekh Usuman Dan Fodio of Sokoto, Nigeria, although an unknown number of Fulbe pastoralists, traders and sedentary Islamic scholars were already living in the region prior to the jihad (Schilder 1994:100). The holy war led to the establishment of the Sokoto Caliphate with an Emirate in Adamawa (now a province of northern Cameroon), which answered to Sokoto and in turn was answered to by a number of hierarchically arranged local chiefdoms. Many of the pre-existing local populations were made into tributary groups of the Fulbe rulers. And many local residents converted to Islam.

Concepts of ethnicity in northern Cameroon are characteristically based on a distinction between pagan and Muslim. As a rule, all Muslims are considered to be Fulbe, and all non-Muslims, of various heritages, are lumped into the category "pagan". The latter are frequently referred to as *haabe* (the Fulfulde word for pagan) or *kirdi* (the term for "pagan" used in the sweeping generalizations of French colonial administrators). Locally, the Mundang, Tupuri, Guiziga, and Guidar are the Fulbe's primary non-Muslim neighbors. Fulbe people I knew tended to look down on members of these ethnic groups as mere *haabe*, an attitude which has its roots in the Sokoto empire.

During the nineteenth century, the outright incorporation of Mundang individuals into the Fulbe population occurred through the Fulbe adoption of Mundang twins, who were considered dangerous to their parents, through slave raids, which often captured young children, and through the Mundang sale of children in times of famine (Schilder 1994:108). These children grew up in Fulbe communities, speaking Fulfulde and knowing only Fulbe culture, though they were always seen as *haabe* captives. Fulbe also participated in the West African slave trade, supplying slaves to Hausa traders, significantly enriching their economy. Paradoxically, the economic success of the Fulbe traders depended on the availability of potential slaves, which were, naturally, their pagan neighbors. The trade thus both thrived on the incomplete subjugation of the Mundang and fostered the persistence of a Fulbe/pagan distinction. Schilder (1994:118) argues that this may have dampened the missionary zeal of Fulbe, as Islam forbids slave raiding among Muslim populations. As long as *haabe* populations lived near the Muslim Fulbe, they engaged in dry season slave raids, which were justified as jihads, or holy wars.

RELIGIOUS AND ETHNIC CONVERSION

With this history in mind, one gets a deeper appreciation of the power of ethnic categories in contemporary Cameroon. As Mal Suudi's case illustrates, ethnicity in Northern Cameroon has as much to do with residence and religion as ancestry. A person who is Mundang might move to a city as a young adult, convert to Islam, speak Fulfulde and dress in Islamic fashion—long flowing robes rather than western, tailored clothes. In this way, he can become Fulbe. He and his acquaintances will not forget that his ancestry is Mundang, but his chosen ethnicity will be Fulbe. Islam favors this process of ethnic conversion as teachers encourage the treatment of fellow Muslims as brothers, without discrimination as to ancestry. "Aren't we all children of Adam?" I often heard *mallums* ask rhetorically. Many residents of Domaayo were married across ethnic boundaries, if those were to be defined by ancestry. A man could easily marry a Mundang woman, I was told, as long as she converted to Islam. During the height of the nineteenth century slave trade, Fulbe men also married Kanuri, Shoa Arab, and Hausa speakers, all predominantly Muslim people who enjoyed free status (Fisher 1978:371). If a woman spoke Fulfulde well, and conformed to local ways of doing things, treating her neighbors as fictive kin, she would be accepted as easily as a native Fulbe woman. The emphasis of ethnic solidarity thus seems to be on the *performance* of ethnicity. Throughout West Africa, the Fulbe have successfully assimilated people of varied ancestry, strengthening their population demographically, as well as facilitating their political rule over diverse populations during periods of empire building (see Willis 1979). Conversion, inter-ethnic marriage and adoption were the principal vehicles for Fulbeization of peoples of varied ancestry in the region. The same views on the process of ethnic assimilation, which were applied to neighboring ethnic groups were also applied to the visiting anthropologist. Having shown interest in Fulbeness by struggling to learn the language, I was encouraged to take on more and more of the Fulbe repertoire and was praised for my efforts. As the Rosaline story illustrates, I was also disciplined when I "crossed over" and mixed with people of other ethnic groups.

My host family teased me about my friendship with her. Rosaline, too, taunted me by ridiculing my "so-called Fulbe" friends and neighbors. Although her claim that Mal Suudi was 100-percent Mandang shocked me, I was curious to hear what he would say about his own identity. Fortunately, Mal Suudi had heard about my inquiries into the ethnic origins of Domaayo residents, and he wanted to tell me his own version of things. Mal Suudi loves to talk, and I quote him below, to give the reader a chance to see how he thinks about himself and his world.

Mal Suudi's Transformation: The Fulbeizing of a Mundang

Mal Suudi spoke to me one afternoon about his Islamic studies, his identity, and ancestral origins. We had been chatting amiably on the side of the road, when my questions about his religion prompted him to give me his educational history in a speech which turned into an impassioned profession of faith:

> I studied the Koran under Mal Nyaako for ten years. When I had read it completely, they sacrificed a large cow for me. They prayed the fatya (a prayer of thanks). I became a mallumjo then! So that others would know I had finished reading the Koran, they gave me a Koran. Amen. They gave me a book. I entered into my own saare then (that is, got married). For ten years, I had carried wood for him (Mal Nyaako, his teacher), gave it to him with my hat off (a submissive pose). The wood was (for light) to read the Koran and to make writing tablets (alluha).
>
> The Arabic books (je deftere Arabia), I studied with Alhaji Bello. There were three books. There too I studied for six years after having finished the Koran. I read laadari, I read dawa I di salaati, I read tawhiidi, I read 'kurdeebi, I read halli mashiiru. These five books were written by Shehu Laadari (an influential Koranic scholar).
>
> Then, I entered the party, I entered the world, I entered the ganjal—I danced the flutes—I entered sukaaku. But now, I have left all that be-

Posing with Koran and baby

hind, I am only praying, I am only doing the work of the religion. (Mi nasti haala parti, mi nasti dunyaaru, nastu mi ganjal—j'ai dansée les flutes—mi nasti sukaaku. Too, jonta kam, mi acci pat, mi don juula non, mi don wadda kuugal diina non.)

Mal Suudi testifies to the labor and hardship involved in becoming learned in Islamic knowledge. Sixteen years of study and submission to the authority of the teacher have made him one who has read (*jangi*) and therefore, one who can act as a spiritual advisor, healer, and teacher. But he is no saint, he lets me know. He became involved in partying, in the concerns of this world and the world of women. The flutes (*ganjal*) refer to the alluring world of *sukaaku* in which young Fulbe men gambled their belongings to "win" a woman for one night.

Fulbe talk about the "temporary marriages" of *sukaaku* often joined fantasy and nostalgia in highly textured stories about beauty, love, and the madness of desire. Griots (musicians), flutes in hand, acted as middlemen in the escalating presentations of gifts and countergifts (kola nuts, cigarettes, money, jewelry) that determined the winner and the loser. The competitive courtship of *sukaaku* would take place when more than one man wanted to woo the same *azabaajo* (free woman). The stakes in this ritualized gamble were high, and men were known to sometimes give away substantial possessions—including livestock—in their determination to "win" a particular woman. Although every man I interviewed about this practice, spoke of it as something of the past, the concept of *sukaaku* survives in the popular imagination as a dramatic example of an un-Islamic and dissipated lifestyle. The villagers talk about it dismissively as senseless, wasteful, and sinful, yet their descriptions carry a wistfulness that betrays the enduring power of these rituals of competitive wooing, if only as fantasy.

In the context of this profession of faith, the *sukaaku* story suggests in Mal Suudi's past, not only a life of sin, but one tinged with glamor and excitement. "Now I have left all that behind," he affirms. It is as if he is saying, "I *know* the world, so I know what I have left behind in order to pursue a religious life." Here Mal Suudi's narrative uses the same plot structure used in stories that describe the lives of Christian saints from Paul to Augustine and, more recently, in the *Autobiography of Malcom X* (Haley 1965). The story of salvation/redemption begins with vivid descriptions of "the life" of sin, only to make the man or woman's conversion more substantial and more convincing (Diawara 1995; see also Van der Veer 1996).

Mal Suudi did not dwell on the topic of *sukaaku*. He wanted to emphasize the significance of the specific texts that he studied, and that he feels made him who he is today. The *mallum* explained the significance of each of the different books. "These books take the language of the Koran and put it in understandable terms. If you read only the Koran, you won't know these things." Thus, the books constitute an exegesis of the Koran. Each book teaches the scholar an additional area of religious knowledge, and attests to his growing expertise and practical authority. The first book reveals the existence of God and gives the names of God. The second "tells you how to do ablutions, how to pray, etc." The third is written by Shehu Usumaanu, the child of Fodi (Usuman Dan Fodio, leader of the Islamic jihad of 1804) :

> *He was blessed. He did many good things* (barkaaji) *for the world. This book praises the prophet.* (Don maanta annabiijo.) *If you read it, it is like you are looking at the prophet with your eyes.* (To a jangi, ban a don lara annabiijo bee gite.) *You fall in love with Him.* (Tu deviens amoureux.)
>
> *The other two are also about prayer—teaching people how to pray.* (Tindingo juulgo non.)
>
> *When you've read these five books, you are a part of the Islamic brotherhood. You can talk to anyone. Before you've read these five books, you don't know.*

The last statements underline another aspect of hierarchy within an egalitarian community of Muslims. All men are "children of Adam" and, therefore, equals before God. But in Islam not all men are part of the learned. As previously mentioned, the average child learns in Koranic school "just enough to pray," and very few go beyond the first graduation, which occurs upon the completion of the recitation of the Koran. Mal Suudi told us that the completion of the five books marked his entry into the Islamic brotherhood, enabling him to "talk to anyone." Those who have not read them simply "don't know." They may be children of Adam, but that does not make them the peers of learned men: Equality with men of that status requires many years of study. Mal Suudi's own life attests to the transformative powers of Islamic learning, and, at this point in his story, he turns to the subject of his own origins to substantiate the point:

> My hair is Mundang. My skin is dark. Not like a Pullo, not like an Arab, not like a nasaara. But my blood is Muslim. My body, my clothes are washed clean. My skin is becoming red (don wooja). I was invited to the mosque in Lara (a nearby town). Those who live in Lara are Mundang. There are those who are Islamicized, but they are few in number. They prayed. The Marabouts were taking turns giving counsel/a sermon (waazu). I stood up. I said that I too had something to say. Instead of speaking in Arabic or in Fulfulde, I spoke in Mundang.
> "I am Mundang 100 percent. I am dressed in white. It is the religion, which has dressed me in white. If you find one person dressed in white, another dressed in black, you are going to sit down next to whom?" So, one of them answered "You will sit next to the one dressed in white." I folded back the sleeve of my gown (boubou). I pointed to my skin which has become a little red (bodeyjum). "The religion has made me red, although I am no nasaara (white person)." I took off my hat and showed my hair. "I don't have the smooth wavy hair (gaasa 'diguka) of the Fulbe, I have 100-percent Mundang hair. But I have changed. I have become red. I dress properly, thanks to the religion. If everyone began to pray (as Muslims do), everyone would become like me: clean and red. (To on donna juula on fuh, on gaddano ba am)." The chief of Lara said, "He has a good point. His words are well marked. I know him. He is my brother. He is 100-percent Mundang like he said. He speaks Mundang so well . . . he knows the proverbs so well, he will give you proverbs in Mundang that even some Mundangs would not understand.

What is perhaps most striking in this speech is the bodily idiom of ethnicity being used to describe an experience of ethnic and religious *conversion*. Although Mal Suudi's ethnicity is fluid (it is an "achieved" status), the new ethnic identity becomes manifest in his very flesh, as his black pagan body "becomes red" and thus approaches the Fulbe complexion. Of course, physiologically, skin responds to solar radiation by tanning, whereas hair does not. So it is sensible to speak of skin tone rather than hair being altered by lifestyle. Unchanged, his hair remains unaffected by his transformation. "It is (still) 100-percent Mundang." Someone who leaves agricultural work behind for work "in the shade" can be observed to become noticeably lighter. But Mal Suudi does not invoke these explanatory links. Instead, he spoke as if his religious and ethnic conversion in itself had become written on his body with the reddening of his skin and the whitening of his clothes. The two processes go together, and the clothes are as much part of Mal Suudi's new Muslim persona as his body.

In traveling to Lara, he returns to a Mundang social space, yet he does this to speak in the mosque—an Islamic space within that Mundang locale. And he does so as an authority in Islamic discourse. He is asked to speak in the Mosque, along with other religious scholars. When he does so, it is in a reflexive manner, baring his Mundang skin before them as he speaks to them in their tongue. He stands before them in a dual identity: Islamic/Fulbe scholar and Mundang man— twinned realities visible in his physical body. His Mundang corporeality persists in his hair, while his Fulbe identity becomes grafted onto his body in the reddening of his skin. Verbally he still speaks fluently in Mundang, while actively wielding Fulfulde and Arabic as part of his scholarly and religious arsenal. Mal Suudi's personal views about the plasticity of ethnicity reflect a widespread belief in the connection between religions and ethnic identities—yet not everyone would agree that becoming Muslim necessarily makes you Fulbe, as we shall see.

Ethnicity as Ancestry: The Case of Usumaanu Lawan

Usumaanu is the son of a former chief (Lawan) and a member of the family, which has recently lost the chiefdom. He always has very strong views on almost every subject; ethnicity is no exception. He believes that people who convert to Islam do not necessarily change their ethnicity as a result.

"All of the people of Domaayo are one race, one lineage. One tribe." When I ask him to define *tribe*, he says "those who speak the same language. "The people of South Africa, Senegal, Mali, Upper Volta—they tell you their name and their race. It is a way of saying: 'We come from over there.' But race is less important here."

Usumaanu translates the Fulfulde word *lenyol* into French as "race," but it would be more accurate to say "lineage." This "mistake" is an interesting one; it is suggestive of how the language of colonial administrators has influenced Africans' own perceptions of their ethnic identities. French colonial administrators, many of whom were also amateur ethnographers, wrote extensively about the Fulbe "race" as inherently superior to other Africans (Amselle 1998; Breedveld and de Bruijn 1996). Such racial "essentialism" (reducing identity to an unchanging essence) is incompatible with the view of ethnic identity as performance, demonstrated by Mal Suudi above. Whereas for Mal Suudi, prayer and other actions can make you Fulbe, for Usumaanu, prayer and ethnic/racial identity are irrevocably distinct, and any confusion between the two is wishful thinking on the part of the convert:

> If a Mundang prays, he is a Muslim. He is not Fulbe. Fulbe is the race. Praying is the religion. One does not become Fulbe I tell you. They want to but are not able to. It is finished. Since the beginning, it is finished.
>
> I ask him, "What if a Mundang woman marries a Fulbe man, what are their children?" "Her children are métis. If a black woman marries a white man, are her children white? No! They are métis." He suggests that it is the same with Fulbe and non-Fulbe marriages. "What is the word for métis in Fulfulde?" "Bakalleejo—neither one race nor another—mixed. "Those who pretend to have become Fulbe are poseurs. I speak the truth. Everyone wants a more elevated name. Anyone wants to say that his race is superior."
>
> I ask him about Fulbe-Hausa marriages. "It is only religion which brings them together (makes them similar). Religion scoffs at race. What counts is to follow the path."
>
> I persist. "O.K., so what if one out of four grandparents is not Fulbe. You are not Fulbe?" He gives an equivocal answer. "If they speak, it is the patoit (dialect) which they speak which you are. If they don't tell you their lenyol (lineage), you don't know. You are the language they speak."

"Not knowing" one's ancestry becomes a way of claiming Fulbeness. Here, Usumaanu, contradicting his earlier statement, equates language and ethnicity. He has completely put ancestry aside. Moments earlier, he had defined ethnicity according to *origins*. "It is finished, since the beginning it is finished." In this way, he implicitly denies Mal Suudi's claim to be Fulbe. This essentialist definition of ethnicity leaves no room for ethnic conversion and limits the consequences of conversion to changed religious identity. Nevertheless, Fulbeness, in the context of northern Cameroon, is defined in opposition to pagan-ness. "Religion scoffs at race" as Usumaanu put it. But the solidarity and mutual respect that Islam demands of fellow Muslims almost requires that Fulbeness (non-pagan-ness) be extended to converts. Islam beseeches members of the religious community to extend to each other the terms of mutual respect that, in the Fulbe context, can only come from Fulbeness itself.

> The ancestors came. They were men. They had to marry the local
> women." "Why did they leave Mali?" I ask. "They left because of wars, to
> trade in slaves, to engage in long distance trade, even to govern, to rule, to
> have slaves. For example, it was our grandfather who came to rule over
> Domaayo with his herd, with his brothers, with his marabouts
> (mallums). The father of our grandfather was Modibbo Jam. This is how
> it is in every place. If they come, it is to gain wealth and power.
>
> "Mal Suudi himself was born Mundang. It is he himself who left his
> pagan village, who became a Muslim, who learned the Fulbe language.
> Mal Juulde (another local religious scholar) is not Fulbe either. Neither
> his parents nor his grandparents were Fulbe, but his people have been
> Muslim for a long time."
>
> "As for me, I don't know what to say that I am," Usumaanu con-
> cludes.

Usumaanu, moving from the conversionist view of Fulbeness to the essentialist version, defines himself out of Fulbeness, although he is the heir to the chiefdom of a Fulbe village. Perhaps here is the key to his early transposition of "race" for *lenyol*. In a village, which is nominally Fulbe—but where each family has its distinctive ethnic and cultural roots—ethnicity, or "race," comes to be about remembered lineage. Not all genealogies are equally remembered. Hausa, Kanuri and Shoa ancestry is more likely to be publicly "remembered" because these peoples were historically Muslim at the time of the Fulbe wars. At a time when all pagans were both military enemies and potential slaves, the religious status of the Hausa, Kanuri and Shoa Arabs theoretically exempted them from both Fulbe aggression and slave raiding. They were like the Fulbe "people who prayed" (Muslims); thus, their descendants can recall their ethnic ancestry without the associated shame of paganism or slavery. Thus Mal Juulde's family is known to come from the Mandara Mountains and was ethnically Kanuri, allowing him to remember his ethnic origins without shame. The Mundang, Tupuri, and Guiziga, on the other hand, are ethnically identified with paganism in the Fulbe view. Their descendants, in a contemporary Fulbe village such as Domaayo, are likely to change the topic when the subject of origins is raised by curious anthropologists. Their friends and neighbors, of course, would know to avoid discussing "lineage" around them.

The various ethnic groups of northern Cameroon are collectively referred to as *haabe* (pagan). This categorization, originating with the Fulbe traders and warriors, came to be widely accepted by German and later French colonial administrators and often by the so-called *haabe* themselves (Schilder 1994). The many mixed marriages that took place were marked by a rule of "hyperdescent," that is, the children of mixed marriages were identified with the group that had the highest socioeconomic status and prestige in the region—the Fulbe. Mundang ancestry is thus much less likely to be remembered than Shoa Arab,

Kanuri, or Hausa ancestry. In ordinary discourse, people of mixed Mundang and Fulbe ancestry refer to themselves and each other simply as Fulbe.

In Fulbe families, which are both patrilocal and patrilineal, women typically move in with their husband's families, and their children are incorporated into their husband's lineage. The social identity of children, therefore, is primarily built on the father's social identity. Chapters four and six will further explore how marriage is experienced by men and women. For the moment, it is useful to note that the women who marry into men's families are considered "foreign"—just how foreign is a matter of degree. Thus, it is not insignificant that "mixing" is most commonly remembered to involve Fulbe men marrying local non-Fulbe women. A patrilineal system is less likely to remember women ancestors anyway. The history nonetheless firmly aligns Islam and Fulbeness with male ancestors, and paganism and *haabe* ancestry with female ancestors. This then resonates with the pattern observed in contemporary discourse in which women are identified with sinful paganism and men with pious virtue.

100-Percent Fulbe

After talking with Usumaanu, I asked my friend Bakari what is meant by the "real Fulbe." As an ethnographer of a Fulbe community, I was dismayed to discover that some of the most central political and religious figures of the community did not consider themselves to be true Fulbe. There was a fiction at the center of the ethnic identity of the people I had been living with for nearly half a year. The real fiction, of course, is in the mistaken belief that there exists anywhere a population of "pure" cultural or racial/ethnic pedigree (with clean boundaries drawn around them). Such a reification of culture and ethnicity has been shown to be a product of colonial and anthropological discourse in its efforts to analyze and ultimately administer and control, the social realities of colonized peoples (Amselle 1998; Schilder 1994; Schultz 1984). Yet it would be too simple to attribute all essentialist thinking to the "bad colonials." The Fulbe seem to participate in this reification themselves. "We are not real Fulbe because we are mixed, but in Mali, there are real/pure Fulbe." Mali is far enough away so that few Cameroonian Fulbe are likely to have been there. Living on the margins of the former Fulbe empire, they imagined that others, somewhere, fit the "type" better then they do. People I spoke with often switched to the French word *Peul* to describe these "real" people, as if the French colonial usage were necessary to endow them with such a distinguished status. It is not unreasonable to suppose that French colonial administrators' concepts of race would have influenced the thinking of Fulbe people with whom they came into contact.

In their alternately brave, humorous, or self-deprecating confessions, there was no room to doubt that Fulbe identity was highly desirable for these men, and

Fulbe boy

yet it was not fully attainable to them. I hoped Bakari could provide me with some illumination:

> *These people (the Fulbe), they come from Mali. I am mixed (*mélangé*).*
> *A real Fulbe, 100 percent, that is hard to find eh? You can even recognize*
> *them. That is to say, by their body type, by their physiognomy. A real*
> *Fulbe should not be fat. Also, he must be light skinned (*brun*). He must*
> *have wavy hair. He must have a long straight nose, not like my nose. He*
> *must also have white eyes. The fingers of his hands and feet must be long*
> *and thin (*chetifs*). Voilà, this is how they can be recognized.*
>
> *He can follow any religion, but he is* Peul *(Fulbe). There are Peuls*
> *who even go to school. They even leave to go abroad to study. Years ago,*
> *there was a Peul in Doumourou, a veterinarian. He was a real Peul.*
>
> *Fulbeness, there . . . there is a Fulbe race. Some are bright (*rouge*),*
> *others are dark (*noir*). All are Fulbe—one race. Within the Fulbe peo-*
> *ple, there are those that feel shame and those that do not. All of them*
> *are Fulbe by race (*asungol*). One person eats anywhere, eats until*
> *he/she is full and is not ashamed. Another person eats only in his/her*
> saare *(compound). He does not eat until he is full. He has shame. One*
> *Pullo (sing. of Fulbe), if you ask him a question, he knows the answer*
> *but he will not speak. Another* Pullo *will tell everything. He is a Fulbe*
> *too. . . . There is nothing more to the Fulbe than this (*Haala Fulbe

kam buray ni'i*). As for the religion of the Fulbe, it is all one. There are
Fulbe who know the religion but who do not pray. They are still Fulbe.
Some of them are extremely discrete. They keep secrets. One person
will not hear anything of the affairs of another. For example, here is an
onion field. Here is a motorized water pump (to irrigate the onion
fields). We can't know to whom the onions belong, to whom the* moto-
pompe *belongs.*

Bakari, like Usumaanu, moves between a reductionistic definition of the "*vrai
Peul*," the real Fulbe whose racial identity is visible in his slender fingers and
physique, his smooth hair, straight nose, and light (reddish) skin, and a more in-
clusive view of Fulbe ethnicity as multiple and pluralistic. The Fulbe are known
for their religious devotion, their modesty or shame, reservedness and self-control in betraying desire for food or revealing information. Yet individuals with
widely different relations to food are still Fulbe: "One person eats anywhere. He is
not ashamed to eat in public or with strangers. He is not ashamed to eat until he
is full. Yet he is still Fulbe (by ancestry)." Thus he will be judged in terms of his di-
vergence from *pulaaku*.

I spoke to the local health-care center nurse one day about my inquiries into
Fulbe ethnic identity. I shared with him several of the contradictory ideas about
Fulbeness that were emerging from my investigation, and I curious to hear what
he thought. The nurse, a recent convert to Islam, had pursued his studies in the
provincial capital and lived in this region for many years. "Fulbe people in
Domaayo?" he asked. "*Mais il n'y a pas de Peuls ici!*" "But there are no Fulbe
here!" he declared, using the French term, *Peul*. He went on to tell me that there
were a few "real" Fulbe people in a nearby village, but none in Domaayo. He
smiled when he said this, with the satisfaction of one who is revealing information he is certain will disturb the listener.

The dismissive statements made by outsiders to the community—such as the
nurse and Rosaline—illustrate the position of non-Fulbe people who look with
contempt at Fulbe pretense to ethnic/racial superiority. When the nurse claims
that there are no real Fulbe here at all, he ridicules every person in Domaayo. He
is categorically "reducing" them, leveling them to the level of the *haabe* (pagans)—the very groups in opposition to which the Fulbe define themselves. And
he is well aware of the irony of what he is implying. Rosaline emphatically asserts
the Mundangness of Mal Suudi who speaks Fulfulde and generally "acts Fulbe."
Mal Suudi reinforces his claims to Fulbeness through his practice of the disciplines of the Koranic repertoire, becoming a noted expert through prolonged
study. What is so radical in the critiques of Rosaline and the nurse is that they
dismiss the Fulbe's claims to be Fulbe at all. From outside the Fulbe world, and
resenting the Fulbe ideology of dominance, they aim their attacks at the foundation upon which this edifice rests—their ethnic difference.

The Fulbe as Trickster and Mediator

*If you find a Fulbe with a poisonous snake (*culaandi*), hit the Fulbe and let the snake go free.*

—*Fulbe proverb*

When you've heard what the Fulbe had done, you can only take hold of your head in astonishment. He is likely to trick you.

—*Fulbe proverb*

These proverbs, cited by Fulbe people I knew, speak of the untrustworthy nature of the Fulbe. Not only will a Fulbe person surprise you with trickery, as implied by the second proverb, but his nature is as dangerous as a venomous viper. These were not told to me by Mundang, or Tupuri neighbors of the Fulbe, but by the Fulbe themselves.

"*To Pullo boo'd'dum, 'yam waandu.* If a Fulbe is good, ask the monkey what he thinks." Noye (1974: 305) cites this poem, which I read to my Fulbe friends to their great surprise and delight. It is as an allusion to a story in which a Peul, dying of thirst, came across a monkey. The monkey agreed to show the Peul the placement of a well, on the condition that the Peul not do him any harm. The Peul accepted, but as soon as he drank his fill, he threw the monkey into the well and covered it so no one else could drink from it. My friends recognized the story and nodded their heads, chuckling. The same people who sometimes expressed great ambivalence about their own Fulbe identities otherwise solidly identified themselves with the Fulbe figures in these proverbs and sayings about the trickster *Pullo*.

The chief's younger brother, Saali, talked to me about the Fulbe position in the pluralistic context of Africa in terms that recall the great ethnic chain of being, only adapted to a Fulbe perspective:

The Arab and the nasaara—*white in color—are in front. The* Pullo *is behind. The kaado, or pagan, of the mountains is farther behind.* (Arab bee nasaara—daneeyjum—don yeeso. Pullo 'don baawo. Kaado don don hooseere 'don 'baawo fahin).

I heard the same expression almost verbatim from a number of other men and women who seemed to cite it to situate themselves in relation to me, defining their position as intermediate between whites like me and the pagan people of the mountains. Again race, or color, is affixed to religion or culture, as whiteness defines what Arabs and European Christians (*nasaaras*) have in common. The *Pullo* is next in line; the pagan (*kaado*) mountain dwellers are last. The redness of the Fulbe is implied, as is their hybrid cultural status. Though not pagan themselves, they are African and Muslim, and are never far from their pagan neighbors or their own pagan roots.

COLONIAL AND POSTCOLONIAL HISTORY

The twentieth century brought the Fulbe into the colonial fold. According to the Dutch anthropologist Kees Schilder (1994:128–129), German colonization, beginning in 1902, favored Fulbe power by ruling local populations through the already established Fulbe political hierarchy and strengthening it with the force of German military power. Fulbe dominance increased during the German period, as Fulbe rule was extended to villages, which had until then largely escaped Fulbe overlordship. The tribute levied consisted of grain and agricultural laborers to work the *karal* (winter sorghum) fields of the Fulbe rulers. Although Germans opposed the slave trade, the Fulbe's punitive expeditions against the villages, which refused to pay tribute or participated in cattle raids, "sometimes resembled the former slave raids" (1994:129). French rule of the Diamare region after World War I (when it became a French protectorate) was characterized by a weakening of Fulbe power and the promotion of chiefs from the *Kirdi* populations whenever possible. Economic opportunities and schooling were unevenly distributed throughout the northern regions of Cameroon, in part because the Fulbe were suspicious of French schools and preferred sending their children to Koranic schools. Fulbe did not value agricultural work per se and, therefore, were unenthusiastic about French efforts to introduce cotton and new agricultural technologies. Schilder demonstrates that the Mundang, with a long and antagonistic relationship to their Fulbe neighbors, were initially reluctant to work with French colonial officials because they assumed the French were like the Germans and therefore "naturally" allied with the Fulbe oppressors. They gradually came to cooperate more actively with French administrators and began to attend French schools in great numbers. Christianity and literacy in the Roman alphabet offered to the Mundang a religion, which was associated with a sacred scripture and a writing system—technologies of power/knowledge, which were alternatives to the civilizing instruments provided by the Fulbe. Schilder thus shows how "following independence, the Mundang people developed into the best educated ethnic group in the whole of northern Cameroon" (1994:210). The strong presence of Mundang civil servants in hospitals and in government bureaus are constant reminders to the Fulbe of their own political losses. The relative success of the Mundang resulted from their more active engagement with French colonial development and, since independence, with the postcolonial state.

The Fulbe have experienced a constantly shifting relation to the contemporary Cameroonian state (Azarya 1978; Burnham 1996; Schilder 1994; Schultz 1981). At independence, the Fulbe Amadou Ahidjo became the head of state. His political party, the *Union Camerounaise* (*UC*), had as its official party emblem the head of a bull, an unambiguous reference to the pastoral past of the Fulbe. Although he ruled through a multiethnic national coalition, his presidency fostered the leadership role of northern Muslims. Non-Fulbe political leaders were encouraged to convert to Islam, supporting the myth of a homogeneous Islamic North.

Taking corn off the cob for planting

From 1960 to 1982, 86 percent of northern Cameroon's top administrators (prefects and subprefects) had Muslim names (Schilder 1994:160). In 1982, Ahidjo appointed Paul Biya to succeed him in the presidency. Ahidjo's subsequent failed attempt to return to power led to a dramatic reversal of Fulbe dominance in Northern Cameroon. Biya set about disassembling the northern power bloc, purging the top administrative positions not only of Fulbe but also of their allies. By 1983–84, the number of top administrators with Muslim names in northern Cameroon had dropped to 26 percent (Schilder 1994:160).

In 1990, under heavy internal and external pressures, prompted in part by the enthusiasm generated by the democratization in Eastern Europe, Biya allowed the formation of opposition parties. In 1991, a coalition of opposition parties organized massive antigovernment demonstrations known as *villes mortes*, which were in effect general shutdowns in towns throughout the country. These met increasing military repression (Schilder 1994:162). The opposition demanded that all of the political parties gather for a round table to discuss procedures for holding the first multiparty elections in the history of Cameroon. In March 1992, parliamentary elections were held but were boycotted by most opposition parties due to the president's refusal of the round-table conference. In October 1992, presidential elections took place. Although the opposition parties did present candidates, the results were highly contested. Paul Biya and his party (the RDPC, or *Rassemblement Démocratique du Peuple Camerounais*) continued to hold positions of power.

The dramatic shifts in Fulbe power over the last two centuries have affected the content of how contemporary Fulbe think about their ethnic identity. During my fieldwork, I spoke to men about their history and ancestry and through these conversations became aware of a deep ambivalence running through the very center of their identities as Muslims and as Fulbe men. Those I spoke with think of their superiority over their non-Fulbe neighbors as being rooted in their Islamic religion and their ethnicity, yet they all have ancestors who were not Muslim and ancestors who were not Fulbe. The "Fulbe" culture discussed in the pages that follow has grown out of centuries of contact, trade, and intermarriage with other West African ethnic and cultural groups. The resulting hybridity and persistent plurality of local identities constitute the foundation for Fulbe cultural pluralism.

Ethnic Tensions between Cattle Owners and "Pagan" Farmers

In May 1991, a young *pullo* student in Kaele spoke to me about Fulbeness. He was a *Lycée* (secondary-school) student, and I often saw him at a friend's house when I was visiting Kaele. Because I spoke Fulfulde, a rapport developed between us. He felt that he could talk to me about things that concerned him. "My parents are from Kolara (a town approximately twenty miles from Kaele). Kolara has a *Peul* majority. Those *Peuls* came and settled there from Chad. They had been migrant cattle-herders until then. They still own many cattle in Chad and (identify with their nomadic heritage to this day)." The proof is the value they place on milk, the student argued. In a land where water is the scarcest resource, "they will choose milk over water (*Kosam 'bura ndiyam*)." Although most Fulbe people I knew did not own cattle, they identified with cattle ownership both as a nostalgic remembrance of a pastoral past and because of the dominance and mastery associated with cattle ownership, which is a potent metaphor for Fulbe dominance over their ethnic neighbors. He told me the following story about tribalism in Kolara:

> Three years ago, a Tupuri man returned there for his retirement and immediately began to politicize the race relations there. He said "why do the Tupuri work for the Fulbe and the Fulbe do not work for the Tupuri?" Tupuri's work involves bringing firewood, building houses, working the fields, washing dishes, all in exchange for food and some money. (The Tupuri are clients to individual Fulbe patrons.)
> He began to beat anyone he found working for the Fulbe with a big stick, to the point of nearly killing a man last year. At the last muskwaari (winter millet) harvest, everyone harvested their millet but him. Their millet stalks were left in the field so that the cattle could graze on them. But his millet was still there, so that the stalks were dry

in the field with the millet heads still on them. Naturally, his millet was eaten. He beat the Peul *shepherd (who he thought was responsible) until his head swelled up to be this big.*" He holds up his hands to indicate a grotesquely swollen head. "*He was taken to judgment in Kaele and fined 500,000 CFA (approximately $2,000 at that time) and was given a two-year jail sentence. But he appealed to a higher court in Maroua, and his case is still pending.*"

For contemporary Fulbe who still own many cattle, yet live in a settled agricultural community, the conflict between field and pasturage is the quintessential metaphor for interethnic conflict. It pits farmer against shepherd in a struggle that recalls historical battles pitting Fulbe nomads and armed warriors against indigenous farmers. The Tupuri today may claim to have historical priority in the region, yet find themselves exploited by Fulbe patrons. In asymmetrical relations of clientage, their fields are "eaten" by Fulbe cattle, which display the same predatory hunger as their masters. In contrast, Domaayo Fulbe are more likely to be in the position of the farmer whose crops are eaten than in the role of the cattle owner/shepherd who gets blamed. The fact remains that in their metanarratives about the history and geopolitics of the region, the Fulbe are the owners of cattle, the masters of pagans. As the following chapter will show, their ideology of mastery is constantly reiterated in their everyday performance of *pulaaku*.

2

Pulaaku and Embodiment
in Everyday Life

The Fulbe take pride in their ability to display high levels of self-restraint and self-mastery, which they have long employed to justify their rule over others. This code of behavior known as *pulaaku* requires that emotions such as anger, joy, grief, and love—as well as feelings of thirst, hunger, and pain—be displayed only among close friends and family. The public denial of physical need and vulnerability shapes how Fulbe men and women approach everyday life, and how they face major life events, such as marriage, death, birth, and sickness. This chapter first discusses the norms of *pulaaku*, then examines several cases in which individuals flouted those norms. Both the individual's rationale and the community reactions reveal the subtle interactions of structure and agency in everyday life.

The moral code of *pulaaku* encompasses meanings of reserve, restraint, self-mastery, and nobility. Closely linked with the idea of *semteende*, the deployment of *pulaaku* in everyday life is strongly reminiscent of the Bedouin *hasham*, which Lila Abu-Lughod translates as "modesty" (1986). My understanding of Fulbe *pulaaku* and *semteende* draws on numerous conversations with my Fulbe hosts, friends, and neighbors who were teaching me how to behave like a Fulbe during my stay with them. *Pulaaku* is a common topic of conversation among Fulbe, who talk about it with pride and often cite it as the basis for their ethnic distinctiveness. As I have shown in chapter one, when non-Fulbes convert to Islam and move into Fulbe communities, they commonly are encouraged to take on the moral code of *pulaak* as the precondition for participating in the Fulbe social world as equals. The seamless performance of *pulaaku* in everyday life by Fulbeized converts erases their pre-Fulbe past, effectively making them Fulbe. As a foreigner who had moved into a Fulbe community and had visibly worked hard at speaking Fulfulde and acting Fulbe, I was treated like a Fulbeizing convert. Everyone, it seemed, had the right to comment on my efforts at *pulaaku* with encouragement, amusement, applause, and even stiff criticism.

The Fulbe Performance of Personhood

The Fulbe performance of personhood rests on the concealment of emotionality and feeling. Pain, anger, grief, affection, and happiness are kept private, and *semteende*, the ability to feel shame, is publicly flaunted. Excessive grief, anger or sensitivity to pain are interpreted as signs of weakness or bad character. Although women may flout *pulaaku* in some situations, they do so in a society that nevertheless holds it as one of its highest ideals.

Pain

At an early age, Fulbe children are taught not to give in to pain. I was especially struck by this when I witnessed an operation being performed on the leg of the child of a close friend of mine. Jaliyatu, a little girl no more than five years old, had an abscess that was causing her a great deal of pain, and the Fulbe healer was going to lance it. She sat in front of her mother who held her tight as the *mallum* prepared himself for the task, washing his hands and setting out the necessary items: water, medicinal leaves, oil, and knife. Solemn and calm, he washed her leg and made the incision. Jaliyatu wailed. Her mother held on. The *mallum* talked to her in an even but authoritative voice, as he pressed the flesh around the incision, directing the pus to move out of the cut. She began to calm down. Her mother looked in awe at the amount of liquid coming out of the abscess due to the directed actions of the surgeon. By the time the surgeon was wrapping the wound with cloth, Jaliyatu had completely gained control of herself. She was shaken but restrained.

Mayramu, the ten-year-old girl being raised by Dija, my host, also suffered from an abscess on her leg caused by an infected vaccination. She had been sick for months and was still in considerable pain when she was found one day sitting out in front of the compound chatting with people as if nothing were wrong. She didn't complain of her leg pain, and when people asked her about it she gave the appropriate Fulbe response. "*Daama jonta kam. Yettugo Allah.*" (Much better now, thanks be to God.) I heard this being recounted by the chief's mother, who was reporting it from a neighbor who had just returned from the well in front of their compound. The story was worth telling, because it illustrates the admirable precociousness of a child. As the narrator concluded, "Now here is a child, who acts better than many adults." She gave a seamless performance of *pulaaku*.

Family Portrait: Co-wives

The Fulbe attitude toward pain is further revealed in their competitive games. The game of *soro* has been documented for some groups of pastoral Fulani of Niger and Nigeria (Dupire 1962; Hopen 1958). It is a game in which a Fulbe man hits his partner on the chest with a big stick. The receiver pretends not to be perturbed and smiles at the audience. Riesman (1975:63) asserts that the demonstration "that one is in control of normal human emotions and above human needs" exemplified in *soro* "is constantly taking place in (Fulani) formal behavior" between members of the same community. The Fulbe of Domaayo, although they do not practice *soro*, do enact its principles in games played spontaneously between male peers in the course of everyday life. For example, it is not uncommon for *nyi-iri* (millet porridge), which is the center of every Fulbe meal, to be scalding when the diners start to eat. The man who is first to put his hand in the millet will be badly burned. Instead of wincing or exclaiming, "It's too hot!" he pretends that nothing is unusual and eats the mouthful quietly. His eating companions will surely burn themselves, and each in turn will have to either cry out in pain and be shamed for so involuntarily betraying their weakness (and loss of self-control), or play along with the game, suppressing his own pain and testing the next one.

Although women also engage in the performance of *pulaaku*, they do not use *pulaaku* to compete with each other as men do. Women often display an impressive ability to pick up hot things (coals, cooking pots) with their hands, but I never saw them play a testing game with heat. Perhaps women don't need to prove their *pulaaku* in such trivial ways because they have the ultimate test of courage in the experience of childbirth. Fulbe women are known for preferring to give birth alone or with only their closes friends or relatives present. They never speak of the pain of childbirth. As I will discuss more fully in chapter five, giving birth is central to the definition of women as adults and as members of a community of women. Perhaps for this reason, I never saw women engage in a competitive game based on the control of their response to pain.

Thus, in response to the pain of sickness and the pain of a cure, as well as in competitive games, Fulbe adults and children make a virtue out of the suppression and even the complete denial of pain. They acknowledge that there is pain in human existence, and they will discuss it publicly. But when they experience physical pain, minor or serious, they learn not to make it visible to others. As children become adults, they internalize their pain and learn to keep it private.

Paul Riesman (in Jackson 1989:201) comments on the Burkina Faso Fulbe's reluctance to express pain: "people talked about it freely and objectively . . . but they did not express it by the language of intonation and gesture." Another anthropologist Michael Jackson, has argued that "To name pain and suffering in a neutral tone is to master them, because the words *do not escape thoughtlessly* but are spoken consciously" (Jackson 1989; emphasis added). So people talk about pain comfortably, in the form of objective statements, but do not express it directly (as in cries, moans, or howls).

Anger

Also men play a game of self-control that involves teasing, mocking, and insulting the other person, who is expected to respond with the same, until one of them loses control and betrays anger. Either a raised voice or a shocked silence constitutes a defeat. This is only played between peers, although it is usually semipublic, as an audience enhances the value of the game. Usumaanu, son of the former chief, was known in the village for having a bad temper. I once witnessed one of these games of verbal taunts in which he ended up furiously walking away. He had told Bakari that he had no influence in the community. Bakari responded that it had been predicted that his own lineage was not destined for success in political leadership (that is, the chiefdom, or *laamu*), but in the area of wealth. This response angered Usumaanu, who had in fact lost a huge sum of money in recent few years and was bitter about it. To make matters worse, Usumaanu had been in the running for the position of *lawan* (village chief) eight years earlier but had lost the election, Bakari explained, because of his bad temper. Bakari's teasing had reminded Usumaanu of the painful truth that he had lost both his fortune and his chance at the chiefdom. Unlike Bakari's, Usumaanu's family was destined for political rule it seems, but he lost the election to his brother, the current chief, who did not have his volatile temper.

These cases illustrate the control of emotion among peers, but it is also important in the context of family relations. The story of Mahmudu and Buulo, a young married couple, shows us that acting out of anger can be severely judged by the Fulbe. Buulo had left her husband after an argument to visit her parents for an indefinite period of time. She had been there for two weeks when Mahmudu went to the compound across the river to get her. He asked her uncle about her coming home with him. He said, "I have nothing to do with it, ask her aunt." Her aunt said, "I have nothing to do with it; ask her." Mahmudu then asked Buulo, and she refused. He picked up a stick to hit her when her uncle intervened. The uncle warned, "If you ever enter this compound again, I'll kill you!" Mahmudu had lost his temper and all common sense along with it. He forgot that he was in his in-laws' compound and was required to be restrained in front of them. Buulo's uncle's authority in his own compound had been violated. Mahmudu's rights to his wife in his own compound did not apply here. This case was brought to the chief, who declared their marriage null and void. Mahmudu's actions illustrated such a shocking transgression, such a complete loss of self-control, that people in the village couldn't stop talking about it. "He tried to hit her in her father's compound!" "What a fool!" "His sensibility is bad. (*Hakkilo maako wo'd'daay*)." "Naa, his mind is not right!" He had completely lost face before the community. No one, not even his family, tried to argue in his favor.

What seems most striking is the fact that Mahmudu losing his temper does not function as mitigating circumstances for his transgression against his in-law. On the contrary, his complete loss of self-control strengthens the case against him and creates a strongly stigmatizing image of him as a man whose "sense is bad." Anger, like pain, is commonly experienced by Fulbe people, but they learn to manage it. They must not let it affect their public behavior. In games and in personal crises, to lose one's temper is to lose face.

Grief

My first encounter with the Fulbe norms about the expression of grief took place at the death of Rugayiatu, the four-year-old daughter of Aabu, who was later to become a good friend. This was my first funeral in Domaayo. Ubbo, with whom I was spending the day, heard that her brother's child had died. She immediately changed into her good clothes, and I accompanied her to the funeral. The men had gathered outside the front door of the compound, seated in a group, looking solemn. She removed her sandals as she approached, holding them in her hand, squatted in front of her brother, head bowed, and mumbled a greeting, a formula of condolence. She went inside, leaving her shoes inside the compound but before the social area where all the women were gathered. There must have been three dozen women sitting in the courtyard. We sat down among them for some time. Then we went inside. The body of the girl was still there sprawled on the floor. I sat near her; her mother was on the other side. The mother was clearly deeply upset, but her face was stolid, not a sign of tears on it. No one there was crying, though there was no smiling either. The atmosphere was formal and restrained. But the women outside chatted on and on about completely unrelated subjects for what seemed like three hours but was probably only about twenty minutes, before we got up to leave. New mourners arrived; others lingered while we got up to leave. I did not know enough to enter into the conversation, but they clearly had other things on their mind than the death they had come to acknowledge.

On another occasion, I visited Zeynabu after her newborn died. She was lying in her house, having given birth to the child earlier in the morning. It seems that the child never took a breath, therefore she was stillborn in the Fulbe view. But no one was there when Zeynabu went into labor; she had not cried out. Her co-wife (her husband's other wife) was right there in her own house, just across the courtyard, and did not hear her. After the baby was delivered, she sent a child to get her co-wife, and they came. The crowd of four to six men at the compound was quite small, and the presence of women inside was only somewhat greater. An old woman kept Zeynabu company, keeping the embers burning in the center of the house so that the air was hot and smoky; this is believed to purify the room and deter malevolent spirits from approaching. Zeynabu was subdued and quiet. She did not appear upset, obeying the instructions of the women around her. They came to show their concern and support, but there were no overt signs of grief.

In *Death Without Weeping*, Nancy Scheper-Hughes (1992) reveals in searing realism circumstances in which mother love can be suppressed. This is manifested in the absence of grief in the face of "natural" and expected death. Fulbe children, like the Brazilian children of the Alto, are never far from death. However, Fulbe parents do feel grief and do mourn their lost children. But social conventions put strict limits on the public expression of grief, so that flaunting one's loss openly is an embarrassment and, if prolonged, can lead to the flamboyant mourner's being discredited as an unbalanced person in the eyes of the community.

The case of Daada May'do exemplifies a deviation from the required acceptance of death in Fulbe culture. She is a victim of an untimely death that has robbed her of the comfortable rest, which mothers of sons expect in their old age. She vacillates between frustration and self-pity. Her son died suddenly in the middle of his life, leaving his family destitute. His wives and children, his mother and his mother's sister—all had depended on him for their well-being. Presently, his mother and aunt live with his senior wife, who chose to stay with her children. "The green fruit has fallen from the tree before the ripe fruit," Daada May'do intones, wringing her hands. She complains to me every time I see her. As she talks about her disabilities—her blindness, her deafness—her voice is habitually fixed in a half-cry; life has betrayed her. Her lot is suffering. When I ask about the health of the children of the compound, she says, "There is no sickness, but there is no health either." There is no doubt but that Daada May'do, mother of a dead son, deviates significantly from the Fulbe ideal of acceptance. But her status as *puldebbo* (old woman) does exempt her from the opprobrium that usually follows from such deviation. The tragic nature of the untimely death also leads others to tolerate her excessive outbursts. "Her story is finished," my Fulbe friends would say. "She will never have more children." Unlike a younger woman who can hope to have more children, Daada May'do is fated to live out her days "alone." Still, I believe that her effusive grief would not be tolerated in a man or in a younger woman.

There was, thus, no public indulgence for young Salaamatu's grief over her daughter Hawwa'u's death. Hawwa'u died when I was gone over the holidays. "Precisely three months and sixteen days ago," she tells me when I ask her how long she had been grieving. The baby was eleven months old. "She was very sick for one day and she died Saturday, while her siblings were at the *kilo* (height and weight clinic) at the hospital." "What were her symptoms?" I ask. "She was throwing up and having diarrhea Friday. Saturday she was breathing very heavily and with difficulty. She didn't sleep at all Friday night. She died Saturday." Salaamatu spoke to me of her struggle to continue living her life since the loss of her baby:

> *I haven't been well since she died. My breasts were heavy with milk, and the milk went back inside my body. They swelled up and became infected, like* caayoori *(an infection), and I got a fever and had no strength. Since then, I don't feel like eating. I have to force myself to eat a little millet and sauce. I haven't been to the* maayo *(river) once since her death. My children go, each bringing a dish full of water at a time. I don't have the strength.*
>
> *I don't go out. I don't feel like being among people at all. I just want to stay here. People say I am thinking too much—that is what is making me sick. But I say so be it.*

Salaamatu's shock may have been aggravated by a mother's guilt that she was not attentive enough to her daughter's sickness. "When my daughter Hawwa'u died, I was taken by surprise. I had been worried about (my son) Annur." Hawwa'u's illness didn't last more than twenty-four hours. Salaamatu is sick with a grief that cannot be publicly acknowledged. Weeks after her loss, people expect her to pull herself together and return to her normal concerns and responsibilities, but her feelings are not so easily confined or hidden.

Parents' Affection Toward Their Children

My research assistant complained to me one day about his neighbors' reaction to the photos of his family that I had given him several weeks earlier. He told me that he doesn't like to walk around the neighborhood with Hammadu, his baby boy, anymore. "People talk. They've started saying, 'Look at how he likes his baby.

He holds him all the time. He loves his child too much!'" People talked about the photos of him and the baby, and they accused him of loving his baby too much. "I don't care, I like to hold my kids. I didn't hold the first one so much, but Hurrey, Jaliya, and Goggo—I held them all. In the old days, a man would never be seen holding a child. They found it shameful. The old men find it shameful *(cemtudum)*, but we young men don't give a damn. We walk around with our babies, hold them, play with them. Still, I don't like to have them talking about me."

Bakari's concerns illustrate the strong social pressure on Fulbe fathers to maintain a certain emotional distance from their children, at least in public. My snapshots of him, taken in the intimacy of his home, show him displaying too much affection for his children. The very nature of photographs, changing hands beyond the family compound, made it possible to betray intimate moments between father and child to those who might judge him harshly.

Such notions about parents' emotional restraint are not limited to fathers. A mother's affection for her children, too, is strongly constrained by beliefs about the pathogenic power of the maternal gaze. The crippling and sometimes fatal nature of sickness caused by mothers' love is discussed in chapter five. Like grief, excessive affection for one's children is not to be expressed publicly.

Excessive Laughter and Happiness

> *It is good (to celebrate), but you will have to think about death from time to time. So then, if you dance a lot, it is because you have forgotten, you have forgotten death.*
>
> **Bakari**

These words encapsulate the contradiction for the Fulbe between celebrating with total abandon and the acceptance of death. The Fulbe view stands in stark contrast to the American injunction to "have fun!" In America, at least in the middle-class America I'm most familiar with, "having fun" means engaging in an activity that is divorced from the daily problems of living and engaging in it without asking questions, without doubts, without distance. This is precisely the state of mind that does not remember death. It is for this reason that Fulbe (and American) attitudes toward dancing and celebration are critical to understanding their ambivalence toward (and our devotion to) passionate love. The following statement from Bakari links the abandonment of laughter with the forgetting of both God and death.

> *Among Muslims, even to laugh out loud, a full-throated laugh, is a sin. What pleasure do you have in this world? Death is here. What joy could you have in this world to laugh so much? To be very happy, that is bad,*

so far as to forget God. This is the reason why, among us, you cannot see a true Muslim dancing.

Fulbe people associate dancing with being out of one's mind. This may be due in part to the presence of neighboring groups who practice ecstatic dancing, trance, and spirit possession. Fulbe people have lived for centuries in contact with Hausa in northern Nigeria and have certainly witnessed or heard of the Hausa Bori cult (Masquelier 2001). Fulbe religious scholars are adamantly against practices that induce trance or possession. In the area of Domaayo itself, Fulbe villagers can, and do, witness the "shameless" dancing of their Tupuri neighbors.

Fulbe experiences with mind-altering drugs also relate to beliefs about dancing. Although Fulbe norms discourage *wuykere* (drunkenness) of any kind, whether caused by alcohol, marijuana, or glue, these drugs are far from rare in Domaayo. Those known to be habitual tobacco or marijuana smokers were shunned by Fulbe elders who refused to share meals with them. But glue sniffing was alarmingly common during the late 1990s, especially among young men in their teens and twenties. My friend Rabiyatu told me about one of these drugs. "You will hallucinate. If you take it, you will spend all day dancing, Helen. *(A wuykan. To a modi a nyallan wamugo Helen.)*" She suggests that dancing proves the influence of the drug on you; that your sense of *hakkilo* (judgment) is impaired, and one's behavior is not tempered by the usual restraint or sense of propriety. Moreover, Rabiyatu's assertion that one "will spend all day dancing" illustrates that the drug does not induce a momentary lapse of reason but one that lasts throughout the day. Excessive happiness, expressed through laughter or dancing, is frowned upon because it involves a denial of death.

Shame

Semteende means alternatively shame, embarrassment, modesty, respect, and deference. Shame is different from all the other emotions. It is the only emotion that is expected to influence public behavior. The Fulfulde dictionary offers the following range of meanings:

> semtugo: *to have restraint, discretion* (pudeur*); semtugo go'd'do: to have respect for someone; a semti: to have shame, to be humiliated; cemtu'dum: to be shameful; semteego: to be respected, to be worthy of respect, to be respectable; semteende: restraint, reserved discretion, shame; semtingo: to make some one ashamed; semtindirgo: to have respect for each other (adapted from Noye 1989:310).*

Semteende is a socially validated emotion. A person is never said to have too much shame. It moves the individual to act correctly, in accordance with the code of behavior. Interestingly, it is both physically experienced in the individual body and shaped by culturally specific rules. Abu-Lughod (1986;1993b) has written extensively about the Awlad 'Ali concept of *hasham* and the complex linkages among modesty, ethics, and power exemplified by it. Many of the things she says about *hasham* could also be said about *semteende*. *Hasham* is demonstrated before strangers and before those with greater authority, one's superiors in the Bedouin social hierarchy. Yet, Bedouin people think of *hasham* as being actively performed or given by those with self-respect. Since it is freely given, it does not erode the honor of those who choose to give it to their superiors. This makes it possible for those with less power to show deference toward those with greater power without losing their sense of autonomy and self-respect.

Semteende not only prevents the individual from acting inappropriately (such as stealing someone's millet), it also moves the individual to action (for example, to sweep the entire compound every day). There is a culturally specific view of what causes shame/embarrassment, and individuals act to avoid it whenever possible. That the Fulbe talk as if not everyone shares the same capacity to feel shame/embarrassment complicates matters. This is sometimes discussed as an individual's obstinate refusal to acknowledge social rules (defiance) and sometimes as an individual's innate inability to experience shame and to display the restraint prompted by the anticipation of shame. Shamelessness is alternatively willful or innate. Sometimes an entire lineage or neighborhood is said to be lacking in this emotion. Remembering the time when Mal Juulde was caught with his neighbor's wife while the husband was away on a trip, a member of another lineage remarked, "*Asli fuh 'be ngalaa semteende*"(All of them in that lineage have no shame). "These people do not feel the dryness in their eyes (*jaaral giite*). They are shameless. *('Be cemtata.)*" The image of eyes that do not feel dry is related to the bodily expression of shamelessness—staring without blinking. Staring suggests both the absence of deference (expressed by averting the eyes) and an inordinate desire for what the eyes are seeing. Here, Mal Juulde and his people are said to show by their actions that they are not moved by the emotion of *semteende*. They do things without blinking, without misgivings, where others would be constrained by their experience of shame.

THE BODILY EXPRESSION OF COMMUNITY VALUES IN EVERYDAY DISCOURSE

Fulbe social life is permeated by expressions of balance and temperance (*hakkilo*) as well as patience and tolerance (*munyal*). The ceremonial greetings that are exchanged daily between all villagers are primarily selfless expressions of membership

Semteende

and participation in the community, and through these expressions men and
women (they are only exchanged between adults) show that they are aware of each
other's condition in the world. Villagers do this by asking about one another's family
members, as specifically as possible, (for example, asking about someone's health, if
he is known to have been sick). So by asking specific questions about the quality of a
person's life and of that of "his people," one shows knowledge of his situation. The
answers given, however, are not themselves necessarily informative. Unless the two
individuals exchanging greetings are intimate friends, the person asked about his
health will always answer "*Jam koo'dume* (Everything's fine)," even if he has malaria
at the moment. If a mother is asked about a child's illness, she will say "*Daama*
(much better)" even if the child is not. Again, this is an expression of restraint and of
self-control. A sick man does not discuss his sickness at every opportunity in an attempt to gain sympathy. Men's greetings to each other were consistently self-effacing
in this way. As if the maxim were: "Show concern for and an awareness of the other,
but do not draw attention to yourself." As Riesman explained for the Fulbe of
Burkina Faso, the greetings also indicate that "whatever messiness there is in my life
is under control; I am a social being. I am one of you" (Riesman 1975:52).

Fulbe gestures and body language also express the Fulbe ideal of the poised, balanced, composed individual, who is always aware of those around him. The Fulbe stride is slow, smooth, flowing, and steady. Although women take smaller steps than men, perhaps as a result of the narrow wrap skirts they wear, both sexes can be said to be extremely graceful. My American pace was often ridiculed for its betrayal of impatience and its somewhat frenetic aspect.

People who eat together are extremely aware of each other's movements, taking turns reaching for millet and sauce from a common bowl. There is also an eating posture children are taught when they begin to eat solid food. While eating, the left leg is pulled up to the chest with the foot resting flat on the ground so that one leans on the left thigh, with the right leg folded on the ground under the left. The left arm is inactive, while the right hand moves for eating. Moving back from the bowl and the washing of one's hands are the gestures that decisively signal satiety. Merely slowing down or skipping a few turns of reaching into the bowl may only signal that one feels that one should not eat anymore. It is tentative, and that person can usually be persuaded to eat a little more. I was startled several times when a host would anticipate my thirst and offer me water during a meal when I didn't ask for it. I gradually realized that my eyes were betraying my desires. I was looking at the water, thinking of asking for it but not wanting to interrupt the conversation, and my host, noticing the direction of my gaze, handed me the water. This suggests a tremendous sensitivity to guests and interest in showing awareness of their needs, as well as showing a keen awareness of the relationship between looking and wanting.

Gestures also express relations of power that require deference and modesty (*semteende*). Fathers and sons avoid eye contact. The chief's courtiers face away from him when he is holding court, even as they carry on a discussion. Women veil (by draping a scarf over their head and shoulders) in front of men other than their husbands. They remove their shoes as they walk by a group of seated adult men. A woman never calls her first husband by his name, even years later, if she has divorced and remarried. Her first husband remains the one who made her a woman. Similarly, a man never pronounces the name of his first born, the child which makes him a full adult, a father of someone. To address his first child, he uses a nickname instead. Fulbe adults are usually referred to as *Baaba Muusa*, or father of Muusa, *Daada Aisatu*, or mother of Aisatu, and so on. Through the orientation of the body, eye contact, veiling, and terms of address, Fulbe people are constantly showing deference/shame for people with power in their lives.

THE MADNESS OF EXCESS

Married men are said to love their wives "too much" when they spend an inordinate amount of time at home when they should be socially engaged with their peers in the male social spaces, such as the main street or the mosque. Women who love their husbands "too much" may be excessively jealous of co-wives or potential co-wives. Generally, people in love tend to flout the rules of availability to peers and deference to elders. Their obsession is compared to the madness caused by spirit possession.

To engage fully in a feeling—be it grief, pain, anger, happiness—is an obscene thing. It is possession. It is a loss of reason or sense and therefore, madness. In this way, Fulbe thinking resembles medieval Islamic medical thought on passionate love, or *'ishq*. The medieval Islamic scholar and philosopher Ibn al-Jawzi condemns *'ishq*: "It exceeds the limit of mere inclination and (normal) love by possessing the reason and causes its victim to act unwisely; it is blameworthy and ought to be avoided by the prudent" (Dols 1992:319). Medical textbooks used passionate love to illustrate the relationship between psychic and bodily ailments. "Human interest in the subject was such that lovesickness also became a favorite topic of popular writers." The story of Qays and Lila and their ill-fated love became a classic in Islamic literature, like Romeo and Juliet in Europe. Both stories tell of star-crossed lovers, but the Islamic tale paints Qays as a "Majnun," a madman. "The customary view is that his madness was a consequence of his ardent love" (Dols:332).

In the same way, the contemporary Fulbe person who loses his or her *hakkilo*, or social sense, to an overpowering emotion will act unwisely. Any emotion, when taken up obsessively, makes a person unavailable to peers, less than fully respectful of elders, contemptuous of convention, and forgetful of death (and of God). "If there is death, there is no pleasure." That is, there is no total pleasure; no passion that is allowed to possess the personality. The literature on love-madness makes clear that there is a resonance between Islamic notions of temperance and emotionality and specifically Fulbe notions of personhood. Love-madness in medieval Islam reveals a stance toward emotions that is consistent with Fulbe views.

In summary, Fulbe discourse about their relation to the community in the language of posture, gesture, and ceremonial greeting continually reiterates the healthy individual's availability to fellow villagers and his or her respect for the power of others. The individual affirms both an egalitarian and hierarchical social order in his or her everyday bodily discourse.

THE GENDERING OF PULAAKU AND THE SICK ROLE

Both men and women value the Fulbe code of moral behavior known as *pulaaku*. Yet, clearly, women and men are situated differently in respect to *pulaaku*. Menstruation, pregnancy, childbirth, and breast-feeding implicates them in the *intentionality of the body* (Merleau Ponty 1962). Women's bodies do things which are beyond conscious control. Their effluences of milk and blood speak of an absence of the bodily restraint, which is available to men. A woman who is breast-feeding her infant may notice her milk seeping into the fabric of her blouse. Women who are having their menstrual periods are said to be "washing" (their menstrual cloths). Significantly, it is these same fluids which symbolize women's reproductive power. Both milk and blood are believed to be dangerous to a woman's husband, who is expected to keep a respectful distance from substance imbued with such life force. Fulbe people thus consider it "normal" that women in their childbearing years are less likely to display bodily self-restraint. Finally, because married women must defer to their husbands, they cannot easily entertain the notion of self-mastery in the same way as men.

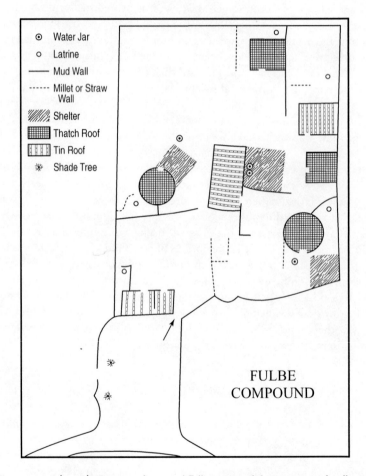

A Fulbe compound (saare). Drawing of an actual Fulbe compound showing principal walls and structures. Most socializing is done under thatch shelters or in front of the entrance, under the canopy of the shade trees. Drawing by Clifford Duplechin. Adapted from an original drawing by Jim Charbonnet.

It follows that the "loss of control" inherent in sickness affects women and men differently. It is men who must continually show that they are deserving of deference by showing, not only that they are masters of themselves, but also that they are capable of providing for their families. Riesman (1992:64) illustrates this phenomenon for the Fulbe of Burkina Faso with the following proverb: "Dad came home, we went to bed without any dinner. Dad left, we went to bed without any dinner. When he dies people will cry out of pity and familiarity only; there's no use in him." He explains: "The force of this proverb is all the greater when we realize that it is a man's ability to take care of the needs of his family (and other dependents) that justifies his dominance over them in the first place. Several people told me that, "There are two who do not know 'I don't have any'—your wife and child. They will just say you refused" (Riesman 1992:64). Men must show that they are worthy of respect by the consistent performance of *pulaaku* and by their effective provisioning of their families. Debilitating sickness undercuts both bases for male dominance simultaneously.

Although men are particularly reluctant to take on the sick role, the expression of pain and need is not unproblematic for women. Women gain negotiating power in their marriages precisely to the extent that they make themselves indispensable to their husbands, as mothers/chief caretakers of his children, as providers of water, food-processing, and cooking, and as virtuous women, whose deference to their husbands' honor gives them prestige. When sickness prevents them from performing this work for their husbands, women lose legitimacy and security in their husbands' home. It is partly for this reason that women often return to their natal families ("their *own* people") during serious illness.

The difficulty for women in taking on the sick role by manifesting pain and need is evidenced in this story of a divorced and childless woman, who is ashamed to beg for aspirin:

> Kajjilde is not yet an old woman; she just looks that way because she is
> miserable and half-dead with fatigue. . . . When she speaks, the whine
> in her voice tells you instantly that she has a sad story to tell, if anyone
> would listen. Perhaps two days out of three she has a headache. She is
> ashamed to ask for aspirin, yet her sense of shame is not strong enough
> to prevent her from asking anyway. Perhaps that is what the whine
> means; it is a combination of shame and pain. Proper Fulbe don't re-
> veal their pain. She feels degraded (Riesman 1992:95).

It is implied in Riesman's analysis that this woman's childlessness in a marriage to a man whose other wife had borne him many children placed her in a fundamentally precarious position in the world and eventually led to her divorce. The chronic headaches are possibly induced by this source of constant stress in her life. In the moment of asking for aspirin, the pain of the headache is compounded by the shame of revealing her vulnerability to pain. The ailment is magnified by its acknowledgment. Furthermore, her begging for aspirin reveals her general dependency on charity for food and clothing, because she is divorced, childless, and without surviving male patrilineal relatives. It is exemplary of her general condition in life, one which, as she ages, is increasingly unlikely to change. A married woman or a woman with surviving male relatives could look within her family for aspirin or the money to buy it with. She would be unlikely to broadcast to the world her general dependency and helplessness, as her own social standing depends on her men's ability to provide for her.

The Fulbe ideal of *pulaaku*—self-mastery or self restraint—emphatically requires control over one's self-expression and one's body. The full acceptance of being sick and taking on the sick role requires an admission that one is not (or no longer) in control of one's body. This embarrassing fact is all the more distressing because it is impossible to take on the sick role privately. To prevent certain people from knowing about this is not possible, because as soon as a man fails to go out of the *saare,* or to leave his house, or to get up from bed, or to go to the market as usual, or to go to the fields—the word will begin to circulate. His neighbors, his close relatives and his fellow villagers will come to see him. To take on the sick role for a man is to be gravely ill. Days are counted, and the longer this goes on the more people are coming from other villages to see him. Relatives who have not come are sent for. People come to show concern, to be sociable, to inquire about the symptoms and circumstances of the sickness, to ask what remedies have already been tried and to offer possible alternative diagnoses and remedies. Close kin stay nearby and care for the patient, reflecting on the visitors' comments and repeating them to others. The immediate family sifts through the information and compare the discourses of each visitor, past and present. If there is a relative known to have expertise in treating "this sort of thing," he or she will be called. Other specialists that are nonrelatives may be called in succession. Every possibility, diagnostic and therapeutic, is considered. The patient is greeted, questioned, engaged in conversation, and watched, never to be left alone. He is discussed in the third person (in his presence) without restraint. This is commonly done to children and anthropologists, but not usually to sentient adults. Finally, the most unsavory bodily processes are analyzed in detail without so much as a grimace. Once again, this would be normal for children (and animals) but not for adults. What emerges from this lack of deference for the sick person is a temporary loss of personhood.

In these circumstances, it is not surprising that many sick people go to considerable trouble to avoid the sick role, as the following excerpt from my field notes can attest:

> *Bakari's* pa'booje *(malaria) is still not over. During these two weeks, Bakari did not miss one day of work or one meeting. He says he does*

not wish to stay home, though he would like to rest. "If I stay home, my
mother will tell everyone, and all my neighbors and relatives and old
women from all over the village will come to see me. Will I get any rest?
No, I won't get any rest! So I prefer to come here (to the anthropologist's
house) where no one will bother me."

Bakari was not reluctant to seek medical treatment from a health clinic or
nurse, but he sought to do this without letting his mother realize that he was
seriously ill. Quinimax, an injectable form of a quinine derivative, is an expensive treatment by village standards but known to be very effective in malaria
treatment. Someone without the resources to purchase medicine would have to
make their illness public in order to solicit resources. A married woman would
certainly try to get her husband's help in paying for the medicine and would
thus be encouraged to "act sick" in order to have her complaints taken seriously. Men seem to avoid making their sickness public in order to avoid announcing their weakness and vulnerability to a world in which strength and
autonomy are prerequisites for respect and social authority. In this context, it is
interesting to notice how women talk about men's illnesses as being more serious than they let on:

> *Ubbo, the chief's mother and my host for a year, talked to me about the*
> *condition of her brother, Oumarou. "He has a toothache. He has had it*
> *for one week. It stopped him from going to the Djigilaw market today."*
> *"Also," says Ubbo "He has pewri cukku. Asthma. He refuses to go to the*
> *hospital for it. I have begged and begged him to go. But you can't physi-*
> *cally force a grown man to go to the hospital."*

Her complaint that she cannot force her brother to go implies that he has no
more sense than a child with respect to what is good for his health. His refusal is
interpreted as headstrong or willful, rather than wise. In fact, his refusal may be
due to his belief that hospital medicine is not useful in treating asthma, or to a
judgment that he simply can't afford it. Many people perceive the clinic's medical
practitioners as being inconsiderate of cost of medicines. "They write you (prescriptions) that you cannot afford." Women were acutely aware of this problem
with hospital medicine, but the issue affected them differently than their husbands.
Women, who received costly prescriptions could complain about the insensitive
nurse or blame their husbands for being unwilling or unable to spend the money.
But men who were given costly prescriptions may have felt that their economic
power was inadequate. They were made to feel impotent, unable to meet what
presents itself as a basic need. Categorical refusal to call on the clinical medical system for particular illnesses was a radical strategy to avoid being made impotent by
that system.

Although several men adopted this stance toward biomedicine, most men I knew simply avoided seeking treatment until an illness became serious. An illness became weighty when it prevented a man from performing his normal work. As my friend Muusa explained to me about his nasty cold: "Since it does not prevent me from walking around, I don't want to be bothered with a remedy." Men have more to lose by flouting *pulaaku*, and they have more to lose by taking on the sick role than women do. It could be argued that men are the most reluctant to take on the sick role because it requires for them a greater deviation from normal behavior. Particularly, it fundamentally changes their relation to social space. They are confined to the *saare* (compound) and deprived of their usual male company in the public spaces they normally move through; and this clear-cut contrast from normal behavior means that their sickness is more quickly noticed and broadcast.

I often heard parents coaching their children in the appropriate responses. During my interviews about health and illness, mothers nudged their children to answer my questions in the Fulbe way:

> *(Field notes, July 1990). A little boy has been sick for several days. He has pimples on his skin and fever, a headache, and a cold. His eyes are also red and dull. He plays a little, then runs home in pain. His mother teaches him pulaaku. "Now aren't you better, Hammadu. Aren't you feeling daama?" "Hmmh," he answers without enthusiasm.*

The denial of illness is a part of everyday life for the Fulbe adult. Everyone has pain, hunger and suffering. But to acknowledge need is to ask for help; to admit the limits of one's independence. And this too is shameful. In practice the reality of disability is socially negotiated, and an individual's claims to special consideration due to hardship is not always met with the most serious or sympathetic response, as the following passage from my field notes illustrates:

> *Mal Bakari, a neighbor of Sarki, is telling me that his back is hurting him. Standing in his neighbor's entrance hall where the women are gathered to weave their baskets and tend their stores of kola nuts, tea, and sugar, he explains that he has suffered from back pain since he fell off his bicycle as a child. The women at Sarki's laugh. "His pain comes from his night work (kuugal jemma)." General laughter. He protests. "A man with four wives doesn't have a backache like this. He gets up in the morning like this (demonstrating a sprightly walk bouncing with energy and vitality)." More laughter. "But my back hurts so much I can't straighten up sometimes. Only after walking around awhile can I stand straight. It's a different sort of back ache."*

Sarki's wives, who are, significantly, four in number, turn his pitiful complaint of back pain into a story of sexual prowess. Chronic pain, in this perspective, suggests an active sex life characterized as "night work." They jokingly transform his disability into masculine privilege. But he refuses their interpretation, insisting that a man with four wives (such as *their* husband, he implies) walks with enthusiasm, while *he* has trouble even getting around in the morning.

CONCLUSION

I have shown how Fulbe concepts of personhood and *pulaaku* shape the display and concealment of emotions and feelings. On one hand, they contribute to specific definitions of normalcy and madness. When strong feelings prevent an individual from acting according to his *hakkilo*, or social sense, he is said to be mad. On the other hand, the Fulbe understanding of adult personhood and autonomy rests on the performance of *pulaaku*. One who publicly fails to master his feelings or bodily processes ceases to be regarded as an autonomous Fulbe person. The taking on of the sick role, then, by involving the individual in the care of his or her family, dramatizes the loss of autonomy and normal personhood, which the sickness causes. The performance of the sick role, like the performance of *pulaaku*, is gendered, with the result that men are considerably more reluctant to take on the sick role than women. It confines men to the female social space of the *saare*. And it requires the graphic discussion of his bodily processes by relatives and neighbors, who speak of him in the third person, as if he had no social sense. If the illness is prolonged, he must endure the embarrassment of being cared for by his relatives, while being unable to provide for them economically, again failing in his role as a Fulbe man. Although women also suffer from the loss of personhood implied in the sick role, they have the possibility of returning home to their natal kin and distancing themselves, at least, from their marital responsibility. With such cultural constructions of personhood, normalcy, and the sickness, is it surprising that men and women have completely different ways of voicing complaints?

In the next chapter, the differences in men's and women's experiences are explored through an examination of their narratives about marriage. Men and women have distinctive ways of talking about their lives, fortune, well-being, scarcity, and dis-ease. What emerges here is the tremendous degree of segregation between men and women and the polarization of male and female worlds.

3

On Cheap Cloth, Bad Sauce, and the Fragility of Marriage

Women are spirits. If you want to construct a shelter, you have to ask your wife whether to put it here or there. You build it in the place of the spirits. A shelter, no matter what you do, is a thing of the spirits. It won't last. But a house, you should put in the opposite place (from the one she chooses). That will tell you which is the true place. (Do wi'ete pelel gonga.) They play with rocks (practice divination). If your wife tells you something, you must not repeat it, or they will laugh at you. They are lies. It is a lie. One who believes the talk of a woman is also a woman. (Tokkido haala debbo boo debbo.)

    Bad sauce. Isn't that a sickness? It is terribly bitter. It will hurt your stomach. It is simply a sickness. Tasi'ba and cukkuri and water. My stomach burns until it lights up like a fire. Meat and butter, these are what is lacking.

Both of these passages reflect the profound feelings of ambivalence and antagonism, which Fulbe men and women express about marriage. The first statement, "women are spirits," is a man's expression about his need to be vigilant: he should never to listen to his wife, or at least never to repeat something she has said to him. Women's choices are misleading, their words false. Things associated with women, like shelters made of millet stalks and slender wood, vulnerable to the wind, rain and termites, are by their nature ephemeral. They are not built to last. By implication, perhaps marriages too are evanescent. One shouldn't become attached to them. They can crumble into dust or collapse without warning. Unlike a house, which might last thirty years if built properly, shelters provide shade and a cool breezy place for sharing a meal and conversation, but they do not protect from severe weather.

The second expression is less transparent. What does bad sauce have to do with marriage? Sauce (*haako*) is a central element in a Fulbe meal. It is the complement to the *nyiiri*, or millet porridge, which is dipped into it. Hawwa, the woman quoted in this paragraph is complaining about a sauce so ill-tasting that it in fact makes her sick, causing her acute stomach pain. Perhaps it is the acidity of the *tasi'ba* leaves, which aggravates her condition. The *cukkuri*, or potash, is a poor-person's attempt to balance the acidity of the leaf sauce when oil and meat are unavailable. But perhaps this is taking her complaint too literally. After all, who is responsible for bad sauce? The provider of the ingredients? The cook? Discord or bitterness between the two?

Paul Stoller and Cheryl Olkes (1986) have written about the discursive power of bad sauce for the Songhai of Niger. Serving an inedible sauce for dinner after everyone had raved about the savory sauce she had prepared for lunch, a young Songhai woman made everyone notice her ability to act in spite of the constraints in her social environment. She let them know in the most tangible way possible that she could have a very palpable affect on their world. The sauce in question was also a very specific expression of her sour disappointment that Stoller and Olkes did not lend her any money.

I don't know whether Hawwa's distress was due to such a specific complaint. Among the Fulbe, bad sauce is contrasted to savory sauces, which are said to be "sweet" tasting (see also Masquelier 1995). The idiom of sweetness can be used to speak of an agreeable or popular person, of happiness or flattery in seeking the favors of a woman, or causing joy or pleasure (Noye 1989:377). In this case, taste can be seen to be related to goodwill as well as wealth (the ability to provide savory ingredients) and skill (knowledge of cooking techniques). The first utterance, then, is a representative example of men's generalizing discourse about women. It stands in sharp contrast to women's particularistic, and usually oblique, complaints about the condition of their lives—and ultimately of their husbands.

CHEAP CLOTH

The following complaint is revealing about how Fulbe women experience polygyny (cultural rule that men can marry more than woman at a time) and marital insecurity. In Fulbe culture, it is considered acceptable (and may be desirable) for a man to marry more than one woman at a time, but he is under a special obligation under Islamic law to make sure that he treats his wives equally. Because equality in human relationships is elusive, some have argued, the Islamic rule may be read as an argument for monogamy. In any case, Fulbe husbands' obligation to provide for their wives materially means that polygynous men labor under significant material constraints at the same time that they seek to walk an emotional tightrope between potentially jealous partners. Hawwa's two-year marriage to Yaya has yet to produce any children. Her children from a previous marriage live with their father in Chad. Her childlessness in this marriage is a cause for concern. It makes her marriage to Yaya fundamentally insecure. This is aggravated by the presence of her co-wife, Hurey, whose long-term marriage to Yaya has produced many children. Hawwa complains about her co-wife, who seems intent on keeping her at arm's length:

> That woman. There is no understanding between us. (Narral wooda.)
> She is always starting trouble with me. Her children are many. She has
> been with him for a long time. She doesn't want anyone else to be here.
> We quarrel and quarrel. (Min jokkira. Min jokkira. Min jokkira.) She
> doesn't want anything to do with conversation. (O yida haala ngew-
> tugo.) She is always insulting me.
>   She won't eat with me. If she has prepared, she eats with her kids.
> (All of them!) I eat all by myself. If I want company, I go out to talk to
> Juleyia and them (women in the neighboring compound). But in this
> compound, I talk to no one.

Hawwa's security in this marriage is tenuous. Her childlessness in this *saare* (family compound) and in this marriage influences every aspect of her experience. She eats alone, while her co-wife eats with her many children. She has no one to send on errands. Her negotiating power is limited because she has no children to worry her husband when she leaves him to visit her parents. What is more, she worries about the fate of the children she might bear him since he already has so many to support:

> "If you have lots of money and lots of kids, they will grow (and survive
> through childhood) (mawnan). But if you have many children and no
> money, isn't that bad? It is better in town," she added, as if town meant
> money and the village (kaywe) meant poverty. "Cheap cloth (abada).
> These wrappers have a wrong side (nyo'i)."

Cloth in Domaayo is subject to a complex ranking system and is a powerful medium of communication about wealth, social status, and affection. All women in Domaayo wear blouses and wrappers, or wrap skirts, which are custom made from a six-yard-length of cloth, known as *wure*. The gift of a wure to one's wife is a yearly obligation for husbands in this community, and a suitcase filled with several lengths of cloth is the essential component of the wedding gifts a groom must offer his bride. The quantity, quality, and price of the cloth selected for inclusion in the suitcase are a central topic of discussion around a village wedding. As Hawwa reminded me, a suitcase full of cheap cloth can make a full-grown woman cry.

At the recent wedding in the neighborhood, Juleyia, the bride's mother, was overcome with emotion. "*O 'don wooka*. She wailed!" In the bridal valise on display at the bride's mother's saare were several Cameroonian prints, but none of the more highly valued "wax" cloths manufactured in Nigeria, Holland, and Indonesia. Juleyia was particularly upset because the value of the cloth not only speaks of the groom's poverty but of his opinion of the bride and her family. She and her daughter were both being insulted or slighted by these poor gifts. Yet she did not send the suitcase back to the groom, refusing the offer of marriage. Juleyia's daughter was "growing up too quickly" and needed to be married off. Perhaps Juleyia was concerned that her daughter might become pregnant before getting married, so it was necessary to act quickly. Without a better offer forthcoming, she had to marry a poor man. If only a few "genuine wax" cloths had been included, the mother of the bride might have found the wedding valise more tolerable, but the conspicuous absence of any of these suggested that the groom did not find it necessary to compliment the bride's family with good cloth.

Cheap cloth, like bad sauce, is an evocative symbol of hardship for Fulbe women. Its crude designs, mechanically imprinted on the cloth, only appear clearly on one side of the cloth, and they wash out quickly. The more highly valued wax prints permeate the cloth, so that its designs are equally visible on both sides. The color and clarity of the design resists numerous washings, and some patterns even appear to improve with age. Cloth not only makes up an important component of the groom's wedding gifts to his bride and her family, but it also constitutes a husband's minimal obligatory annual gift to his wife or wives. A husband's failure to provide his wife with one length of cloth (usually for the feast ending the month of Ramadan) can be grounds for divorce. The quality and beauty of this cloth varies widely, and many women may receive much more. As women visit each other to offer greetings on the holiday, wearing their newly sewn outfits, their husbands' economic potency and generosity are publicly displayed and evaluated. By decrying the cheap cloth that the women of Domaayo receive from their husbands, Hawwa insults her marital home and, indirectly, her current husband. She criticizes her husband for producing so many children without being able or willing to spend money on them. As the second wife in this already large household, she worries about her ability to secure resources for herself and for the children she may have with him. For the moment, she has second-rate cloth, a mean woman for a co-wife, and no children of her own.

POLARIZED WORLDS

Writing about the lives of women and men in a society deeply segregated by gender, I share with many ethnographers the desire to avoid the arrogance and ethnocentrism of Western feminism, which has often been judgmental of gender relations in non-western societies (Abbenyi 1997, Abu-Lughod 1993, Behar 1995, Boddy 1989, Cole 1991, Raheja and Gold 1994, and others). Framing women's discursive practices solely as protest and resistance sometimes has the effect of reifying male dominance. The work of Michel Foucault cautions against too easily locating power in one social space, group or person. Power is more diffuse and works through a great variety of practices. Fulbe women have taught me that power can be exercised through such seemingly insignificant acts as cooking, through particularly ways of using clothing and through speech, as well as in formal political institutions, laws, offices, and administrations. Janice Boddy, in her study of women's spirit practices in northern Sudan, has written that "within Hofriyat, there exists no controlling hegemonic group, only the fiction of one—men. (And they, contrary to appearances) are equally subject to cultural constraint and no freer than women to alter the fundamental conditions of their existence" (1989:185).

Fulbe men and women inhabit highly polarized worlds. Not only are they routinely segregated in social space, but they have remarkably different ways of talking about their lives, marriage, fortune, scarcity, well-being, and dis-ease. In this chapter, I aim to show how Fulbe men and women talk about marriage and about each other. Male privilege and dominance over their spouses is seemingly ensured with patrilineal and patrilocal patterns as well as by Islamic legal traditions that give men the right to marry up to four wives, to divorce, and to require wives to be secluded. In practice, however, women have considerable influence on their husbands and their own quality of life. They assert their autonomy through an evocative discourse of complaints that reminds women themselves as well as their husbands that they may also leave and seek happier marriages elsewhere. Through their complaints women build dyadic relations of sympathy, affection, and reciprocity, upon which they may draw in times of need.

FERTILITY AND SEXUALITY

I learned of the significance of marital status for women very early in my stay in Domaayo. Still learning to speak Fulfulde, I spent most of my days visiting women in their family compounds (*saare*), talking and taking notes, and gradually expanding my vocabulary. However, one woman, Diddi, spoke some French and invited me to come back and visit her. I discovered that she was a pleasure to talk to. She had a wonderful wry sense of humor and an independence of spirit that I admired. And I found it a great relief to be able to speak French with her, after a long day of Fulfulde lessons in Domaayo's saares. It was Diddi who first outlined for me the rules that govern Fulbe marriages. For instance, a woman cannot call her husband by his name, but he can call her by her name. She was aware of these rules, and could speak about them, almost with an outsider's perspective. I was living with Dija and her family at the time and whenever I returned home from a day of visiting, they would ask me to relate to them who I had seen for news from their households. I usually ate the evening meal with Dija, Jaara, and Juleyia (Dija's husband's brother's wives), and whenever I returned from visiting with Diddi, they would make some comment that I didn't understand but that I sensed was negative. They clearly didn't like her and didn't like my going over to her house, but I couldn't understand why. Finally, I pressed them to explain. The called her an *azabaajo*, a term I did not understand. In the flurry of explanations that followed I finally picked out a word I recognized—*bordel* (brothel; in local usage, prostitute). I was stunned. Diddi, my friend, was a prostitute?

Girls and Women: Married, "Free," and "Old"

It was some time before I came to fully comprehend the meaning of bordel, or azabaajo, in the Fulbe context. It refers to one of the four possible structural positions which Fulbe women can occupy. Although there is considerable room for negotiation between these positions, women are nonetheless influenced by these terms of debate. Most Fulbe women live in dramatically different conditions depending on their status: virgin, married woman, free woman, postmenopausal woman. Though the older woman may recall her days as a free woman fondly, the virgin and the young married woman are more likely to view her as a competitor for the attentions and resources of their men. The free woman, *azabaajo* (plural: *azabaa'en*), is a woman who is "between husbands." She is neither secluded nor sexually inexperienced and is thus by definition "available." Some free women derive a considerable proportion of their income from gifts left by their lovers as a token of their appreciation. Others earn their food money by making beignets and selling them on main street. A few, mostly younger women, live obediently with their fathers, while waiting to remarry. They are closely watched and are expected to behave with modesty, deference, and restraint. They might see lovers, but only with the greatest difficulty and in conditions of the utmost secrecy. Often, their behavior is beyond reproach, yet these young divorcées are still called *azabaajo*. Both women and men refer to the sexuality of *azabaa'en* openly and with impunity. The *azabaajo* label describes their liminal status, but not (in many cases) their practice. They are widely regarded as sexually available but many of these women prefer to exercise patience (*munyal*, as Fulbe would put it) in seeking a courtship that might lead to marriage. Those who entertain casual relationships with lovers while maintaining their autonomy are particularly sub-

Family portrait: Diddi (center), an azabaajo, with her brother and his wife.

ject to criticism and are most likely to have their actions labeled *azabaaku*, or prostitution. Practicing *azabaa'en* are viewed as a threat to established relationships of lineage and marriage, yet they may act to reinforce the existing village social order. I often heard them being called "bad" women or shameless women. Ultimately, all divorced women are called *azabaa'en*, regardless of their behavior.

One might imagine that a group of women so negatively portrayed would constitute a small portion of the population. But that does not take into account the high divorce rate among the Fulbe. In a survey of twenty-five women over the age of forty-five, the average number of marriages was 2.6 marriages. This means that women commonly live through two or three marriages and separations (through divorce or death of a spouse) in their lifetimes. Most Fulbe women have the experience of being "between husbands" (and inhabiting the *azabaajo* status) several times. The irony is that every married woman who speaks negatively of *azabaa'en* has likely been or will be an *azabaajo* herself at least once in her life. If she has remarried, however, she is currently benefiting from the respectability afforded by her marital status and has seemingly "forgotten" about her *azabaajo* past. Thus, although the stigma is very real, it is a temporary mark and does not constitute a permanent stain on a woman's reputation.

I was very disturbed by this negative view of divorcées. Though women differ widely in their sexual behavior, all are at one point compared to (if not identified with) the prostitute. The married woman's current status gains meaning from the fact that she is "not an *azabaajo*," whereas the *azabaajo*'s status is defined by the fact that she is "not married." Yet, the *azabaajo* can only be this because she was, perhaps recently, a married woman with all the legitimacy and respectability that status bestows on a woman. The married woman, "not an *azabaajo*" in the moment, is only one divorce away from becoming what she is not.

The asymmetry (or double standard) in gender roles in this respect is striking. Men too, differ widely in their sexual practices, but, as we shall see, their status is defined according to rather different criteria. Although some men may be negatively viewed if their behavior strays from the moral norms, such men are not seen to embody some essential (and negative) quality of manhood. Men sometimes spoke of the *azabaajo* as if she represented the essential woman, stripped of all veils, of all claims to honor, piety and legitimacy. When a free woman engages in *azabaaku*, or prostitution, (for example, has lovers who give her gifts of money, clothes, perfume, or food), this is never seen as morally legitimate, but it seems to be accepted as understandable and even appropriate or somehow "fitting" behavior. Because that is how women *are*. From the perspective of the *azabaajo*, however, each courtier or lover is a potential husband, and therefore a possible means to a life of respectability.

Significantly, there is a widely shared sense that there is a natural progression to a divorcee's experience, which ought to bring her back into the fold of patrilineal structures. There always comes a time when, as my Fulbe friends put it, a woman begins to think about her own death. Then she will put aside her ways and she will remarry. For the Fulbe, the life of a "free woman" (*femme libre*) is a life of sin, for she is assumed to be sexually active, and sex outside of marriage is forbidden. "Prostitutes" are always urged by relatives, friends and acquaintances to remarry, at which time they can begin living according to God's laws once more. Thus, in the same way that every woman is a potential prostitute, so is every prostitute a potential respectable wife, daughter, or mother. The fluidity and immateriality of women's status and of women's character is continually before the eyes of Fulbe men and women. The following conversation (which I have reconstructed from my field notes) between Adda Habiiba and a male admirer illustrates this fluidity:

> *Mal Aadama leaves his* saare *(compound), where his wife is pounding the millet for the evening meal. The afternoon is heavy with the April heat, which tempers every stride, every gesture. On his way to the mosque, where male elders gather to talk in the late afternoon, he passes by the evening market on the main road, where the young virgins and free women have already begun to lay out their goods for sale. Men returning home from the market will buy these treats* (digeege) *to consume with friends or to bring to their families. It is Ramadan, the Muslim month of fasting. Everyone is hungry and thirsty, and dusk is still nearly an hour away.*

Aadama eyes Adda Habiiba, a middle-aged azabaajo (free woman) for whom he has a great deal of admiration. She supports herself and her adopted daughter on what she makes selling beignets. Every day, she is up at three in the morning to mix her dough and to let it rise. By six, she is on the road with her beignets which make up the breakfast of many villagers. During Ramadan, her schedule is eased, as her sales shift to the afternoon, when fasters begin to imagine their next meal and the freshly fried beignets she makes. "Jam 'bandu naa, Adda? (How is it, older sister?)" "Alla woonene Baaba Maamudu. Walla koo'dume. Himbe maa fuh yambe?" "Alhabdulillaahi. Jam ni tawon kam." They exchange the customary greetings. Are you in good health? God's blessings be upon you. Everything is fine. Are your people all fine? etc. "Noy? Adda am. A tammaake bangugo naa? Malli a don tammi? Naa Alla 'don laara kuugal maa? (So, my older sister, aren't you think-ing of getting married? Or are you considering it? Now you know God is watching your work?)"

He teases her about her unmarried status. But Habiiba contests his classification of her. "I am an old woman, father of Maamudu. Don't you know these things for me are finished? I am a puldebbo (an old woman). Now there is only my family and my older brothers. I am happy to live among them and to see their children grow up. What do I want with a man?"

The older brothers in question are actually her father's brother's sons. Patrilateral cousins are classified as "brothers," revealing the continuing signifi-cance of patrilineage in the village. They are the children of her *bappa* (paternal uncles) and she theirs. This makes them *bi'b'be bappaybe* (children of paternal uncles) and thus *derdiraa'be* (siblings).

Adda Habiiba, by calling herself *puldebbo*, was claiming for herself the fourth status of Fulbe womanhood. This term resists translation. What term in English conveys a woman's aging in positive terms? In Fulfulde, *puldebbo* connotes a woman who is a veteran of life's battles (including marriage and motherhood). She is well versed in the difficulties of life and perhaps also knows something about how to overcome them. The English word "crone" is too witchy; "dowa-ger" implies royal status; "matron" suggests physical heft; "matriarch" suggests one who wields power heavy-handedly. "Elder" is the most neutral, but it im-plies masculine gender, and in Africanist ethnography it usually suggests a polit-ical role, as in a council of elders or as an adviser to the chief.

When Adda Habiiba calls herself a *puldebbo*, she claims the only respectable status available to single women. It requires giving up (or graduating from) sex-ual relations with men, and all the entanglements these involve, and confers the legitimacy and respectability that is otherwise only accorded to men. Ideally, a woman would have the ability to become a *puldebbo* as soon as her male children are grown. In the logic of Fulbe patrilineages, a grown son can replace a husband, both as a provider and as a purveyor of legitimacy. Adda Habiiba, without children of her own, asserts her right to live with her brothers' children in the same way. She claims the legitimacy, which she argues is her due as an "old woman," even though she has no children of her own.

In order to fully understand Adda Habiiba's claims, it is necessary to examine the four categories of women's social status in terms that are typically discussed in Domaayo. These four statuses constitute a seemingly rigid structure, which organizes women's experience in this society. In practice, however, these categories serve as a starting point for women's efforts to negotiate their social relations, and to take them at face value would conceal much of women's richly varied experience. But this "negotiation" can be said to take place around socially shared definitions of the "structure."

What determines a woman's status? Her age, her marital status, her fertility, her relation to a patrilineage (as Adda Habiiba's case suggests) and her sexuality all come into play in some way, but no single variable can completely exhaust the meaning of the categories. Although sexuality plays a big part in how Fulbe people talk about women's status, the categories might be best understood with respect to fertility, as Rose Oldfield Hayes (1975) has argued with respect to Sudanese women. With this perspective in mind, the four statuses of Fulbe women can be viewed as follows:

1. *'bingel/budurwa* (child/virgin): potential fertility;
2. *debbo* (wife/woman): fertility channeled to husband's lineage;
3. *azabaajo* (prostitute/free woman): disrupted/unchanneled fertility;
4. *puldebbo* ("old woman"/crone): completed or exhausted fertility; identified with her sons' lineage and *their* fertility.

Although both the *azabaajo* and the *debbo* are generally assumed to be fertile, only the *debbo*'s fertility is usefully channeled in the service of a patrilineage. The *azabaajo*, if she conceives, produces a child that belongs to no patriline. Her fertility is "useless"; therefore her presence is fundamentally disruptive for that reason. Whether or not she is sexually active, her potential fertility is not being channeled usefully to build families. It is said to be going to waste. *Azabaa'en* (plural of *azabaajo*) are often described in those very terms as having chaotic or undisciplined (*hanyam*) lives that are not useful to patrilineages. The *puldebbo*, theoretically infertile or postmenopausal (whether she in fact is or is not), is "useless" to family building in a different way. Her fertility is behind her and her days of married womanhood are over. Her accomplished fertility, through her grown sons— or men she assimilates to grown sons (like her brother's sons)—give her standing

Adda Habiiba with henna

as an old woman worthy of respect. She no longer needs to be "useful" to a husband, because she can find respectability and legitimacy elsewhere. Although a woman may become a *puldebbo* while remaining married, she gains increased autonomy and mobility within the marriage as she assumes this status for herself (and as others begin to attribute it to her). Adda Habiiba's case illustrates how a women who does not "fit" the ideal structural definition of *puldebbo* can nonetheless claim to be one in order to gain its respectability, autonomy, and the ability to refuse a playful marriage proposal. "Don't you know these things for me are finished? I am a *puldebbo*. . . . What do I want with a man?"

Bachelors, Strength, and Millet

Fulbe cultural logic posits complex interconnections among marriage, food (especially millet), strength, and social adulthood. Marriage is axiomatic for the Fulbe. For a Fulbe woman not to marry is simply unconceivable; For a man not to marry is extremely rare. "Only two men in Domaayo have never married," I was told. "There is Bappa Ji'birilla, (who) eats his brother's millet" and Maygida, who lives a life of leisure in his brother's compound. Although I never met him, descriptions of Maygida by others conjure up the image of a pleasant, harmless madman. He is always immaculately dressed and eats with enjoyment, but he never leaves the *saare* and does not concern himself with anyone, seemingly living in a world of fantasy. There are many men in their twenties and thirties for whom economic hardship has meant postponing their first marriage. People think of these men as wanting to marry, and their bachelorhood is seen as temporary and circumstantial. However, the men in their forties and fifties who have never married and have no intention of marrying are usually described, as the men above, as mad, living in perpetual childhood and dependency. Their lack of enthusiasm for marriage is matched by their total disregard for economic matters. Lacking both economic potency with which to buy millet and the resource of a woman to cook for them, they eat the millet of their brothers. Their infertility is unstated, but implied by their bachelorhood. Unlike the bachelors of circumstance—those men who do not yet marshal enough resources to marry—men like Bappa Ji'birilla never will experience the social adulthood or fatherhood, which can only be accomplished through marriage.

But there were other bachelors in Domaayo. "What about Alhaadi, who hasn't married although his younger brother has?" I asked Bakari. "Ah yes, he and Maamudu both. They cook ('*be don defa*): *nyiiri* (thick millet porridge, the staple of the Fulbe diet), *gaari* (a delicate millet porridge thin enough to drink), brochettes, and *gato* (cake)." In the Fulbe view, one hasn't really eaten if one hasn't eaten *nyiiri*, the millet paste which, along with a thick sauce, constitutes the typical Fulbe meal. *Nyiiri* is the substance of domestic reciprocity. It is prepared by a woman for her husband and his relatives. A bride's first *nyiiri* is considered to be the first true step in the inauguration of her marriage, more than the sexual initiation of the relationship. And a young girl is said to be ready for marriage when she has the strength to stir the *nyiiri* for a family meal. Being "able" (*waawugo*) to stir this thick gruel in quantities required for a household of ten people takes not only strength but considerable know-how. Experienced cooks know when to add a little water or flour to achieve the right consistency. The millet flour must be tender but fully cooked, or else it will cause stomach aches.

In this context, for a man to cook millet is to appropriate for himself the role of a woman. The *samarooka* is defined by the Fulbe not by his sexual behavior or desire but by the fact that he cooks millet. Alhaadi and Maamudu are not discussed as bachelors in conversations, because they are not considered male. "They do not have fields?" I ask. "How could they?! Would they have the strength to farm?" is the response. The answer to my question is clearly, "no—these men lack the strength to grow millet." In the same way, women are often described as lacking this "strength," but the symbolic nature of this strength opens it to contestation, as one conversation with a would-be millet farmer illustrated.

My neighbor Goggo Aisa, a *puldebbo*, who lived alone in her parents' *saare*, complained bitterly that, although she should have inherited her deceased parents' fields by Islamic law, they were taken away from her and given to a man because "women do not have the strength to grow millet." Childless, and having left her husband to take care of her aging parents, she scoffed at the rationale "they" (the chief and his council) gave for taking away her livelihood. "Do the men work their own fields?" she asked rhetorically. "Aren't they going to hire Bananna'en (migrant laborers from Chad) to do all the work for them? Can't a woman do that equally well?" Goggo Aisa makes clear that "strength" is the product of her community's gender ideology, and is not practically related to the backbreaking work of growing millet. Like Goggo Aisa, the *samarookas* lack not actual strength but the symbolic strength, or manliness, which only manly men can have. These "womanly" men buy millet with the money they make providing food and lodging for travelers and selling snacks on the roadside on market days. Like the *berdache* role that is common among Native American cultures, the *samarooka* concept provides Fulbe society with a third gender, an option to take on a gender role that is neither fully male nor female in that society's traditional gender norms but something rather different (see Herdt 1981, 1997, 1999; Murray and Roscoe 1998; Nanda 1999). These men are considered a bit odd by other members of the community, but they are in no way ostracized or burdened with a weighty stigma. Alhaadi, who lived in his father's saare along with his father's wives and their children and his divorced older sister, was an integral part of the social life of Domaayo. He could often be found along the main road, talking with ordinary men and with the various roadside vendors. What is more, his father, who has traveled to Mecca, is the most respected religious scholar in the community, and has made no move to disavow publicly his son's social identity as *samarooka*.

Is the samarooka homosexual? Neither Alhaadi nor anyone else ever discussed (in my presence) samarooka identity in terms of sexuality. These men may be queer, in the sense that they diverge considerably from Fulbe conventions of masculinity. But I avoid translating samarooka as "homosexual" or "gay" to avoid colonizing them with labels not of their own choosing.

Although there is room for womanly men like Alhaadi in Domaayo, the social condition of ordinary bachelors falls something short of full social adulthood. Marriage is what makes Fulbe men social adults. Not only do they first *become* men through marriage and fatherhood (as females become women through marriage and motherhood), but their continued social adulthood depends on their ability to marshal the services of women (that is, wives) to cook for them. A man must be able to invite people to share meals with him, and since he cannot cook for himself (or risk being called *samarooka*), he must be married or hire a woman to cook for him. The embarrassment of the bachelor in being unable to invite friends to eat with him is multiplied for the father of many children who is temporarily made a bachelor when his wife leaves him suddenly to visit her family following an argument. He is left with children and an "empty" compound— empty, that is, of food, water, and his wife. He must then call on his relatives for help, often paying them to cook for him and his children. My friend Bakari hired his brother's daughter to cook for him, his children, and his guest (the anthropologist) when his wife made an unplanned trip to her mother's after an argument between them. He was literally helpless without her. It is partly for this reason that the Fulbe say that a poor man is ruled by his wife. He is more likely to have only one wife and to be entirely dependent on her labor and good will for food, water, and the care of his children. The sudden departure of a wife in a monogamous household makes her man a bachelor, whereas the departure in a polygamous household only frees up more of his time for his other wife or wives. Men's feelings about women's travel are further discussed below.

A SHARED EXPERIENCE OF WOMANHOOD

Married women sometimes talked to me as if I were a fellow married woman. After all, I was the same age as many women with three or four children, and I had moved there to that village from somewhere else and had come to live among strangers, as if I had come for a marriage. The building of community for Fulbe women residing in patrilineal and patrilocal villages hinges on the performance of dramatic demonstrations of suffering and hardship. "As for me, this chest . . . my body is finished," Jebba Hawwa told me. The effects of hardship and suffering of women are located within their chests (*suwire*). "There is nothing, it hurts, it is simply finished. So I don't know what sickness it is then." The clavicle, like the chest, is an important locus for suffering. Women often point to it to show their thinness. The gesture is a common accompaniment to the complaint of "my body is finished." Thinness is demonstrated in this one gesture that condenses references to emotional pain, disappointment, loneliness, physical hardship, fatigue and pathos. Yet, in these performances of suffering by women I knew, along with blatant self-pity, I sensed a triumphant undertone to these declarations. It was as if women were strengthened in their declarations of weakness. Could it be that in bemoaning the wasted condition of their chests, they were simultaneously boasting about successful fertility? The chest is, after all, the prime site of women's nourishing fecundity. Breasts which have fed numerous babies commonly become worn, flattened, and distended. But these women did not use the more specific term *en'di* (breast) to form their complaints, nor did they point to their breasts, as several women did on other occasions when speaking of specific breast ailments. The gestures, which indicated their chest or clavicle, speak to a more general wasting of bodily resources due to the struggles of life in this village.

Sometimes women's self-pity was expressed through humor, in joking interchanges with friends and neighbors. Thus, Rabiyatu's neighbor and confidante greets her with this taunt: "Have you gained weight? (Has your body filled out like a baby?) (*A woofini na?*)" Rabiyatu's response is sarcastic. "I'm as fat as a cow in the dry season! (*Mi woofini ban nagge ceedu.*)" Complaining about skinniness

Goggo Hajja

and the suffering for which it is emblematic is a way of averting the evil eye. It is as if women were saying: "You cannot be jealous of me. I am suffering. This body is proof! Look at these bones!"

Rabiyatu insults her neighbor and friend Daada Abba: "She is as skinny as an *entaa'do*." An *entaa'do* is a child who is prematurely weaned because the mother became pregnant again too soon. The *entaa'do* is frustrated by having his mother's breast taken from him too soon. The milk of an expectant mother is thought to belong to the fetus inside her. A nursing woman who discovers that she is pregnant must wean her baby immediately, lest it become sick for having stolen its younger sibling's milk. Here the reference to skinniness is pitying and affectionate. The insult, ironically, shows the lack of ill will between these women. Rabiyatu says to Daada Abba: "I am not jealous of you. I know your suffering. I look upon your body with sympathetic eyes, not with jealous, hurtful eyes." Through this insult, she tells her friend that she has noticed her suffering and that they share the hardships of life as friends.

When women treated me as a married woman too, they commiserated with me about my exhausted bodily resources as evidence of the genuine suffering I had experienced since my arrival in their village. "Look at you, you have become skin and bones, you have truly suffered, you have drunk the suffering of Domaayo." And when I left for two weeks for a trip to the capital, several women, misunderstanding the nature of my trip, thought that I had gone home to my mother for a visit. Upon my return, they greeted me with cries of "How fat you've become! Did you suckle at your mother's breasts?" Here, they again use visceral bodily metaphor to speak of womanly experience. In this case, the comfort and nourishment of mother love serves to condense the essential dimensions of a married woman's visit home to her people (see Scheper Hughes 1992). Just as the hardship of life among strangers is manifested in women's bodies, through protruding clavicles and the overall wasting of the body (and sometimes they are compared to the child prematurely deprived of his mother's breast). The emotional and material sustenance of home is actualized on the rounded curves of a woman returning from her family. Her bodily resources are replenished (metaphorically) at her mother's breast. When women comment on each other's bodies, they are telling each other that their joys and difficulties are not invisible but are a part of a common idiom in which metaphors of kinship, place, and nourishment speak to a shared experience of womanhood.

GIRLS, FRESH CONVERSATIONS, AND WOMANLY POWER

A children's song, loosely translated, reads as girlish reflections on men's evaluations of them, as they themselves mature into women and become objects of desire to the men who once insulted them:

> White plate
> My husband is a well of money.
> My co-wife is the bottom of a mortar
> While I am a white plate.
> My husband is a well of money.
> When I was a child,
> he said to me "snot nose."
> Now that I am grown, he said to me
> "come and let us talk."
> That conversation—
> The conversation on top of the bed.

The white plate is the stuff of wedding-gift exchange. The plates are stored on a young bride's shelf in her house as symbols of her social worth. Before her marriage, they are stored on her mother's shelf in anticipation of her com-

Gifts for the bride.

ing betrothal. In the song, the young girl who sings of being a plate is identified with the potential fertility of the virgin, sitting dutifully on her mother's
shelf, waiting to be married. She is an object of value and of exchange. Her co-
wife, on the other hand, is a well-worn mortar who has been used repeatedly.
Sexuality, fertility, and food preparation are merged in the image of the mortar, which stands in contrast to the pristine state of the delicate enameled plate
used for serving food to guests, or to store a woman's precious belongings, including money, medicines, and prized clothing. A mortar is provided to a wife
by her husband or his family. It is a necessary tool for women's work in food
processing, but it is not an object of beauty or ceremonial exchange. A new
bride will likely use a mortar already in her husband's *saare*. She does not usually get a new one.

The young girl describes her husband in song as a "well of money," meaning that he is an unending source of lucre for a young bride. A man who has become successful in trade could opt to take a second wife, chosen for her beauty and her ability to adorn his life with pleasure and the prestige of polygamy. The first wife is now as well worn as the bottom of a mortar through childbearing, breast-feeding, and arduous labor; she is functional but unattractive. The new wife, a virgin like the unscratched white plate given to a bride on her wedding day, has a body, which is unmarked by sexual or reproductive labor. Unlike the old wooden bowls that were handcarved and passed down from generation to generation, acquiring a smooth patina with time, the newly manufactured dishes of enameled tin imported from Nigeria and China are easily chipped and become rusted, discolored, and cracked with use. Purchased for cash in local markets, they must be replaced frequently. Furthermore, these enameled dishes are manufactured with imprinted designs that change from year to year with the tides of fashion. This further distinguishes them from the wooden mortars that, like the wooden bowls used in the past, are unadorned.

Interestingly, this song speaks of *conversation* as the substance of marriage. "That conversation on top of the bed" is a euphemism for sexual intercourse. The song also chronicles young girls' increasing awareness of (and play with) their growing attractiveness to men and the knowledge that this power of youthful beauty and desirability will wane with old age. Above all, this songs attests to the fluidity of life situations. What is true today will no longer be tomorrow. A girl becomes a woman, and a wife becomes a widow. The once slighted is now desired. The awkward and unattractive girl becomes a woman engaged in conversation of all kinds. Insults are exchanged for the sweet language of courtship.

Foreshadowing their possible futures, nine-year-old girls sing of things they cannot yet know from experience. The rhythm of the songs and the tone of their voices are playful and girlish, yet the lyrics speak of womanly power. Cynicism and innocence meet as snot-nosed girls sing of conversations upon the bed.

The Desirability of Girls

> What is good is to marry a girl. Otherwise, you have many problems. The girl, everything you give her, everything you bring to her in the home is foreign to her. She doesn't expect anything. She's easily pleased. A woman may have been married to a rich man. She compares constantly. She may leave you for it. A woman cannot accept that you go out at night. To play cards, to walk at the maayo (river), to chat with friends. A girl knows nothing.

Thus Bakari speaks about the advantages in marrying a virgin. What precisely is it that a girl doesn't know? She doesn't know about other men; the possibilities of other marriages aren't yet real to her. Unlike Rabiyatu, Bakari's wife, whom experience makes bold with the confidence that she can get another man, a young girl doesn't know her own value. At least, she has no way of comparing her first husband to her other husbands. She cannot complain about his habits, having no one to compare his habits to:

> *A girl knows nothing. You can go out. You teach her yourself, or you find an old woman to teach her to cook. You instruct her: "At such an hour, I want water, I want coffee." She does it. A woman, if she orders you to buy something and you do not buy it, leaves! A woman searches your pockets, wants your millet, she steals. It is bad. You hide the money. One does not trust a woman. I mean all women, not just the older ones.*
>
> *Women of other tribes go to market. Here, the religion forbids it. One must keep women in the compound (saare). If they go out, it is a great sin. We do not trust in women. If a woman goes out everyday, one beautiful day, she will not return.*
>
> *"So, when are they allowed out?" I ask.*
>
> *Even going out to draw water is a sin before God. They can go give their condolences in the event of a death. This is done at night, usually, or during the day if it is a close relation. Women can ask permission to go give their condolences, and they do not go there, they go elsewhere.*

Here is a humorous admission of the bargaining power of women when contrasted with the docility of girls. "A woman, she orders you to buy something. If you do not buy it, she leaves." The deceit of women is boundless. Even when they claim to be going out to a funeral, they may go elsewhere. Ultimately, the husband is frustrated in his efforts to control the movements of his wife. And yet it is of the utmost importance for men of a certain social standing that they claim to have this control. The mobility of women threatens the control of the patriline.

Men Talk about Women

> *It is only that our women here are wild (sauvages). If I tell her that I have no money, she gets angry with me. She is wild, very wild.*
>
> *She has her own money. If her friend gives birth, she will bring a gift (to the naming ceremony). It is a credit. Her friend will give back. In the event that she doesn't have the money to buy a gift, you (the husband) are obliged to give it to her. She is your responsibility, is she not?*

If you refuse, she will have to bear it and wait (supporter). But in
twenty months she will go to her friend's house with her gift. Not be-
fore, not empty-handed. There are women who have an understanding.
They cannot even to go to a marriage. If someone gives you a gift and
you do not give back, the friendship will be severed.

Inside the saare, household expenses, even for her own body, she can-
not accept to spend her own money.

When a woman complains that she is lacking something, the young
men will buy it for her; the elders refuse. They do not buy it. Special
treats (digeege) like salads, cucumbers, etc. that women ask for.
Certain men are very severe. They do not even laugh with their
women. Especially the old ones.

A woman may own animals, plates (taasaaje), money. She may ask
her husband for money, or she may do small commerce such as braid-
ing hair, embroidery, knitting or sewing children's clothes.

The husband is the one who pays for the food, bananas, millet,
meat. If she braids hair or she sews—any money she earns is her
money. I reimburse her for all her expenses. She has money. She does
not spend it. She simply waits for me to give her money (for household
expenses).

Thus Bakari presents the tensions between husbands and wives in matters of
money. For contrast he presents another scenario, which demonstrates the subtle
power plays that unfold in the intimacy of marriage.

She demands money. I have none. She stays dirty. Because she knows
that it will make me angry. I do not want her to be dirty. The woman
goes out. She is dirty or shabbily dressed. People will see her and say
'Whose wife is this?' She doesn't give a damn. She can stay dirty. (The
woman puts pressure on her husband to give her the money by sham-
ing him publicly.) It is the fault of the husband since he does not buy
soap. It puts pressure on you. If your wife is well dressed, that also
helps the man. If he wants to get married, he will be able to get women
easily.

The implication is that a woman's appearance when she is in public has an important effect on her husband's reputation. Therefore, her ability to make him
look stingy in front of her peers will affect his future marriageability. Women in
the village are very interested in men's willingness to treat their women well, and
the parents will be reluctant to marry their daughters to a man with the reputation for being miserly. A man with wealth who is unable or unwilling to share this
wealth with his wife is indistinguishable from a poor man. The only way for a

man to demonstrate strength and wealth is through generosity. Wealth is, thus, not "real" until it is shared, circulated and made visible, in this case, on the body of his wife. Thus, the seemingly mundane matter of a woman's grooming and appearance embodies a potent weapon for shaping public opinion about her husband. This opinion is not trivial to him if he thinks he may ever wish to marry within his community again. Women therefore are not without weapons in the struggle for influence over the allocation of resources in the household.

Mobility

"A woman only has three journeys: birth, marriage, and the grave," I was told. All other travel is superfluous. The men whom I heard quoting this proverb nostalgically all had wives who were only moderately secluded. Men longed for greater clarity than they really experienced in their lives. In fact, every journey taken by a married woman is potentially ambiguous. Outside of her marital compound, her status becomes more negotiable and indefinite. Although arguments between men and women could be about money, provisions, or clothes, they often are centered around the movement of women through space. "Her wanderings are more than you can stand! (*Yilaaru maako 'buri maa sembe.*)" is a complaint I heard frequently from men about their wives. '*Yilaaru* was first translated for me into French as "promenades," or leisurely strolls. It also means visiting. In this case, it refers to illegitimate, excessive or even illicit movements of a woman outside her husband's *saare*. Such visits violate the idealized norm of seclusion. As I was told, "A woman. She should go out only with the permission of the man. But if she goes out just like that, she has "stolen" the road (*o wujji laawol*)." In other words, she has taken a path that it is not her right to take. Therefore, she stole it, and with it the mobility that should remain under male control.

In a general way, all roads are conceived to be male social spaces and activities, but the more frequented the road, the more it should be avoided by married women. In Domaayo, the main street, or *buwol*, where young girls and free women market their snacks, is nearly a "market." Men traveling to and from Chadian markets get off the transport trucks to buy food and drink from the local vendors. In the context of Domaayo it is the most public of all spaces. The *buwol* is thus the least acceptable thoroughfare for a married woman, who will opt for more circuitous yet more sheltered paths away from the main street and the gaze of so many strangers.

Another term used to describe women's movements critically is *njaan-njaangu*, It resembles *jahaangal*, which refers to an important and legitimate business trip performed by a man. The duplication and simplification of this morpheme underlines the repetitiveness and illegitimacy of women's movements, suggesting travel without value or purpose. In a general way, the amount of a woman's movements is inversely related to her husband's prestige in the community. In my observation, men of modest means often have wives who travel to the fields to farm and even to the markets to trade so that they can contribute to household expenses (in spite of Bakari's assertion that women do not spend their own money to help their husbands). I knew several women who were devoted wives and traveled widely. Their husbands were unpretentious and were not criticized for their wives' movements. On the other hand, a man with pretensions to high status in the community whose wife nonetheless traveled extensively would be the object of ridicule. The lack of fit between his pretensions and the reality of their travels would be pointed out to him. Many men of modest means, who practice moderate versions of seclusion (e.g. they provide for their families, but their wives engage in some visiting), fantasize publicly about the ideal of seclusion.

When a woman goes home to her natal family, her presence there will raise numerous questions. Is she leaving her husband? Did he divorce her? Or is she simply going home for a visit? But the question, even if posed outright, is not simply answered. A woman just divorced may deny that this is the case, out of modesty or shame or embarrassment (*semteende*). A woman who has left her husband in anger may refuse to acknowledge the argument and simply say she came for a visit. A woman who truly has just come home for a visit may smile and let others think what they will. She may even take advantage of the ambiguity surrounding her trip to flirt with men as if she were a free woman. The refusal to clearly define the purpose of the trip home is at once *semteende* and a desire to maintain privacy, or at least to delay the widespread knowledge in the community of her status. If she stays a few days, of course, her story will come out, in time, and her status will be clarified. Married or divorced? Free or belonging to someone? If she has left her husband in an argument, the ambiguity may be drawn out as negotiations for reconciliation are undertaken, dropped and taken up again. The argument could end in divorce or her return to her husband. Women's travel is by definition polysemic and therefore "suspect" from the perspective of their husbands. The sighing of men about the unattainable ideal of female seclusion becomes more understandable in light of such complex meanings of womanly travel.

Roads, motorized transport, and the availability of buses, cars, and "*moto taxis*" for hire have made it possible for men and women to travel farther and more quickly than ever before. The moral ambiguity surrounding women's mobility may partly reflect changes in the structure and meaning of travel since the colonial period. For men whose wives come from distant towns, commoditized, motorized transport has made visits home to the parents a financial burden on cash-poor husbands. For them, travel has become another sinkhole for their money. A young bride who marries far from home now expects her husband to pay for her taxi fare home. Women's travel, thus, becomes yet another focus for men's experience of cash scarcity and ultimately, of their lack of control. Motorized travel also has the effect of placing mobile women in the symbolic space of modernity, money, cars, tarred roads, urban life-styles, anonymity and, as discussed previously, prostitution. But men's grumblings about women's mobility have more to do with their longing for an unattainable Islamic ideal than with nostalgic memories of a less mobile past. To the extent that they identify with a pastoral Fulbe past, their ancestors traveled continually, and pastoral women made daily trips into towns and markets to sell butter, yogurt, and milk to settled communities. To the extent that their past is Mundang, their women were active contributors to the farming economy and were certainly not secluded. Thus male discussion of female mobility encodes in a different way their difficulties in embodying an Islamic identity. More, conflicts over mobility reveal unresolved contradictions of a hybrid and non-Fulbe past for people who today nostalgically identify with the historical prestige of Fulbe dominance.

THE PROPHET SAID "MARRY"

Men often talk of women as if marriage to them could materially affect their fortune. This goes beyond the tangible effects of women's tactics to shape a man's reputation to some ineffable power that women possess to alter the course of men's lives for better or for worse. The following story was told to me by Sayihu, a man of modest means, who was married to two women and whom I visited frequently as part of a monthly health survey. He enjoyed teaching me the subtleties of the Fulbe language and world view.

> A man lived in the times of Mohammed, a very poor man. Every day he walked miles looking for firewood to sell, so that he could buy millet to eat. Every day he brought back a bundle of wood. He could not rest even one day, or he would not eat. He talked to Mohammed of his suffering. The prophet told him to take another wife. He protested. "I can hardly manage to feed myself and my one wife. How will I ever feed two?" The prophet said, "Marry."
>
> Now they were three. Every day he went out into the bush to get a bundle of wood to sell to buy millet, so they could eat. And it sufficed as it had before when they were only two. Nothing had changed. He returned to Mohammed saying, "You see, now I have two wives, and I have neither more nor less. It is as before." The prophet told him to take another wife. The man protested. "I can barely feed the three of us. How can I possibly marry another wife?!" But the prophet only said, "Take another wife, and your life will improve." He did so and found once again that his wood gathering brought just enough millet to feed them. He was neither better nor worse off than before. But he still never had a day off from work. He returned to Mohammed, telling him,

"Prophet, nothing has changed. I have not been enriched nor have I
been impoverished. All is as before." The prophet said, "Take another
wife." Now, he did this. They were now five in the compound. A single
bundle of wood was sufficient to feed all of them. But he could never
take a day off.

One day, his women gathered to talk. They said, "We have a husband
who never gets a rest. Every day he is in the bush. If we were to go out
once and each bring back a bundle, we would have five bundles and he
could rest for four days." Thus, they decided to follow him into the
bush, returning with five bundles of wood. But it turned out that the
bundles were not of ordinary wood. When put into the fire this wood
released an exquisite perfume. It was alud—incense.

The word got around town that their compound had the most fragrant incense. He sold to all comers a tiny piece for a lot of money, and
he became very wealthy.

The story over, Bakari turns to me, explaining:

This is why they say that you should consult a Marabout before marrying, so that he can counsel you whether or not the marriage is favorable.
Some say it is a sin before Islam, but . . . that is why it is good to marry
from time to time, so that one day you may become wealthy. One
woman can make you lose all your money. Another brings good luck.

A rich man will marry often. He can afford to. Why suffer at the
hands of a woman if you can afford to marry another? You can even divorce four women at once. A poor man, no matter what his wife does to
him, can only be patient/endure. What can he do? (Il va supporter par
que faire.)

A favorable marriage will be fruitful, harmonious, and long lived and will
bring good fortune to both parties. Success in trade or in cultivation may be attributed to a man's wife. For most men of modest means, who, like the wood cut-
ter do not believe they can support many wives, trying one's luck at marriage requires an occasional divorce. A man who has not been able to prosper financially
or who has never had children may persist in believing that the problem is not
with him, but with his wife. Although people I knew acknowledged that infertility can be caused by problems in the male body, it was generally the case that
women were blamed for their failure to produce children. "What are the reasons
for divorce (initiated by a man)?" I asked Bakari.

(1) a woman fools around (se promene); (2) she refuses orders; disobe-
dience; (3) she gives her husband an ultimatum: "If you don't give this,

this, and this, I will leave you" and she leaves. Then you may as well divorce her. With the economic crisis, there are fewer divorces. Many women are "unemployed" (au chomage). Girls are given away (in marriage) for free.

Bakari goes on to point out that although women cannot technically initiate divorce, a marriage may be "untied" by civil or religious authorities under certain conditions. "If the husband fails to provide food or clothing, the marriage can be dissolved before Islam." Sayihu interjects. "There is a saying: 'Three things are never found together in one compound: a man, a woman and poverty.'" A poor man can lose his wife easily. If he wants to keep her, he will go out looking for work, or else it is she who will leave. The discourse of men about women and marriage links women and fortune in complex webs of interrelation. Women can bring wealth or misery. At the same time, poverty can lead to the loss of women, while wealth gives men more opportunities to marry. However, as the story illustrates, marriage itself, even in conditions of poverty, can bring good fortune and wealth. Left out of Sayihu's or Bakari's exegetical commentaries is the generosity of the poor man's wives. Reaching out to him across the boundaries of gender and status and choosing to overcome their situational antagonism as co-wives and their prerogatives of seclusion and leisure in the normative Fulbe marriage (in which the husband is supposed to provide for his wives), they decide to go out into the bush and each bring back a bundle of wood, so that he may rest for four days. Their generosity, initiative, and feeling for him are what brings about the transformation in his life, from simple woodcutter to wealthy incense merchant. Poverty, like marital antagonism and discord, is as common as firewood. But exquisite wealth, like cooperation among co-wives and generosity of wives for their husband, is as rare as incense.

Culinary Know-how as Power: The Sauce of the Mature Woman

Fulbe men talk about the marriage of younger men to older women as being determined by "sauce". They say, "Their sauce is too good." It spoils their younger husbands, giving their women control over them. Although this might seem to suggest that ingredients with highly specific action (for example, sorcery) are invoked, such is not the intent. Rather, what is being underlined is the expertise of the cook, gained from experience. Good sauce concretizes power or influence over the husband *in and of itself*. The power of sorcery and the power of fine cuisine both stem from know-how. Both "work" on the gourmand victim through direct contact with his body. Because it is a scarcity of money that often leads a young man to marry a mature woman rather than a girl, it leads to a marriage in which his wife's superior knowledge gives her more power in the relationship.

With a combination of culinary skill and goodwill, an experienced woman may prepare surprisingly good sauces, in spite of her husband's modest resources. Using inexpensive ingredients, she expresses her appreciation for her young husband by valorizing his contribution in a tasty dish. The phrasing, of course, is also suggestive of an older woman's greater sexual experience and hints that her ability to please her husband goes well beyond the culinary arena. The raised eyebrows and suppressed laughter that often accompanied men's discussions of older women's sauces reinforced this interpretation of the metaphor.

Also implicit in men's talk about the virtues of older women was the idea that they were grateful to their husbands for providing them with the comfort and legitimacy of marriage. Having spent some time as free women (*azabaa'en*), and having suffered the difficulties of life alone, they appreciated the benefits of marriage and would do what was necessary to make the relationship work. Thus the grateful older woman whose sauce is "too good" contrasts with the one who complains about her husband's inadequate provisioning. Like the woman quoted in the beginning of this chapter, she bemoans the absence of rich ingredients, like meat and butter, in what turned out to be a bitter tasting sauce. In both cases "sauce" is discussed as an indicator of the quality of reciprocity between man and woman in marriage. Whereas millet (*nyiiri*) is what makes a marriage exist, it is sauce (*haako*) that provides the sensory inspiration for a nuanced discussion of the sweetness or bitterness of marital exchange.

Men's social adulthood depends on the presence of submissive female bodies; this submission is always, to some extent, voluntary and dependent on a morally grounded reciprocity. The flow of material substances between husband and wife is a constant subject of negotiation in the Fulbe household. Although I was only privy to the more public of these exchanges, they seemed to be structured in such a way as to maximize the number of interchanges between husband and wife. Items and sums of money were always given for particular items or specific requests and never given as a lump sum. On a daily basis, men provide millet, money for oil, salt, meat, and the ingredients for sauce (leaves or vegetables), sugar, tea, and also money for the grinding of the millet at the diesel mill. They are also occasionally expected to provide sewing money, "hair-braiding money," cloth, soap, and henna. In addition to child care and their quotidian labor of maintaining the household by sweeping, cleaning and fetching water, women produce prepared food and children. Although men appear to dominate their wives completely, if they fail to provide the items women request, the latter may refuse to cook or to go to the river for water, or, as Bakari complained, they may simply leave. As water jars run dry and uncooked meat spoils on its plate (or as his children cry for their mother), a man will feel the bargaining power of his wife. The utter dependence of men on women in the domestic realm of everyday life sheds light on the common male complaints about women's chaotic, disorderly nature and excessive jealousy.

These refrains are employed by men as a way of minimizing particular conflicts or dismissing particular demands.

TALKING ABOUT MARRIAGE

Though men use generalizing talk about the world (*dunya*) to discuss personal, intimate problems, women rely on the bodily idioms of bad sauce, cheap cloth, wasting flesh, and restless nights of longing to speak of their experiences of scarcity and dissatisfaction with particular marriages. In these laments and complaints women remind their husbands, as well as themselves and each other, that they know of other life possibilities and that their engagements in their marital homes are always contingent on their own willingness to defer. Although both men and women experience the constraining force of culture and live in a world that often resists their efforts to bring about desired outcomes, the ways in which they express these experiences are fundamentally different.

My analysis of "marriage talk" in this chapter both builds on and modifies the approaches of previous scholars. A number of writers have questioned the homogeneity of "culture" in favor of ethnographies that emphasize a multiplicity of voices, including the subaltern groups and from the margins of a social order. Cleavages of age, gender, social status (class, caste, and so forth), ethnicity, race, and religion often produce tremendous heterogeneity, even within small communities (see for example Tsing 1993). How much of a culture is shared by all members of a society? How much is subject to negotiation, debate, and contestation? How significant are these differences? The marriage talk analyzed in this chapter reveals some rather stark differences in how Fulbe men and women engage with this social institution. Some anthropologists, such as Janice Boddy (1989), Shirley Ardener (1975), and Brinkley Messick (1993), have described women's complaints as muted expressions of an alternative reality. One could characterize Fulbe women's talk in the same way. But for whom are these expressions muted? Women know exactly what they are saying. And their subversive complaints are not necessarily best figured as muted critiques of male hegemony (or social order), rather than as incisive, surgical strikes at particular men's reputations—effective uses of their power. Fulbe women's complaints are not expressed as generalized critiques of a male-dominated social order; they are particular utterances about particular husbands, that effectively undermine their husbands' power. Narratives of longing and complaints about "bad sauce" work to destabilize the current couple, calling into question the apparent immutability of their hearth, and to remind their husbands that their deference is voluntary and could be withdrawn. The discourse of scarcity, in which women criticize their husbands' provisioning, has the effect of shaming particular men, shaping their reputations, their marriageability, and ultimately their leverage in that particular relationship.

When women speak of the constraints on their own mobility, they are simultaneously sharing an experience of isolation and frustration and declaring their virtue by the fact that they are contained by their husbands' lineages. Yet when they speak of scarcity in the idiom of exhausted bodies, bad sauce, and cheap cloth, they declare their membership in a community of suffering at the same time that they criticize particular husbands, particular marriages and remember the possibility of other husbands, other villages, other lives. When men speak of women as spirits and liars, they demonstrate a bravado that claims to be invulnerable to women. Yet when the same men talk of messiness and the chaotic nature of women, they declare their membership in a community of men living in a world that does not always give you what you want; because that world is a womanly world, they indirectly give expression to feelings of powerlessness, frustration, and vulnerability in their relationships with women.

4

Forging Islamic Manhood

The ancestors came and they were men. They were forced to marry the women who lived here.

Ji'birilla Lawan

During the holy month of Ramadan, men often gather together in the late afternoon waiting for nightfall, the evening prayer, and the first sip of drink with which they will break their fast. Older men usually gather outside the Mosque while groups of younger men cluster along the roadside. From sunup to sunset, members of the Muslim community participate in a holy fast, abstaining from food and water as they go about their daily activities, in a display of devotion, sacrifice and solidarity, which profoundly marks the life of Domaayo. During Ramadan, the social fabric is strengthened through this shared experiences of thirst and hunger, of hardship and devotion. As my own experiences during the month of fasting made clear, it is impossible to be a full member of this community without being a Muslim. When I tried to fast in solidarity with my fellow-villagers' hardship in 1990, I was told by my friend Ji'birilla: "Have you converted to Islam? If you do not pray, you are not fasting—you are just starving yourself!" His joke at my expense, turning on the contrast between a holy fast and mere starvation, underscores an important point. Local experiences of community are founded not only in shared cultural practices but in a common faith.

In everyday conversation, Fulbe men I knew spoke of their common bonds in terms of Fulbeness and Islam. In local religious practice, Muslims are defined as those who pray and who fast during Ramadan. By this standard, 99 percent of Domaayo residents are Muslim. By 1997, the religious unity of the community was increasingly challenged by the growing popularity of religious brotherhoods.

69

Still, most Domaayo residents agree, Islam is one, at least in theory, and any doctrinal divisions that appear are superficial compared to the deeper thread of a shared faith in God.

As the following discussion on Koranic education, *lakol*, Islam, and the circumcision school will illustrate, the social fabric is not, in fact, a seamless one, but a patchwork of nicks and tears. Government sponsored schools continually pull at the minds of young men, and there are generational differences with respect to many cultural practices (such as marriage, scarification, medicine). Growing concern with money, consumerism, and individualism increasingly undermine social solidarity. Some young men seek a different relation to the cosmopolitan world (*dunya*) than their fathers had forged. Islamic scholars, at the same time that they critically examine modern, or foreign influences (that is, French language schooling), argue against elements of Fulbe culture which they deem un-Islamic, remnants of a pagan past.

Fulbeness, Islam and the institution of circumcision are important elements in the construction of a community of men in Domaayo. However, the solidarity of these men is not monolithic. It is constantly being negotiated in verbal and bodily discourse: in greetings, in communal prayer, in the commensality of millet and sauce, in the fasting month of Ramadan and in the shared experience of circumcision. As we saw in chapter one, the responses to my requests for "origin" stories and many long conversations about Fulbeness revealed some major cracks in the wall of solidarity in this community. When ethnicity was defined as ancestry, some villagers were more Fulbe than others. Yet ultimately, membership in the community rests on the quotidian practices of Islam and the performance of *pulaaku*.

As we shall see, the schooling and discipline they receive from the circumcision school are also important in creating bonds of relatedness between men. The specifics of the proceedings of this bush school are shrouded in strict secrecy. It is generally known by all that the process is filled with pain and hardship. During my fieldwork, when a man in his thirties, a non-Fulbe client of a prominent Domaayo figure converted to Islam and was to be circumcised, I overheard Fulbe men talking about his "conversion" with broken voices, full of empathy, then bursting out in nervous laughter. As a woman, I could not judge how frequently this subject might come up in conversations among men. But in talking with my research assistant, I learned that the memory of circumcision is very strong between men who went through the ordeal together, and that they do not discuss it with men of other generations any more than they discuss it with women. All of these idioms—Fulbeness, Islam, and circumcision—are interrelated in forming the masculine community.

The communal experience of fasting, the experience of circumcision, the textual initiation into the religion of Islam through the pupil's Koranic schooling—these are the three major processes which serve to build male community. Throughout this chapter, one can see the tensions in Fulbe society between those practices closely associated with Islamic orthodoxy and those that it judges to be un-Islamic. Thus, although I am primarily concerned here with discussing the ways in which men demonstrate and reinforce their membership in the community, I also discuss how they exclude those elements, which are judged to be antithetical, heterodox, or peripheral to this community. The processes of solidarity building and exclusion are inextricably linked, and they work simultaneously through gender, ethnicity, religion, and cultural orthodoxy. The discourse of relatedness and commonality is ongoing and incomplete. It never succeeds in producing a homogenous community.

READING THE KORAN

Young children of both sexes begin going to Koranic school between the ages of six and eight. They can be found at nightfall, refilling their petrol lamps and cleaning their glass domes as they prepare to run to the teacher's house. Koranic schooling is remarkably decentralized, and even a small town like Domaayo has numerous small schools organized around extended family and neighborhood. Anyone who has read the entire Koran can teach small children, and most parents send their kids to the teacher in their neighborhood, who is often a relative. Boys and girls classes may be separate or together, depending on the teacher and age of the students. Kids often perform chores for their teacher, or *mallum*. For example, they bring firewood from the bush or carry water for him. If they fail to do what is asked, or if they skip classes, they are severely punished. Middle aged men vividly recall the beatings of their first Koranic teachers. The relation between teacher and pupil is a vertical one in which the child gives respect and obedience to the teacher. Discipline is a large part of the curriculum. The learning techniques involve repetition, memorization, recitation and copying of Arabic texts, usually from a printed page to a wooden slate, or *alluha*. These wooden boards are washed and reused for decades so that they are worn smooth and thin with the years (see photo).

Every Fulbe child attends Koranic school, at least to learn "the minimum needed to pray," but the goal of every child is to one day complete the Koran. One who has read the entire Koran can genuinely be called *mallum*, though the word is used to show respect toward any adult male, somewhat like the word "Sir" in English. Only the most devoted students go beyond the Koran to the *hadiths*, or traditions, religious texts associated with the Koran. Most girls quit school when they marry, usually between the ages of twelve and fourteen. Boys continue for several more years into their late teens, when, Fulbe wisdom suggests, their concerns may lead them away from religion for a time. It is not uncommon for men in their thirties and forties to resume their religious studies. At this age, men are said to become "serious" and begin to think about death. One such class was held in the afternoons during the dry season in the entrance hall of a prominent

Young Scholar

Alhaji's compound. It was a course on the translation and interpretation of the
Koran in Fulfulde. All of the students were men in their thirties and forties, many
of them married and with children.

Like men, women also are thought to become more interested in religion later
in life, but if they are married, the conventions of seclusion and the demands of
caring for young children may prevent them from studying formally with a *mallum*. As married women, they often learn from someone in their immediate social sphere, such as a close friend, a spouse or a relative (often a brother or
nephew), who is learned in religious matters. Increasingly with age, they begin to
pray more intently, fast extra days and perform other devotional rites (such as
drinking scriptural water to break a fast). Although both men and women are expected to begin thinking of their own death as they age, only women have their
religious piety linked with their sexuality and fertility. As we saw in chapter 3,
post-menopausal women and especially women who are no longer having sexual
relations with men are believed to be more capable of religious devotion than
women who are fertile and sexually active.

POWER, INDIVIDUAL WORTH, AND THE ETHICS OF RESPECT

Fulbe society is at once egalitarian and hierarchical. Deference to one's superiors
is one of the fundamental elements of children's education, yet mutual respect

also is stressed, particularly in the egalitarian community of men defined by Islam. *Darja* and *neddaaku* are key concepts in the Fulbe understanding of worth and respect. *Darja* means "the worth of a man" (*la valeur de l'homme*). Although all men are worthy of respect, not all men are of equal worth. *Darja* is a multidimensional concept. It can be based on learning, wealth (e.g. money, clothing, a motorcycle), chiefly power, and the power of *gendarmes* or of bureaucrats (*fonctionaires*), which is tied to the contemporary state. As one young man, a modest market trader put it,

> No one equals the chief. To enter his compound, you have to take off your shoes. A jawro, or neighborhood chief, may have many fields but he must show respect for the village chief (lawan) by removing his shoes when he enters his compound. A gendarme requires that you respect him, that you address him politely. The government official, who strolls through the markets levying taxes—the merchant surpasses him in monetary wealth but fears him. Every man has his better. And every man, no matter how poor, surpasses someone else. Everything that breathes has its equal. (Ko foofata fuh bee ko fondata).

Acknowledgments of other men's *darja* come in many forms. One can show respect through gestures, such as removing one's shoes. There are also ways of showing deference in greetings. A subordinate will usually extend greetings first and then respond to the other's greetings with more questions and blessings, rather than answering any inquiries about his own health. When the chief speaks, his subjects look away from him and convey their attentiveness with backchannels of "*naam*" (like the American "uh-huh" but with the added respect and deference of "yes *sir*").

Regardless of their worth, men are required to speak to each other with consideration (*neddaaku*), always recognizing the other's presence as a person worthy of respect. "*Mi 'don wolwane bee neddaaku* means that I speak to you softly (with consideration), so that we make come to an agreement." The reverse is to destroy someone's "face," to humiliate someone (*wilgo mo neddaaku*). As one young man explained,

> In the Muslim religion, all men are equal. If you are respectful, God will look upon you with favor. A polite man will not hurt another man. To humiliate someone is sinful. (Wilgo neddaaku—woddaay).
> Neddaaku is self-possession, self-restraint, self-control. It is mindfulness, dutifulness, obedience. First of all, it is a question of values. Someone who knows how to live among people, without losing his temper, who can speak with others without annoying them—that is the sort of person who has neddaaku. But someone who is raised poorly

and without values doesn't have neddaaku—*he is mostiido. It is a question of being well-brought-up, well mannered.* Mostaare, mostugo *(means that) you insult, you exaggerate, you refuse to run an errand for an elder, you do things that shock people,* n'importe quoi *(whatever)! Take the Minister of Women's Affairs, Madame Ya'u Aisatu. Her husband is from Guidiguis. She can give speeches in Kaélé (the administrative center), and people will stand up and clap for her. But in Guidiguis, if she finds a group of men sitting down, she takes off her shoes.*

When she is acting as Minister, respect is given her, but when she is acting as daughter-in-law to her husband's kin, she gives them the respect any woman would give. She humbles herself before these men by removing her shoes, taking on the role of woman and momentarily leaving her prerogatives as minister in order to show respect. Each person has respect from others in some role and gives respect in other contexts. "Even our chief, when he is in Kaélé, is no longer chief." He has his elders too.

Kulol Allah *means the fear of God. Equality among Muslim brothers lies in fear of God. One should not harass another, bear a grudge or look down upon another Muslim. Each Muslim is forbidden to (cause harm to) another Muslim.* (Juuldo fuh karamdo dow juuldo.) *Hurting him is (a violation of the code of conduct—*haram*) tantamount to eating pork. A wise person is very near death always. In the next hour, tonight, tomorrow—anytime death can be upon me.*

Whereas death is the great equalizer (as all men die, and mindfulness of death has a moderating influence on people, reminding them to be humble before God), deference toward one's superiors/elders is something that must be taught. In Domayo the principal institution for instilling respect for elders is male circumcision. During the ordeal, fear of elders is collectively experienced by the group of young boys. Their fear and respect is literally inscribed on their bodies with the razor blade and continuously reiterated during their confinement. The food that they are forced to eat to the point of vomiting serves as a visceral embodiment of the cruel authority of the elders, which can never be forgotten.

CIRCUMCISION

During my field stay, a circumcision camp was located across the *maayo* (river) from my compound. I heard the flutes of the circumcised boys in the evenings as I wrote up my fieldnotes, and often wondered aloud about them. As in many societies, circumcision for the Fulbe is a rite of passage, a profound physical, so-cial, and moral experience, through which all boys must pass in order to become men. The process is surrounded with secrecy, and I learned that, as a woman, I could not legitimately ask questions about it. My friend and research assistant, Bakari, was at first amused by my curiosity. In time he began to reminisce about his own experiences of circumcision with a mixture of bitterness and nostalgia:

> *They will teach you to respect. All the old men come to beat you.*
> *Someone will come and put a rotten bone under your nose. You smell*
> *it. "Hmmm it smells good." You are forced to say this. You take the* nyi-
> *iri, you eat it. A huge ball of millet and you eat it all! A large calabash*
> *of* bouillie *(millet porridge). They force you to drink it. You vomit, you*
> *drink. (He tells me he was twelve years old; it was 1968.) They made*
> *me do it. Now, it has gone out of fashion. (C'est démodé.)*

Bakari continued to speak of the circumcision camp that initiates boys into man-hood through an intense process of moral education and ritual humiliation. Boys learn the special rules governing behavior during this liminal period in their lives.

> *If you see a grown man, you bend over. You do not look a superior in*
> *the eye. They have secrets. Animals that don't exist. Like that they fool*
> *women and children. Now, this has gone out of fashion. The old women*
> *know (the secrets). Who does not know?*
>   *The* bouillie—*that they still do. Even if they are full, they are forced*
> *to eat a lot so that they will become fat. They force you to drink* bouillie
> *until you vomit. They want you to come home in good health. There*
> *are even those who gain weight. You go hunting in the bush, to kill fresh*
> *meat. Birds, quails, squirrels, rats. Even in the village, there are certain*
> *meats—dead chickens even. Sometimes trucks hit and kill chickens.*
> *They give them to the circumcised. They eat everything. They come*
> *back fat.*

Ritual inversion, in which initiates do things they would never do in ordinary life, is a characteristic feature of initiation. Bakari struggled to explain the contra-diction. How can brutal force-feeding be healthy? How can purification be achieved by its opposite, eating taboo foods?

> *That means, it is (pause) to facilitate purification. If you are pure, you*
> *are holy, you will pray easily. If you are in the bush, you will become*
> *holy (or saintly)—so you will say good-bye to bad things. If you return*
> *to the village, that's it—until your death, you will not do those things*
> *any more. The initiates can refuse certain things—donkeys, horses,*

pork—it is the worst! Better to eat a dead sheep than live (properly sac-
rificed) pork. Some of the circumcised can drink milk, but it is a ques-
tion of means. If your father is rich, you can get it.

The information embedded in this narrative is complex. On the one hand, the
initiates are abused, made to suffer physically, being forced to eat both repugnant
things and good foods in such quantities that they begin to vomit. They are
beaten and abused. Yet, on the other hand, they are meant to come home healthy
and fat. Their bodies are the vehicles for learning respect, but they are not to be
seriously harmed. They learn about becoming Muslim men, about praying, and
about which foods are forbidden to a Muslim. Pork, for instance, is universally
forbidden, as is any meat from an animal that has not been slaughtered in the
Muslim manner (that is, by a Muslim man who utters the prescribed prayer before cutting the animal's throat). The roadkills, which Bakari says are offered to
the boys, thus, constitute part of their ritual abasement. Then they are humiliated
by being forced to eat forbidden foods for the last time. After this period of seclusion is over, they will never again taste of these forbidden foods.

The flutes, handmade from local clay by the circumcised boys, serve as a
means of communication between the boys and others who have been circumcised. They also serve as constant reminders to the whole community that the
"education" of young boys is going on just across the river. For the uninitiated, it
recalls our exclusion from the structures of authority, knowledge, and prestige,
which privilege adult males.

As the whistling of the circumcision flutes continued over the next few weeks,
Bakari's reflections on the process continued. He knew I was interested in the institution, and I suppose he enjoyed being able to formulate his thoughts about it
to an outsider. I cannot judge to what extent his understanding of the institution
is idiosyncratic, because I did not have access to other sources on the subject. But
I believe many of his doubts and ambivalent feelings would be echoed by other
Fulbe men of his generation.

> *Early June 1990. "On Wednesday, they were circumcised. Wednesday is*
> *an auspicious day. They play the flutes. Their fathers can understand*
> *what they are saying through their whistling. They can ask for food*
> *sometimes." In a pause in the conversation, we could hear the eerie*
> *sound of the flutes in the distance. "Luwalji 'don fufa. (The flutes are*
> *whistling.)*
>
> *"The whistles of the circumcised are made of earth: stick shapes, made*
> *hollow with a straw. The are used only during the circumcision, they are*
> *broken on the way home (at the end of the stay in the bush).*
>
> *"The man who guards them, the* jaagori, *is like their father. He*
> *watches over them at night. Among us, the circumcised must not sleep*

*on their side. They sleep on their backs. For ten days. They must heal a
little before they can sleep on their side. They can talk to their "father."
"Now Jaagori, forgive us, forgive us, excuse us. We will never do it,
never will we do it."*

"Have they been doing something wrong?" I asked.

*"No, because they are beaten always, they are treated roughly (ils
sont malmenés). So that you will be polite, each 'superior' comes to
beat you. Once returned to the village, you are obedient, you know how
to be respectful. (In the circumcision camps, if) you see a superior who
is coming, you sweep his path . . . things like that. They bring you food
with sauce, they pour out the sauce, tell you to eat the nyiiri dry. Two
plates full, they force you to eat, until you have finished it. All that is a
way to educate them: Respect your superiors!*

*"In the past, they even killed children in the bush with these trifles
(brimades). In this very village, they have killed two children."*

"The people who did this, are they still around?" I wondered.

*"It was over forty years ago. Umaru, Ji'birilla, Aadama, those who
are sixty, seventy years old, they are still around, are they not? They are
alive. It has gone out of fashion. If I have a son, and he is beaten in the
bush or he loses weight from fear. This is terrible. I will file a complaint
(Je vais porter plainte)."*

"Where?" I ask.

*"Even with the gendarmes, with the chief. The jaagori will go to
prison."*

The topic of circumcision becomes an occasion for discussing generational
differences within the village. Bakari had been very critical of the violence of the
circumcision rites. But there is something good in it, he adds, to respect common
rules, for all the people—not just the parents—to have a role in disciplining children. He regrets the loss of community spirit which communal parenting implies.

"Now, there is no love. You live alone. It would be preferable to live communally. That is what is good." It is clear that he has something specific in mind, as
he laments the loss of "commonality." The story which follows clarifies his feelings. I took notes as he spoke, filling out the story in my notebook later that day:

*Bakari tells the story of his poor years. "Two years ago, I had two children and no money. I had gotten married in 1982. I used to eat with
my brothers at night without bringing a dish." Normally, each man
brings a dish prepared by his wife, and they eat each dish together, in
turn. "My older brother took me aside and said: 'Don't do that anymore. If you want to eat, you bring a dish.' I went home and cried. I*

cried until I resolved never to be in that position again. Last year, I
harvested my onions before anyone else. I sold each bag at 13 to 15,000
Francs! God has looked upon me. And I have done O.K. ever since. I
never have less than 15,000 in my house. No matter what! Even if I
have no money, I know what I can do to get it.

Eight years later, he still struggles to talk about this lesson in self-reliance. There is still pain in his voice as he recalls coming to the realization that "you are all alone in the world." The world of the circumcision school stands out in his memory as a time when he was not alone. There he shared the hardships of initiation with other boys, who became his closest friends. There, he explained to me, you learn to fear your elders, but you also learn about true intimacy and trust from those who go through this ordeal with you.

Collectively, the circumcised are called *juulnii'be*, which is formed from the root *juul-*, to pray. It suggests something "made prayerful" or "made holy (or religious)." They have been taught about prayer and the holy and forbidden things in Islam. And they have been taught to respect their elders through bodily rituals of pain and fear. And the process in its violent concretization of hierarchy has created the feeling of being "of the same rank" among the boys, who suffer together. Although the Fulbe do not have age grades, they do have age classes formed at the circumcision schools. This feeling of coevalness and intimacy between fellow *juulnii'be* outlasts their boyhood and continues to shape their lives as they become men, take on wives, father children, and eventually have their own boys initiated.

Other constructions of community occur through the relations of reciprocity, which unfold at rites of passage, especially baby-naming ceremonies, weddings, and funerals. Though the circumcision camps isolate boys from women and, thus, concentrate in older men the power of educating boys in the ways of Muslim adulthood the *nastirdu* ceremony celebrates the return of those boys into the mixed community. Literally translated as "coming in" the *nastirdu* is a kind of graduation, which marks the return of the circumcised. Because they are now potential husbands, fathers and adult men, their usefulness to the women of the community is underlined. As we shall see in the next section, the *nastirdu* reincorporates these boys into particular lineages, and publicly features important roles for the boys' paternal aunts (*goggo*) and other women. The principal emphasis in circumcision, however, is on building up and molding the next generation in the community of men.

The "Coming-In" Ceremony

The Koranic school experience can be seen to reinforce some of the key lessons of the circumcision school, though in a more diffuse and sustained manner.

However, there are some aspects of the circumcision process which are felt to be antithetical to the religious ethos. The circumcision school customarily ends with a celebration of homecoming for the young boys. Fattened and healed from their physical and moral shaping, they are dressed in fine robes and feasted by their families. Sheep are slaughtered, musicians are hired, and friends and family are invited to attend, partake in the feasting, and admire the circumcised. The boys are now not only "true Muslims," capable of praying and observing the rules of *haram* (avoiding forbidden things), but they are also potential grooms, husbands, and fathers of children. Their mothers and their paternal aunts (*goggo*) are especially prominent in the "coming in" ceremony of *nastiirdu*. In one ceremony I attended, the paternal aunt put aside all restraint, dancing wildly and singing in a full-throated voice, which I had never before heard coming from a Fulbe woman. Her overtly sexual dance seemed to be an expression of a woman's joy for her nephew's new status and a celebration of potential fertility for her patrilineage. The other women smiled, laughed, and giggled at her performance, while a few maintained a stern, even severe expression. On the trip home it became evident that the women I had come with felt that the aunt had gone too far in her expression and had exhibited "shamelessness" for which they judged her harshly.

There is a tension running through the center of this ceremony—between the restraint prescribed by Fulbeness and Islam and the playful celebration of fertility implicit in the moment and embodied in the *goggo*'s dance. The boys are symbolically likened to brides. They are dressed in newly sewn clothes, their eyes are rimmed with kohl. Their heads are covered in Saudi-style "cheches," which partially cover their faces, as they peer shyly at their admirers. The women I had come with criticized the shamelessness of the boy's *goggo*, but there were other complaints coming from men about the use of drummers for entertainment.

I learned that several of the most learned *mallums* in the village opposed the presence of drums at the *nastirdu* ceremony, just as they objected to them at weddings and naming ceremonies. Drumming, they argued, is un-Islamic:

> The mallums *do not like drums. They consider it a great sin.*
> Me: *Who is in favor of the drumming?*
> Les illétrés. *Illiterate people. Or even to dance the traditional dances. It is bad. They let the children and the young ones do that. When we grow up, we ask God for his forgiveness.*
> The Marabouts *do not like music. If they must like something, then it would be singing—singing the songs about Mohammed or songs which praise God. Like Hajja who sings the night of the Laylatuure (the 27th day of Ramadan). She sings the songs of the life of Mohammed (basur-a'u).*
> The father of Yaya, the Alhaaji, *didn't want for Yaya to have drums for his wedding. He only closed the front door of his compound. So it is*

Griots

> *Alhaadi, Yaya's older brother, who played the role of father and mother*
> *(since the child has no mother). The* alhaaji *is old. He wants nothing.*
> *Only he gave money. Everything he could.*

The opposition stated here between illiterate people and the *mallums*, masters of the pen, echoes the opposition between drumming and singing the praises of God, and between children and adults, pagans and Muslims, women and men. Although all residents of Domaayo consider themselves to be Muslim, there is a tendency among men to ascribe pagan qualities to women and children. Children are pagan because they do not yet have social sense (*hakkilo*) and therefore, cannot be expected to act like Muslims. Why are women linked to paganism?

If Fulbe men married local women who were pagan before their marriages, then it would be literally true that in those relationships, the women would be less learned in Islam than the men (see Boddy 1989, Mernissi 1987). But the association of women with paganism is not reducible to such specific marital histories. Women are symbolically conceptualized as being more easily overpowered by bodily processes and sexual desires than men. Blood, milk, and children flow out of them, and they are more vulnerable to spirit attack, especially when they are bleeding (during menstruation or childbirth). The permeability of their bodies is contradictory to the norms of self-control contained in Fulbe conceptions of *pulaaku* and Islam. These symbolic linkages between women and paganism gain support in the schooling of circumcision.

As boys leave behind the world of women, they simultaneously abandon all that is *haram* to the Islamic religion. They are no longer simply their mother's children, but are now knowledgeable about their religion, their responsibilities as men and their place in a world, which is external to and emphatically separate from the womanly world into which they were born. Is it any wonder that as men they attribute the "pagan" beliefs and practices to that womanly world from which they were torn in order to become men? As husbands and fathers, they welcome their children into the world through blessings of the *mallums* at the naming ceremony. Otherwise, they keep their distance from the womanly world of birth and infant care. They lavish affection on their children only in the privacy of their homes, away from the gaze of elders who frown on such indulgences. Men are kept far from the visceral process of birth and from the medicines, which women use to monitor their reproduction.

Conversely, women are excluded by the communal practices of Islamic prayer. Women who are menstruating cannot enter the mosque. Reproduction and piety are thus constructed as antithetical. Just as men cannot enter the birthing house until their child has been blessed by the *mallums* at the naming ceremony, which serves as its "coming-out" party for the entire community, so women cannot have any contact with the circumcised boys until they have been blessed by *mallums* at the "coming-in" (*nastirdu*) ceremony, which celebrates the return of these boys to their lineages and to communal life.

The separation of male and female spheres parallels the mutual exteriority of blood and prayer. During the month of fasting, menstruating women neither pray nor fast. Though they may eat and drink discretely, they nonetheless occupy the symbolic space of "pagans," who eat while others fast and are absent while others pray. Premenopausal women's exclusion from the mosque routinely reinforces their exteriority to the community of religious men. As long as the segregation of male and female space is maintained, and blood and prayer remain mutually exclusive, women remain a "divisive" and "chaotic" force interfering with the solidarity and harmony of the male community.

Here, the exclusion of women and pagans from the community of Muslim men is viewed as only one dimension of the multiple oppositions and fissures that run through Fulbe culture: Drums are opposed to Koranic chanting; illiterate persons are contrasted with *mallums*; dancing is opposed to praying, as youth is to maturity. I interpret these oppositions as, in part, indicative of a tension running through Fulbe culture between the Islamic and the un-Islamic (or anti-Islamic). Sometimes, this plays out in everyday conversation as an opposition between the Islamic present and the pagan past of the Fulbe. In other contexts, the opposition is voiced as being between the Fulbe present and the *haabe* ancestry of Domaayo's residents. Since most Fulbe I knew have at least some non-Fulbe ancestry, the tension between Fulbeness and Islam on the one hand and non-Fulbeness and paganism on the other makes ethnicity a crucial issue in the life of the community (as shown in chapter one). The intensity of the criticism of the circumcised boy's aunt and the *mallum*'s fervent opposition to the use of drums in the boys' homecoming ceremony are symptomatic of a struggle running through the center of people's identities as Fulbe and as Muslims. These issues run through every dimension of Fulbe culture from ethnicity to medicine, gender, Islam, and the world of spirits and motivated affliction.

CONTRASTING EDUCATIONS
OF *JUULNII'BE* AND *BIKKOY LAKOL*

Age mates (lawaala amin) never forget one another—even if they come back to the village after having been away for a long time, and even when they grow old. They are always camarades. Lawaale'am means my friend, my homie. We say, "He is of my age group. (Min lawaale.)" They wash together, dress together, eat together, have secrets between them . . . they never forget one another. That's where you make a close friend, a best friend. Soobaajo am koolaado. Bana ami intime. Gorgi am koolaado. (Close friend of mine.) Amaanaajo am. (My confidante.)

Thus the *juulnii'be* become lifelong friends through their shared experiences. The subject of *amaana*, which Bakari translated as *confiance*, or trust, reminds me of another conversation with him on the topic of government schooling:

Our older brothers, our parents, they do not recognize those students. They say they are not, that they do not have . . . (he searches for a way to explain). They do not help others, they are not trustworthy. They have no amaana. For example, there are Tupuri people who come here to Domaayo, stay with a (Fulbe) family . . . while going to school, they eat there, sleep there, etc. But then, when they have finished their schooling, they leave, get a job, and do not give anything back.

In this narrative, the social rule of reciprocity is broken by a schoolboy who leaves without ever giving anything back. Here, the trust-building of the circumcision process is contrasted with the trust-eroding effects of schooling. Circumcision strengthens communal values, whereas schooling promotes individuality and selfishness. These statements were recorded on two separate occasions. No one ever explicitly contrasted these institutions to me in one statement. However, the language used to talk about both suggests a fundamental

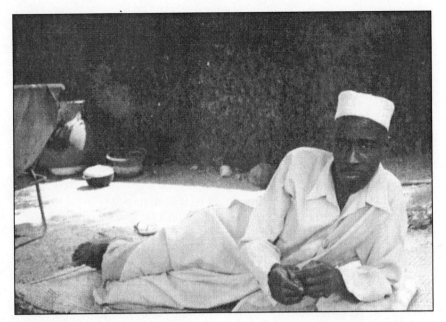

Mal Oumarou

opposition between the two institutions. In circumcision "school" one forms lifelong friendships of trust and intimacy. One makes a best friend (*amanaajo*). But children who go to the government school are characterized as lacking *amaana* (trust). They are untrustworthy. They forget their obligations to people and their debts. They leave Domaayo and never come back. *Bikkoy lakol* (schoolchildren) learn to disrespect their elders in school through the schoolteachers' contempt for local customs and traditions, which are explicitly and implicitly contrasted to the enlightening powers of schooling, science, and civilization. One begins to see how the production of *juulnii'be* and the production of *bikkoy lakol* run in opposed directions and promote contrasting ethics of work and value.

One educational process is community centered, designed by village elders to instill in young children respect for their religion and their social hierarchy. The other educational process, that of *lakol*, or government school, is designed by elements outside of the community with other interests in mind (that is, those of the postcolonial state). The teachers of this school are from elsewhere and often feel themselves deeply alienated from the local culture. Not only are they non-Fulbe and unfamiliar with Fulbe language and culture, but they also identify in a general way with the cosmopolitan and "modern" ways of the city, rather than the local and "traditional" ways of the country. Their "secular" training and cultural estrangement translate into a highly critical stance toward local structures of traditional power and prestige. Children at *lakol* learn to disrespect their elders and their traditions.

THE SCHOOL, THE SUPERMARKET, AND THE MORAL IMAGINATION

Many of the young men I knew in Domaayo had gone to the *lakol* (government school) where they learned to speak, read, and write in French. Indeed, in spite of official statements about English and French sharing the status of official language, the latter is by far the dominant language in most parts of the country. Both French and English were introduced to Cameroon after Germany lost its African colonies (such as Togo, Cameroon, Namibia) at the end of World War I, and the territory was divided into French and English protectorates. In the far north of the country, however, few people speak French or English outside of urban and semiurban areas. And then it is boys who have the greatest exposure to public schools and are therefore most likely to speak French. The language comes to have a special meaning for those boys who are initiated, through the government schools, into a strangely attractive world of Eurocentric learning. In the early years of the colony, schoolchildren were recruited by force, as colonial officials confronted village chiefs with enrollment quotas. Men of high status sought to spare their own children, and sometimes sent the children of their slaves instead. In Senegal, an early colonial school was known as *"l'école des hôtages,"* or the school of the hostages, where the children of chiefs were educated (see Bâ 1991; 1994). The implication was that chiefs, who had signed treaties with French colonial authorities, were beholden to French administrators for the well-being of their "captive" children.

Collective memory of the close relationship between government schools and colonization affects how Fulbe parents feel about contemporary postcolonial schools. Although staffed by African instructors, they are still perceived as essentially "white" schools, which exist to brainwash their children into the values of a foreign culture. Fulbe parents observe that their children return from school with attitudes of contempt for their traditions and with a longing for foreign things, which take them out of the community. Parents complain that most children leave school without having acquired the necessary skills to actually succeed in that world, while those who do succeed have been observed to leave and never come back. They are left wondering why they should invest in the costly school fees, uniforms, and textbooks to send their children there. Thus, public schools are perceived as linked to whiteness, foreign values, and postcolonial politics. They are also viewed as a masculine space. This is a space into which I entered because I shared a language with those schoolboys. Most women, however, are excluded from the world of French, because it is perceived as an immodest language.

IMMODEST KNOWLEDGE

Men often spoke to me as if they identified with me as an "honorary male" in certain situations. This was often encouraged and reinforced by our common knowledge of, and use of, French, which in Domaayo is a gendered language. Indeed, French is the language of men, particularly of young men. It is a language of the world (*dunya*), in the sense of the secular world of travel and markets and chance meetings (and, to a lesser extent, of schoolbooks; a world outside the moral constraints of the mosque and lineage. Women who know French will often conceal their knowledge of it, so as not to be suspect. Fluency in French, for a woman, smacks of a history of travel, of markets and cities and prostitution. In practical terms, most markets (from Garoua to Maroua to Ndjamena) are dominated by the use of Fulfulde. But French symbolizes the mobility and promiscuity of travel, markets, roads, and cities.

In northern Cameroon, French is not only the language of cosmopolitan travel and modernity, it is also the language of schooling. As one young father explained, he was deeply concerned about the possibility of sending his daughters to middle school. Although he would like for them to be educated, he worries about what would become of them in the hands of strangers:

> A girl who goes off to school. She is an intern. No one watches her. If you send your girl to boarding school, in Kaele . . . or in Mindif or Mokolo or Garoua and she becomes pregnant, everyone will laugh at you. Everyone is against you. And it is certain that she will not hold herself back. It is certain.

He went on to share the current gossip that the *sous-prefet*'s interpreter's daughter was pregnant at the time. She attends school in Guidiguis. Most schools beyond the fifth year are boarding schools. Stories like this one are important because they all see the same lesson in it: Do not send your girl to school or she will become a *bordel*." Carol Delaney (1991) writes of a similar construction of school girls as prostitutes in rural Turkey. In both contexts, the knowledge acquired in government schools, like the social space of the schools themselves, is the province of males and loose women. Although such associations are less problematic for boys than for girls in Cameroon, they nonetheless have significant effects on how schoolboys think about their experiences.

CIRCUMVENTING SEMTEENDE: THE MORAL GEOGRAPHY OF FRENCH

If my feelings are hurt (To bernde am naawi), *I can explain that to you in French, while I cannot in Fulfulde. For example, if my wife is giving*

*me a hard time at home, I leave to go to my friend's house. I tell him,
"This is what happened" (literally: this is what they did to me). I tell
him everything. I can speak to him of my pain. While in Fulfulde, there
are certain things I cannot say.*

*If I have problems, I express myself well in French. Not in Fulfulde. I
go to my friend's house. I tell him my situation. He can understand so
far as to feel my pain. In Fulfulde, he hears, but he is not sympathetic.
He will say "Yes, but this sort of thing happens all the time. You will
have to bear it." While in French, it can shock him as it did me. He will
comprehend my suffering. He will understand the state I am in.
Because the French language specifies (détermine). French explains
everything. It can interpret the heart of man.*

In these quotes, from two young men, both of them former *bikkoy lakkol*
(schoolchildren at the French language government schools), reveal how they use
French to circumvent *semteende* (modesty/respect). They are reappropriating the
social space of the classroom, where ethnic identity was theoretically suspended,
and using it to allow for the expression of certain sentiments which Fulbe iden-
tity/language normally proscribes.

One day, I was talking with my friend Muusa about some strange letters I had
been receiving. A Mal Baabikir's had been writing to me in exceedingly formal
and persistent letters of courtship in French. Given the one-sided nature of the
interest (I did not share in the mallum's enthusiasm), I was unsure about Fulbe
etiquette would have me respond in such a situation and I hoped Muusa could
offer some advice. I reflected since my arrival in northern Cameroon I had not
experienced any sexual harassment from Fulbe men (in contrast to what I had
experienced elsewhere) and I suspected that this had something to do with
Islamic norms of *semteende*. Muusa's response was surprising: "What prevents it
is that the villagers do not speak French. There are certain phrases (*paroles*)
which you do not want to say in Fulfulde. But in French, you say everything!" I
persisted in arguing that it was my experience that non-Muslims and southerners
(for I had internalized these categories) were more "shameless" than Fulbe men,
who generally struck me as respectful if not averse to flirtatious banter. But
Muusa disagreed vehemently: "No. They are not any calmer. If they spoke French,
they would all be pursuing you." Muusa's argument underlines young people's
use of French to gain a new kind of autonomy from the values of their elders.
French in Cameroon is the language of power at the national level. Even at the local level, the use of French symbolizes the power and arrogance of the state towards ordinary people and its disregard for local concerns and values. Thus, although the anthropologist had internalized Fulbe stereotypes and their ideology
about moral and emotional norms, Muusa reminded me that local youth do not

accept these ideals passively. Indeed, when Domaayo's young men use French to speak of things which Fulfulde silences, they also harness its power, cosmopolitan arrogance and disrespect for the values of their elders.

Though free women flaunted their knowledge of French, their access to cities and knowledge of the larger world, married Fulbe women often deny having any knowledge of French to avoid raising questions about their past. In a way, the young men who used French to circumvent the constraints of *pulaaku* and *semteende* were also displaced from a Fulbe moral center by their use of French. Like the free women, the *bikkoy lakol* use French to flaunt their autonomy from the moral constraints of Fulbe elders.

If traditional Fulbe society is a gerontocracy, as the circumcision school suggests, it is nonetheless under considerable pressure from numerous institutions, which compete with it for boys' imagination. Indeed, it seems even rural Cameroon is witnessing the growth of a distinctive youth culture, which situates itself somewhere between the Mosque (and the world of Fulbe Islam it signifies) and the increasingly fickle global market place, exemplified by the modern *libre service* (self-serve) supermarket.

Strong friendships between men are formed during circumcision schools as they learn to respect their elders. Through shared notions of respect, worth and *pulaaku*, men learn to weave a communal discourse of identity as Fulbe men and as Muslims. Yet even in the community of men, there are divisions: maleness is not homogeneous. It is permeated by hierarchies defined by age, education, and ethnicity, as well as prestige. And it is creatively interpreted by young men strongly influenced by French language education and media, and the moral imagination of the global marketplace.

In addition, it is profoundly shaped by men's ambivalent relationships with women, who are by definition on the margins the androcentric community. The complex role of women in discourses of witchcraft, sorcery, and spirit possession play no small role in this tension, a topic explored further in chapter six. First we turn to the experience of motherhood in order to examine how women gain social authority in Fulbe society as they face the joys and perils of being a mother.

5

Dangerous Affections: Mothers and Infants

A BABY BOUNCING SONG

In a world full of danger for a newborn child, where wild animals glimpsed in the past by a pregnant mother can cause grotesque, fatal illness, where prosaic sicknesses like malaria and worms are endemic and no less fatal, where the admiring glance of a neighbor and the complimentary phrase from a passerby can induce extreme fevers, weight loss, and death—a mother requires a combination of fortitude, a large network of friends and relatives, and the ability to face the possible loss of her child. Mindful of these things, a woman sings to the baby she bounces on her lap to the rhythm of her words:

> My *Ndendewru. Ndendewru.*
> *Ndendewru* is like a tamarind flower.
> It blooms, it stinks, it produces fruit, it tastes bitter.
> It ripens, it becomes sweet.
> There the ugly thing is, it eludes your grasp (you thought you would get it but didn't).
> There it is, it was brought by the headwaters of the river.
> Whoever wants it—come and look at it!
> Who doesn't want it will wake up sinking;

He will avert his eyes and go blind.
He will click his tongue in disapproval,
      and his tongue will be cut.
Who says of it that it is ugly,
Over the top of the straw screen he has looked at it;
In the shadow of night he has looked at it.

These words are recited by mothers to their children as they bounce them on their knees in joyful moments of intimacy and affection. In contrast to the secrecy of some of the medicines discussed later in this chapter, this "medicinal song" is recited in broad daylight, within hearing range of anyone who wants to hear. In fact, the song, though apparently sung *to the child*, is actually addressed to those who might be looking over the compound wall, staring at her child with longing.

It is a protection poem, telling the spirits, witches, envious neighbors, and any other sentient beings wishing her baby harm that the child is ugly and thus undesirable. "Do you desire my child?" the mother asks. "You can't have it." It was brought to the mother on the edge of the flood waters. It came like flotsam and jetsam, garbage carried on the waves of the flood. Like the Western stork story, this image detaches the mother from the infant. The baby simply arrived. It also suggests that the baby was not wanted by the mother, perhaps, by extension, hinting that undesired, it is undesirable (and thus beyond harm). The poem expresses a mother's fears about her child. There is also a denial of the child's value, in the use of the pronoun *nga,* which means "it." *Nga* could refer to a "big ugly dog" (*dawanga nga*), which belies the woman's sense of her child as in fact precious and worthy of protection, as desirable to envious, admiring eyes and praising tongues. This verbal strategy is similar to that mutual recognition of suffering and hardship between women discussed in chapter three. I argued that these verbal self-deprecations serve to deflect potential feelings of jealousy, because there is nothing to be jealous of. Here, the mother similarly denies that her child is anything desirable at all. The vehemence of the denial speaks volumes about her true feelings.

Women usually treat their babies casually, as if they did not love them quite so much. Unlike many Western women, Fulbe women are with their infants constantly and do not need to concentrate their love and attention in intense and all-too-scarce "quality time." The Fulbe mother, though constantly caring for her youngest children, exhibits an apparent nonchalance about her child, simultaneously breast-feeding and busying herself with tasks, such as sorting rice or cleaning vegetables for the evening meal. Only in the moment when she is making the baby dance in this way (*wamdugo bingel*) does she allow herself to focus completely on him or her—singing as she "makes him dance." The scene could appear to a naive outsider as an idyllic scene of innocent harmony between mother and child. To such an observer, the words to the poem are appalling, at first. But understood in the context of Fulbe culture, the mother's odd words make a lot of sense. She sings about how she is not overly attached to this child, didn't even yearn for him but found him on a trash heap. It is a defiant denial of maternal attachment, superimposed on a physical performance of motherlove. The mother smiles and stares into her baby's eyes, singing, "The big ugly thing is beyond your reach."

I have already described the Fulbe wariness about emotions and, in particular, their awareness of the potentially harmful effects of mother love (Scheper-Hughes 1992; Rebhun 1993). In this chapter, an examination of some common children's illnesses will further expand our understanding of the scope of the Fulbe's ambivalence toward the mother-child bond. Everything mothers give their infants is potentially harmful. From an adoring glance to the intimate gift of mother's milk to the blood of the womb itself—all may have potentially harmful effects on the child. Of course, many negative effects can be alleviated, cured, or even prevented with the application of appropriate medicines. For example, when a mother protects her child from *garsa*, a sickness caused by an excessively admiring look from the mother, the communication going on becomes complex indeed! Through the visible display on a child of a medicinal amulet against *garsa*, she is announcing to all who may see that her baby is loved, since he requires protection from her admiring gaze. The baby's vulnerability, protection, and desirability are all simultaneously evoked in the display of medicines for *garsa*.

Eye and Mouth in Motherhood: Pregnancy, Birth, and Postpartum

Pregnancy accentuates the permeability of women's bodies (Boddy 1989; Popenoe 1997; Schmoll 1991; (Masquelier 1995) and increases the risk of their becoming vulnerable to outside influences/substances. A woman who suspects she is pregnant guards her condition closely. There are restrictions on what a woman can take into her body, not only through her mouth, but also through her eyes. She should already begin caring for her child by avoiding tabooed foods and sights. But she should also avoid drawing attention to her condition, as the envious feelings of other women could cause her to miscarry. There is also a less mechanical modesty about pregnancy that leads a woman to demure when asked about her condition, averting her eyes in silence. She will let her body speak for her, in time, or let her neighbors and co-wives inevitably spread the news throughout the village. It is not so much that it is shameful to talk about pregnancy, but that a woman does not want to claim to be pregnant overtly. It might be taken as boasting, causing resentment and jealousy in other women. Perhaps too, early in her pregnancy, she is unsure that she is truly pregnant (perhaps she fears miscarriage) and wants to avoid the embarrassment of a false claim. If she truly is pregnant, the silence can only postpone her exposure to the harmful effects of envy. The Fulbe believe that the envious gaze itself has the power to cause miscarriage.

An unborn child is extremely vulnerable to what his mother takes into herself through her eyes or through her mouth. A pregnant woman should not eat ribs, for example. She should not set eyes upon a wild animal, such as a rabbit. *Kujje ladde* (wild animals), when seen by a pregnant woman, can cause the sickness called *musub'*, which is characterized by fits in which the child gets a wild look and has trouble breathing. *Musub'* is usually cured by "hunters" (*gaw'en*), who possess hereditary knowledge about the bush, the wild animals it contains, and the sicknesses associated with these animals. Seeing a lizard, or preparing a sauce in a pot that has had a lizard in it, will give her child a sickness called *huutooru* (a large lizard). The illness of *huutooru* occurs in young infants, usually in their first few months (*'Bingel keccel wa'data*), and is characterized by extreme weight loss, or *marasmus*, in which the child's skin hangs on the body so that it resembles the skin of the lizard.

The eyes can also transmit or inspire positive outcomes. Looking at an *'el'eldu* (antelope) when pregnant will make the child's fingers beautifully long. Long, thin fingers and a generally linear build are central to the Fulbe definition of beauty. As was discussed in chapter one, these traits are considered characteristic of the "real Fulbe." The Fulbe of Domaayo, having intermarried with local populations, resemble them more than they do the nomadic cattle-herding Fulani (Woodabe, Mbororo, Fulbe na'i), which the settled Fulbe sometimes called, "Fulbe of the bush" (*Fulbe ladde*). Perhaps the nomadic Fulani's connection with the "bush" resonates with the antelope's slender, graceful build. But the three bush animals cited here have radically different effects on the child, which the expectant mother carries when she sights them. Both the rabbit and lizard cause serious sickness, whereas the antelope causes the development of long and slender fingers. In each case, physical characteristics of the bush animals become marked on the body of the developing child. Wild, frightened eyes, loose, distended skin, and slender fingers are explained in reference to a past event—a sighting during pregnancy. Yet how could such a sighting be avoided? Could women avoid all ventures into the bush? All travel outside the village's immediate surroundings? Perhaps. But what of the pot in which a lizard has been cooked? This image is puzzling, for Fulbe people I knew do not eat lizard. Perhaps this strange culinary practice metonymically refers to, or stands for, un-Islamic practice generally.

As the *juulnii'be* (circumcised) boys learn during their initiation in the bush, those who pray (Muslims) are differentiated from those who don't pray (non-Muslims) by what they eat. During their initiation, they are forced to eat "bush" animals, which, after their return to the village, they will never eat again. Although I never heard of anyone eating lizard, Fulbe people joked about their "pagan" tendencies to eat termites and grasshoppers during the rainy season when they are plentiful. Neighboring Tupuri and Mundang people deep fry them and sell them in the local markets, with salt and cayenne as condiments. Many people I knew had tasted them but claimed to have given them up since childhood. Although not proper foods for a Muslim, they are not heavily marked as *haram* (forbidden) in the same way as pork. Lizard, however, is clearly outside the Muslim repertoire of edible food. A woman who has been cooking lizard is "up to no good" in a disturbing way. Of course, it is possible that a woman's cooking pot might be tainted with lizard by someone else. Neighbors or co-wives all might have access to a woman's cooking pot without her knowledge. Thus, it is possible for a pregnant woman to have her child affected by contamination with a wild animal without her knowledge. The cooking pot, which momentarily contains the lizard, mirrors the mother's womb, which now also contains a lizard or a child, which will gradually come to resemble one.

The mother's pregnancy can also affect the child she is breast-feeding. A woman who is nursing a child must wean it immediately when she learns she is pregnant, as her milk now belongs to the child who is preparing to be born. The child who is allowed to continue "stealing" its younger sibling's milk can become violently ill. Yet mothers feel sorry for their infants who are abruptly weaned in this manner, especially if they are much under two years of age, when children are normally weaned. The image of the pitifully thin, prematurely weaned child (*entaa'do*) was humorously deployed by Rabiyatu (see chapter three), when she teased her friend and neighbor Daada Saidu, by saying that she is "as skinny as an *entaa'do*."

If it is her first child, the mother-to-be will normally go home to her parents to give birth, staying "at least six months" I was told and sometimes up to two years. The two-year postpartum taboo has little chance of being observed if the young mother returns to her husband. Both men and women suggested to me that they no longer wait this long to resume sexual relations. There seems to be a contradiction between the relaxation of postpartum taboos and the continuing view that it is preferable to wait until a child is ready to be weaned (at about age two) before becoming pregnant with his/her junior sibling. "We say that two years is a good amount of time to pass between births." Thus the two-year birth spacing is still desired, yet in my observations, women who gave birth more often were not criticized but admired. Abortions are not considered a legitimate practice, but medicines that can cause abortion are not unknown. Given the sensitivity of the issues involved, information about abortion and birth control (as well as infanticide) are not easily available to anthropologists, and have consequently been understudied and underreported in the anthropological literature. Nonetheless, I've heard of some who use *kucce* (calabash seeds), as "it kills, it is bitter, even more than Nivaquine (chloroquine, a common antimalarial drug)." Leaves like *dubaajo* and *haabiiru*, are also said to be effective. Although women control information about such topics, even men are aware of these practices: "Certain women drink medicine to abort or the day of the birth, they kill the baby." Because women often give birth alone, the decision not to keep a baby they do not have the strength to feed, may be made without the knowledge of others (see Scheper-Hughes 1992).

Of course, enforcing postpartum abstinence is not the only reason for a new mother to stay home for a while after giving birth. At home the young woman will learn her own mother's recipes for *dollere*, a millet broth, which serves as a food supplement for infants, and is also considered a remedy for many childhood ailments. Also, prior to giving birth, she can be assured of her natal family's compassion and their desire that she not hurt herself or her unborn child in the advanced stages of her pregnancy. In her marital compound, she is not guaranteed a respite in the weeks leading up to her term, even if she has a co-wife who could take over some of her more strenuous work. Thus Ubbo commented on her son's wife Zeynabu's pregnancy: "One co-wife, if she has a heart (*en'dam*), will take over the cooking during the ninth month, but it's up to her. There's no rule that a woman should be relieved of work at a certain time in her pregnancy. Look at Zeynabu, she is nine months now and has Astajam [her co-wife] lifted a finger to help her? No! She has no heart at all. (*O walaa en'dam sam!*)" After the miscarriage of the baby, who would have been her grandchild, Ubbo reminded me of our earlier conversation: "You see? You were asking me whether a woman late in her pregnancy was spared strenuous work? At nine months, Zeynabu was left alone to cook and draw water for her husband. And last night, she made two trips to the well! You saw what can happen." A woman, who is able to return home to her parents, can avoid such dangerous circumstances. Her home stay gives her a chance to rest from domestic work, distances her from the potentially worrisome domestic politics of her marital *saare*, and incidentally protects her and her child from the envious glances of co-wives and neighbors.

Pregnancy both dramatizes and accentuates the permeability of women's bodies. It calls for heightened vigilance on the part of the expectant mother, who must protect herself and the child she carries from the dangers of the bush, as well as that of her closest neighbors. Furthermore, she must protect a nursing infant from the consequences of stealing her junior sibling's milk by weaning her immediately. She is thus not only vulnerable but also capable of causing harm, as her bodily resources are shifted from the children she already has to the one she awaits. After giving birth, she will have to follow other precautions.

GIVING BIRTH: HAWWA AND BUULO

There are no midwives in Domaayo—that is, no healers whose specialty is to deliver children for a fee. However, there are several older women who seem to appear after a birth to help with the baby and tend the embers, which are kept burning in the house of a new mother. Shortly after Rabiyatu gave birth to her son, Hammadu, she talked to me about their postpartum practices:

> When a woman gives birth, she does not drink cool water. She does not walk in cool places. If it is a little cool in the house, she lights a fire. She washes the child twice a day with a calabash of hot water for a year. This is done from day one. The first week, it is always the aunt or grandmother who does it. This is to strengthen the bones and the joints (haa saatina i'e bee jokke). [Sa'ati means strong, to become strong. It can be used to mean "to scold" as in a don saatanammi (you scold me, literally, you make me tough/strong).]
>
> They say that scarification "forbids" (prevents) illness. Even shaving the head. Me, I had forbidden it until [my son is] three months old. Among the elders, they split the gums with a small knife, so that the teeth come out well. I have forbidden this.

Most women give birth alone, or only ask for assistance after the child is born. This has several consequences. There are no witnesses to the mother's pain, and there is potentially some ambiguity around the condition of a dead baby. Was it a stillbirth? Or did it die after being born? The possibility of infanticide was never raised directly with regard to a particular "stillbirth," but more than once I heard men allude to their inability to know what really happened at the moment of the birth in which a baby died. New mothers usually send a child to get their co-wife or neighbor. This person will put the first drops of water in the baby's mouth, a ritual gesture thought to impart the child with the temperament of the woman doing it. "You always want to chose someone calm and stable," said Rabiyatu, who had just given birth to her fifth child. "Or else it will give you no end of trouble."

> Rabiyaatu talks to her friend and neighbor about her baby: "O nyatdo Daada Hawwa! Ba Yerima Usumaanu. He doesn't ever laugh, Daada Hawwa. Like Yerima Usumaanu." Daada Hawwa is the one who gave him water. She took water in her mouth and spit it out on the child, spraying his face with it. This is done if the child comes out and it doesn't cry right away. Then they cut the umbilical cord. Daada Hawwa did it, with the help of Daada Abba. Then Daada Hawwa put a few drops of water in his mouth with her fingers, three times (with cold water). After that it's only hot water. All this is done immediately after the birth. Last time it was Daada Abba who put drops of water in Goggo Peetel's mouth. This is why those people are blamed (jokingly) for the child's character. You are supposed to choose someone who is quiet, calm, never lets anything bother them (even tempered). (Go'do bee hakkilo de'udo). Others say you should get someone, who doesn't always find fault with others.

(*Go'do je yida yawaare.*) *Friendship and mutual support between these*
three women is strengthened by the fact that Daada Hawwa, Daada
Abba and Rabiyatu are all wives of brothers.

The mother and child stay inside the house for seven days, until the day of
the naming ceremony, when the baby is brought out of the house by its father's
sister or her representative. Smoke, talismans, and medicines protect the mother
and child during this period when they are known to be especially vulnerable.
The danger which threatens them at this time is never named aloud. Yet this
cluster of practices points to the invisible but no less powerful predatory forces
of spirits. Calling them out by name is believed to attract them to the speaker
and is therefore strictly avoided. Women are always more vulnerable to penetration by spirits than are men, but their condition after they have just given birth
makes them especially permeable to alien influences. Among the Berti of Sudan
and the Hofriyati (Boddy 1989; Holy 1990), women's attractiveness to spirits after childbirth is explicitly linked to their bleeding, which attracts spirits. No
Fulbe person ever made such explicit connections, but they could very easily be
implied. In any case, the house and fire offer maximal protection. Spirits tend to
dwell in cool places and on the margins of the village. The mother avoids these
places until she has recovered her strength and a greater degree of impermeabil-
ity.

The Millet Stalk and the Razor

We are a group of women in the compound of Saali'en, talking about
tetanus in newborns. Nenne, the mother of four sons and two daugh-
ters and many grandchildren, asserts: "The ancestors (boyma'en) *cut*
the umbilical cord (jaaburu) *with a millet stalk. But people don't want*
the old." So they use razor blades (lazoir) *which are not sterilized, and*
thus may cause tetanus. Says Laadi: "you should heat the blade over a
fire, boil it in water. Then cut the umbilical cord with it." Nenne adds,
"the dabboje *(sugar cane stalk) is sharper!"*

The colostrum (*murla*) is expelled and the breasts washed in medicine to protect the newborn. The father's family is usually responsible for providing the pa-
paya (*dukuuje*) and *barkeeje* leaves used in this washing, which will continue for
seven days until the *indeeri* (naming ceremony). The mother does not breast-feed
for the first three days. Earlier feeding is believed to make the child sick. The
mother washes in hot water twice a day and drinks only hot water. Burning logs
keep her house hot. The baby drinks water until he or she can begin to drink

milk. One month and ten days after the birth, the baby is given *dollere*, a millet broth, to supplement the milk diet. Administering the *dollere* is a daily ritual for mothers, usually in the late afternoon before the evening meal is prepared [see photo]. The *dollere* is continued until the child begins to fill out (*haa o wuufini*). I do not know if there is a standard age when *dollere* is stopped, but I do not recall seeing any child over a year old being fed this broth. Recipes are passed down from mother to daughter and exchanged only between close friends, if at all. There are differing views on *dollere*: how to make it, when to start giving it to a baby, how long to give it as a supplement to breast milk.

Rabiyatu told me that because she had given birth immediately before the fasting month of Ramadan, she would only wait one month before giving her infant the broth. Giving the child additional food presumably eases the physical strain on the mother who is breast-feeding while fasting. Her mother-in-law advised her not to fast for forty days after giving birth, but Rabiyatu would not accept this "reprieve" from fasting. She would have to "make up" the missed days of fasting later in the year, alone and without the camaraderie of communal fasting.

I visited my friend Hawwa shortly after she had given birth. The following excerpt from my field notes evokes the atmosphere and concerns of that room. Hawwa is married to Yaya, a man who is wealthy in cattle and children but poor in cash (see chapter three). He is also married to Hurey, who is well-established in this *saare*, having given Yaya many children. Although Hawwa has been married before and has four children who live with their paternal relatives, this is her first child with Yaya. Since she has had children before, it is expected that she will stay in her husband's *saare* to give birth. She is originally from a town across the border in Chad (perhaps 10–15km away), a distance short enough to be traversed on foot but far enough to discourage a woman from rushing home without due cause. In fact, her visits home during this pregnancy reflect her quarrels with her husband, not a typical visiting pattern. Her co-wife has recently given birth to twins who both died only a few weeks ago.

> A baby girl was born to Hawwa on October 12, yesterday.
> She looks strong. Has a lot of hair. They say that's why the mother has heartburn during pregnancy, because of the hair. "Asee (look!), she had hair even inside my stomach. So that's why my heart (bernde) hurt."
> I notice Hawwa has a cloth belt tied around her still-big belly. The child has kohl streaked down the front of her head, from her forehead to her nose, right down the middle. "Dija President came over yesterday after the birth and did everything for me! She lit a fire, cleaned up, drew water until my water pots were filled, etc."
> I notice that they keep the newborn covered with a length of cloth, that the belly button and drying umbilical cord is well covered so that

flies do not land on it. The drying jaaburu *(umbilical cord) is tied to a cloth belt "so that it will not be lost when it dries off" [it will be useful to her later].*

There are three logs smoking up the room, lying on a tin tray in the middle of the room. Hawwa keeps distancing the logs from one another to reduce the smoke. Her sister keeps moving them back together. The burning in my eyes is becoming unbearable, so I am extraordinarily attentive to this charade. Daada Alhaaji (a neighbor) comes with something she has just pounded outside. Perhaps some medicine.

Hurey, Hawwa's co-wife, acts cheerful enough and greets incoming visitors, but she stays aloof from the main event. The baby. Even if they were best of friends, she would feel some jealousy, having just lost both of her fragile twins. But they are not apparently such very good friends. There seems to be some very live tension here. I wonder if that is not perhaps why Hawwa had run away last week. The Ladan (the village muezzin and Daada Alhaji's husband) had mentioned it to me, saying the whole neighborhood was discussing how to bring her back. Implied was the importance of her giving birth in the best of conditions. She gave birth by early morning. Having begun labor at the first hints of dawn. Alone. Finally, I step out to escape the smoke. My eyes streaming with my tears. Hurey laughs "Curde! (smoke!)"

The *Ladan* was concerned that husband and wife should be reconciled before the birth, so that the child would strengthen the marriage, rather than weaken it. When I look at Hawwa, surrounded by her neighbors, who came to help, to give thanks and to witness the birth, I saw a woman who was making her presence in the village more real. Witnessing the fact of the birth is the first significant step in building this community of women as a community of pain and suffering. This community of suffering, discussed in chapter three, can only truly be entered through the process of giving birth. The pain of childbirth, endured now in this place, makes Hawwa a real woman to her neighbors. While it is a woman's first child which makes her a woman, a previously married woman who is a mother still has never given birth in that town and, thus, has not yet become "a woman of that town."

I rarely heard women discuss the process of childbirth itself. Perhaps they discuss it only with other women who have experienced it or with their expecting daughters. But the pain, risk, drama of it were often referred to in passing by both men and women. A male friend once told me in awe, "a woman in labor has one foot in the grave." Further, it is said that no one is completely free of sin, as Muslims are born with the sin of having caused their mother's pain, which they must atone for, in order to get into heaven. Some women talked about wanting to give birth in a hospital, in order to be able to get help in the event of a complica-

Rabiyatu and friend feeding their infants dollere, *a medicinal broth. Married to brothers, they share family recipes.*

tion. But I never heard a woman describe what her birth was like in great detail, as, for example, some American women do. It is very likely that my own status as a woman who had never given birth affected what I could easily learn about the process among Fulbe women.

Had Hawwa given birth in her home village in Chad, she would have no doubt received the support of kin, but there would have been the uncertainty about her future and the future of her child. Was she still married? Or had she left him for good? Would he ask her to come back? Would she accept? These questions, though unspoken, would be on everyone's mind, including Hawwa's. If she returned to Domaayo weeks later, with her baby, there would be visiting, of course, as friends and neighbors would come to see her with her new baby. But she would return with a child already named and celebrated elsewhere. The moment of glory for the new mother would have happened elsewhere without the participation of the women of Domaayo. She could never make up the lost opportunity to create and strengthen her networks with women in this town.

Now this baby, the first that Hawwa has brought into this *saare*, was actualizing relationships of reciprocity with the women of this village. She had visited them and come to their nomination ceremonies, bringing gifts and good wishes. Now it is their turn to come to her. There was an unmistakable satisfaction on Hawwa's face the day of the birth that I read as being, not only about her physical accomplishment, but of its acknowledgment and affirmation by her women co-villagers.

Hawwa's sister, Dija President and Daada Alhaaji formed the core of Hawwa's supporters during her recovery. Their willingness to help her now reflects her ongoing relationship with them. I lived in Dija's compound during my first two months in the field. So I was able to observe up close the network of friendships between women of this neighborhood. Hawwa and Daada Alhaaji were frequent visitors to Dija's *saare*. Hurey also came to visit, but never at the same time. Although Dija and Daada Alhaaji never took sides in the quarrels between the two co-wives, they were well aware of Hawwa's difficulties with Hurey. Dija, who is herself childless, might have felt particular sympathy for Hawwa's predicament as a "useless" woman next to her prolific co-wife. Hurey did not have an easy life herself, but her suffering was the joyous suffering of a "mother of children" (*daada bikkoy*). Daada Alhaaji's children are full grown, and she is once again alone with her husband. Both Dija and Daada Alhaaji had the leisure as well as the inclination to help their neighbor after she gave birth. Juleyia and Jaara, who live in the same *saare* as Dija and, thus, are equally close neighbors to Hawwa, did not volunteer to come help her after her birth, though they came for a brief visit. Dija and Daada Alhaaji demonstrated their friendship and intimacy with Hawwa by simply coming as soon as they heard and doing what was needed.

In contrast with the tense situation in which Hawwa gave birth, my friend Buulo's child appeared in a more serene and ordered environment:

> Buulo gave birth yesterday. I find her this morning drinking gaari kilbu
> (millet soup with natron). Her aunt, who is acting as her mother, ex-
> plains: "She won't eat nyiiri (normal millet porridge, the Fulbe staple)
> until tomorrow maybe. There is no hunger in the stomach. (Weelo
> wooda haa reedu). Only gaari and meat. (Sey gaari bee kusel) "her
> aunt informs me. Buulo looks at her baby, pointing to his wrinkled skin
> and his umbilical cord. "You eat sweet things. (Kuje belde yakka.)
> When it has been three days, I will eat nyiiri. Coffee, you can't drink
> until the day of the nomination (indeeri) [which takes place] seven
> days after the birth.
>   Her aunt teases her. "Buulo puldebbo. Buulo naywi! (Buulo is an
> old woman. Buulo has gotten old)."

This is Buulo's first child, and it is the child that makes her a mother and a true adult in Fulbe society. It places her in the community of women, who have felt the pain of childbirth, who have endured the hardship and suffering of a woman's life. When Buulo's aunt seemingly insults her, calling her an old woman, she is really congratulating her on her entry into the world of womanhood.

The foods she eats are "sweet," meaning tasty, special foods like *gaari*, the fragrant drink made by women during Ramadan, which is used to break the fast. It is delicate and aromatic, nutritious without being too rich. All *gaari* is easy to digest, and the *kilbu* (natron) added to a new mother's *gaari* is said to calm her stomach. "Meat gives her strength" I am told. And it is not insignificant that women, who are normally given smaller portions of meat than men, get to have their own special meat dishes during the post-partum period, which they are not obligated to share with their husbands or anyone else. The meat is said to give them strength. According to Rabiyatu, the husband is obligated to "buy" the mother's milk with the meat of sacrifice. "It is in the book [the Koran]. You give the mother good things to eat for forty days so that her milk will be plentiful."

> *In the house where Buulo sits with her child, people are commenting on the child's looks, as cheerful insults and scandalous laughter fill the room. To my great dismay, my presence inspires a commentary on the superiority of whites. "The strength of one white person equals that of three black people." The insults also take the form of "racial" commentary, focusing on nose shape. "Look at this nose. Kine wooda! He has no nose!" exclaims a woman who has come to visit him. She blesses him by touching her fingers to his forehead, mouth and chest, while saying a prayer.*

Fulbe people are "supposed" to have long straight noses, whereas local Africans, whom the Fulbe sometimes call *baleybe* (blacks), do not. But most Fulbe people I knew found that their looks departed substantially from the ethnic ideal. This was the source of extensive teasing between people who were related in joking relationships, like cross cousins and the younger brother of a man and his wife. Here the joking had the value of deflecting harm from the child. By insulting the baby's looks, women not only avoid uttering dangerous compliments, but they also send out a message to anyone who might hear that it is not a "desirable" child, and therefore not worth harming.

THE NAMING CEREMONY (*INDEERI*)

The naming ceremony, as the following excerpt from my field notes illustrates, is characterized by the same radical sexual segregation which marks Fulbe weddings and funerals. As a foreign guest and a woman, I am able to move from male to female space through this highly polarized ritual.

> *Tuesday, February 26, 1991. Bakari's new baby boy is being named today. Mats are neatly laid out in an L-shape in front of Bakari's compound. His brothers sit on the downhill end on several mats under the*

shade of the neem tree. A group of teenagers sit on another mat, closer to Bakari, with a few young (ages eight to ten) boys among them. Two old men sit on a mat uphill, under the shade of Bakari's jawleeru, or entrance house. One of them is Dija Kawo's father, Kawo Paho—a barber who traditionally shaves the child's head on the nomination and "coming out" of the boy after his circumcision and confinement. Bakari doesn't trust the old man's shaky hands on the child's tender head. He will pay him nonetheless. People are served by age classes on the mats, in conversation groups. Bakari is very quiet and still, which is revealing of his ambivalent position in the ceremony. As father, he is featured and congratulated, yet the elders and religious leaders are the ones who accept the child into the community. Bakari can't do that. Today is the child's entry into the community of Muslims. The slave, Falama, holds a tray of red and white kola, which he distributes among the guests. The father of Baaba Rey (Yaya Siddi) gets red kola and chewing gum from Nigeria. Others get white kola and gum. The older men get white kola. Jim [an American] and I got white. How does the slave decide to whom to give white kola? And to whom to give red? And whom to leave out? Since Bakari does none of the serving, the rank/status distinctions seem not to be made by him, but by the community at large [represented by Falama].

Later, the slave came with his goat head and skin (his pay for attending and butchering the goat) and sat by the mawbe, *the important middle-aged guests. He made conversation but never took the lead in telling a story or expounding a point as the others did. A young girl brought the tea on a tray and set it down. The griot/slave served it, in a very specific order. A spoon-shaped calabash ladles the tea from the enamel bowl into the glasses. There clearly wasn't enough tea to go around. The first glass went to Jim. Then the older men to Jim's right (the barber and his peers) were served. Then the middle-aged men were served selectively, while those young men sitting downhill from the tree were left out. The men drank quickly and set their glasses down on the tray or handed it to a child to set it down, so others could be served. Then, the other middle-aged men, including the brothers under the neem tree, and a few young married men were served from the bowl.*

Njaayo are gifts of money presented at a marriage, nomination, circumcision. They are ritual gifts, usually presented publicly. Many of the guests came to sit by Bakari as they were leaving and handed him a bill of money or some coins. (Jim, who was sitting closer to him than I was, estimates that the amounts given ranged from 125 CFA to 1000 CFA.) This occurred upon leaving, so that it was not the reason for the amount or quality of kola or the serving of the tea. Perhaps the kola was distributed according to the strength (sembe), or wealth, of the man, his ability to give money and thus, what was expected of him.

The tea may hàve had nothing to do with that but rather was a marker of age, respect, lineage (not strength or wealth).

The men assembled before the entrance to the compound never saw the baby. Never mentioned its mother.

Inside the compound, a very different ceremony was unfolding. It's as if there were two different nomination events, totally unrelated to each other. One centered around Islam, the elders, the men related to Bakari (his brothers). Another centered on the baby, his mother, his mother's mother. Women came into Rabiyatu's house, each in her best wrapper, carrying an enamel dish filled with millet grain, with perhaps a coin or two stuck in the grain. They entered, sat down, put their bundle down (their dish and perhaps that sent by a co-wife or neighbor who was unable to attend) wrapped in a cloth and tied at the top. They were handed the baby, one by one. They touched the baby's forehead and mouth with their index and middle fingers, then touched their own forehead and chest. This they repeated three times. This is a sign of acceptance of the child into the community. The child is admired, held, touched and passed on to the next woman. All women present are married. No girls come to this ceremony; Rabiyatu's own girls are scolded when they enter the house, crowded as it is with women. Goggo Peetel, two and a half years old, is also scolded, but more gently. She is allowed to linger a little before going out. She is trying to talk. She understands everything but cannot yet formulate words of her own. She does not know that her favored position as the youngest of Rabiyatu's children has been usurped by this creature.

Rabiyatu or her mother would pour the millet into a large enamel bowl and thank the person, pulling out the money and placing it in a special plate, then place a kola and gum in the dish and hand it back to the woman, who then got up to leave. "Allah mawninmo. God raise him." Grant that he grow to adulthood (that he live through the dangers of childhood). The whole routine is repeated again and again. The newcomer arrives with a dish, puts her bundle down, sits down, greets people one by one, starting with the most important, hands over her dish and eventually asks to have it back. The pouring of the millet into the bigger dish, noticing the money, returning the dish with kola. Final blessings, getting up to leave.

These are very carefully dressed women. They all wear "wax" cloth (superior to ordinary "prints"). The cloth is new. All wear matching outfits—no mixing and matching. The women are serious in demeanor, overall, yet they are in good spirits. They talk about there being no money around in these times. The price of leaves, of peanuts, of oil. People barely getting by. Having very little to give. They seem to be saying their gifts are small because of their conditions of economic *hardship, rather than stinginess. They want to participate, be a part of it, give what they can. The women are really into holding the baby. Praising God. "O he'bi! She has received!" A boy. Now she has a boy, she can rest.*

The next day, I asked Bakari about the events of the nomination. "How does Faalama, the slave, know to whom to give red or white kola?" "*Il y a des gens valeureux, il y a des gens pas valeureux. Comme les Marabouts, les Yerima,* etc. (There are people of value, there are people without value. Like the *Mallums*, the Princes (sons of the chief), etc." Those who came early and *gave* the name, received ten kolas and some candy (*shokolat*). Normally it is not a slave, but a griot who does the distributing. But Saalisu was traveling, so he asked his brother to take his place. To slay the goat, the slave butchers it, but the actual cutting of the throat, the sacrifice, is done by the head of the compound, according to Muslim tradition. In this case, it was Bakari's older brother Usumaanu who did it. It can really be done by anyone, so long as he is a faithful Muslim man, one who prays five times a day, who knows how to sacrifice.

Sacrifice is a very important part of the nomination. Women feel very strongly about it because it signifies appreciation and recognition of the mother. When Rabiyatu, who is sitting nearby, interjects a few words, her voice is adamant, challenging. "When was the last time you slew an animal for me? Wasn't it two years ago that you last sacrificed a goat for me? And that wasn't without good reason [a reference to the birth of her last child, Goggo]. Now you slay one for Mohammadu. It is not a gift. It's to *buy the mother's milk.*" It is clear that she feels that the slaying of the goat is for the mother, in acknowledgment of her "work" in bringing this child into the world. When she hears Bakari talking to me about the events of the nomination, she does not trust his rendition and challenges it, re-centering the attention from the ritual work of the father and his slave/griot to the reproductive work of the mother. The conceptualization of the nomination sacrifice as a purchase of the mother's milk underscores the importance of mothers' physical sacrifice of their bodily resources to their newborn children. The combative tone of the interchange is a frequent aspect of my visits with Rabiyatu and Bakari. I am friends with both of them. Being of a younger generation and a schooled child (*bingel lakol*), Bakari doesn't practice the extreme segregation between the sexes, which is characteristic of his elders and many of his peers. He sometimes eats with his wife and often spends time in the thatch veranda with her and their children as they work on different tasks. Because of this, I participated in frequent triadic conversations in which both Bakari and Raabiyatu expect me to sympathize with their distinctive perspectives.

"It is in the book [the Koran]," she says. "You give the mother good things to eat for forty days so that her milk will be plentiful." On another occasion, Rabiyatu's husband shared with me his sense of birthing being excessively costly:

Family portrait: a properous mallum *with his children.*

Giving birth is very expensive for us. You must give good meat to the woman during the first week, and for the nomination, there will be gifts, and it is necessary to sacrifice an animal. If you don't, you will have to listen to your mother-in-law or your in-laws. Whereas I see that among the Mundang and the Tupuri, they give birth and the very next day, they are working in the fields. They go out [to work] without requiring special food.

If these women, the Fulbe's ethnic neighbors, can do without special diets and rest, then, he suggests, Fulbe women could conceivably do without these privileges also. They are not necessary, he implies. Fulbe women are troublesome, placing an unduly heavy burden on their husbands, who often can ill afford extra rations of meat and firewood to heat water. But any man who wants the goodwill of his in-laws must conform to their expectations regardless of his doubts. Even when his wife is staying with her own parents, he is responsible for her upkeep and for supplying an animal to be sacrificed for the nomination. The notion of cost is not an exclusively male viewpoint. Rabiyatu also spoke of payment. The husband's sacrifice "buys" the mother's milk for his child. In fact, she disputes his notion that it is optional, or "extra." After all, the Koran requires it! For once, it seems, the scriptural text can be cited by women to their advantage.

After the nomination is over, the child will begin to move in the world, outside of the house into which he was born, and he will thus be exposed to a wide variety of stimulations and dangers. He will require the protection of a variety of medicines to deflect harm. A woman's kin and her affines will give her infant *layaaji* (talismans) to protect it from various illnesses. Displayed around an infant's neck, a copious string of *layaaji* announces to any viewer that this infant is not only well protected, but also well connected. This infant is part of an effective network of kin who have contributed the various pouches of protective medicine. The *layaaji* string is a concretization of its kin.

Protective amulets for children are used by all. Infants usually have a conspicuous necklace of them during the first two years of life (while breast-feeding). Mothers usually do not want to talk about them out of fear of attracting the sicknesses they are intended to repel. Speaking the name of a thing or person amounts to calling it. Bakari told me about his baby's amulets (*layaaji* Mohammadu), pointing to each in turn and telling me what he knew about them: The first one, made of red plastic, is called *sittanaayel*. "*Be nga'dan non.* They just put it on for no reason." The second one is a *tattadinaare* (a coin) "useful for damp cold (*nafan pewri*)." Other *layaaji* include: A tiny pine cone which is ornamental; the toe of a hyena, so that the child will learn to walk early. Two others are "perhaps for talk (*teema je haala*)." Here "talk" (*haala*) refers to the potentially harmful effects of people's talking admiringly about a child. They come from Aamadu, the baby's father's brother and a severe religious man. Another one is for *mistirii'en* (witches). It is a flat square leather pouch, which suggests that it contains writing! This surprised me at first because the religious *mallums* are said not to believe in *mistiraaku* (witchcraft). The writing of Arabic for *layaaji* (often using verses from the Koran) is typically done by male clerics. Women use and manipulate Arabic writing also. The fact that the *layaaru* contains writing does not necessarily indicate that it was produced from within the "orthodox" terrain of the mallums. I discovered that medicinal writing (*bindi*) is shared among women and recopied again and again, often by people who have very limited knowledge of Arabic. Another talisman is *kohi*, a hard wood tree useful in the prevention of *dem'de* (admiring speech, which can cause harm). One is from Hawwa, the baby's paternal aunt. "She just sent it. She didn't say what it was for!" Bakari speculates: "*Haala mistii'en na? Haala dem'de na? Haala giite non?* Is it for cannibal witches? For tongues, or simply for eyes?" All of them are brand new, costing about 200 CFA to cover in leather (50 CFA each). If they consulted a *mallum* to do the writing, they also paid him (or her) a fee, which varies with the medicinal content and the ability of the client to pay.

The talismans, which are not based on Arabic writing, seem to rely on metaphorical and metonymic associations between some attribute of the talis-manic object and the desired effect on the child. For instance, the *kohi* tree, known for its hard wood, works medicinally to help the infant resist the assault of "tongues" (*dem'de*). The toughness of the wood makes the child's body tough, so that pathogenic vectors will bounce off from its resistant surface. The hyena toe transfers onto the child the mobility of the hyena. The association between a coin (*tattadinaare*) and the ability to ward off damp cold (*pewri*) is unclear. Among other "Sudanic" populations, such as the Berti of Sudan (Holy 1990) and the Tuareg of Niger (Worley 1992), iron and silver are used to ward off spirits. Although *peewol* (damp cold) and *ginnaaji* (spirits) were mostly deployed as dis-tinct etiological registers in Fulbe conversations of sickness, they did occasionally seem to merge imperceptibly into one another.

Michael Dols discusses a connections made in Medieval Islamic medicine be-tween humoral imbalance and spirits (*jinn*) (Dols 1992:81) in which the spirits cause the humoral imbalance, which is itself the cause of melancholia. In the Fulbe context, the connection may be found in the environment. Spirits tend to reside near rivers, watering holes, and trees whose deep roots tap into the water table for nourishment. Water is the ultimate in "damp cold." When walking in the sandy riverbed of seasonal rivers, one sometimes comes across pockets of cool air. In the hot dry climate of northern Cameroon, these cool spaces are evocative of another, unseen dimension of reality, reminders of another plane of being in which spirits live lives parallel to those of humans. Invisible, yet always near human communi-ties, they are easily provoked when their dwelling places are disturbed. Calling them by name (*ginnaaji*) can draw them out, and humans resort to euphemism and indirection in indicating their influence. Wind (*heendu*) is the most common synonym, but damp cold (*peewol*) is also used. More often, people simply refer to spirits as *kanjum* ("that matter") which seems impossibly vague, but in the right context, any Fulbe person would understand the reference.

"Cold," talk, tongues, eyes are all vectors, which transmit the dangerous pow-ers of jealousy, envy, and excessive admiration. The elicitation of these vectors of sickness filled me with a sense of foreboding, imminent danger and an anxious awareness of malevolent forces in the world. I imagine that Fulbe women are al-ways somewhat aware of these forces and constantly work to keep them at bay. Perhaps this is why mothers do not discuss the purpose of these amulets, but merely display them, as shields.

These amulets, while proclaiming the worth of the child and the value at-tached to it by its relatives, evidenced by the number of amulets on his/her necklace, simultaneously, and somewhat ironically, also function to protect the child from the negative consequences of such admiration. *Demde* (tongues), *gite* (eyes) and *garsa* are all childhood maladies caused by excessive admiration, however well-intentioned. Its effects can be devastating. *Garsa* can cripple a child's arm or leg. *Demde* can cause dramatic weight loss and fevers. *Gite* can afflict the whole body, causing pains, fever and anorexia in young children.

Eyes Can Pierce a Baby Like Arrows

Hawwa's baby daughter is suffering from fever and diarrhea. "She has diarrhea. Perhaps it is this sun which causes it. She's lost weight. Maybe it's her teeth coming in—she used to be fat. A remedy for this is a recitation to stop the child from getting sick. My grandmother gave me a chloroquine tablet which I dissolved and gave her to drink. Mi dolla dollere bee kilbu. Nafan gildi haa reedu. Kilbu naa katdum?! Nafan. I boiled up some dollere (millet broth) with kilbu (calcium carbonate, or natron). It is useful for worms in the stomach. Isn't kilbu bitter?! It will be effective."

 Aminatu wears beads of wood around her neck. "Lekki dem'de. It's medicine for "tongues." If someone says, "Look at this beautiful child," the bead will break off. (To go'do wi'i: "Ayee, 'bingel do boongel—dum feetan. Allah tufiihoy)."

 Eyes can pierce a baby like arrows. (Gite fidata 'bingel.) A good looking child, you will surely look at it. ('Bingel bo'dum do kam a laaran).

 "This sickness is different from garsa. Nyawu man feere bee garsa. Garsa is lopsidedness. Garsa kam wuraago. It twists the body. Like Saali in the saare of Goggo Duuduu'en. His leg is ruined by garsa. It strikes the head, feet, or arms. Garsa kam haa jokkude—seeka i'al. Garsa [strikes] the joints—it splits the bone. The medicine for garsa is Koranic/magical. They go over the body with thumb and fingers, then utter a prayer."

 This narrative from my field notes captures the panoply of etiological frames and medicines being employed by Hawwa as she thinks about the condition of her infant Aminatu. I insert it here to demonstrate that no single diagnosis stands in isolation as a mother confronts her ailing child. The image of a bead bursting from the tongues recklessly praising her child powerfully suggests the sacrifice of the bead, which protects the body of the child. One can imagine the satisfaction of a mother, finding a broken bead on her infant's necklace, knowing that she has prevented the pernicious effects of *demde*.

GITE AND "THE EVIL EYE"

The Fulbe conception of *gite* (eyes) bears close resemblance to the well-known concept of "the evil eye," which is found in widely varied cultures from Scotland to Sri Lanka (Maloney 1976b:143). In some contexts, such as among the Amhara, the power of the evil eye is attributed to a particular population who are known for their possession of the disease-causing eye (Reminick 1976:87). In many other regions, the evil eye is attributed to behaviors of which everyone is capable, such as excessive staring, particularly envious staring. Crapanzano has written that in Morocco "a whole range of misfortune may be attributed to the evil eye, but a gradual wasting sickness . . . is the characteristic effect" (Crapanzano 1973:185 cited in Dols 1992:290). According to Brian Spooner, in his overview of evil-eye beliefs in the Middle East:

> *The main characteristic of the evil eye is that it relates to the fear of envy in the eye of the beholder, and that its influence is avoided or counteracted by means of devices calculated to distract its attention and by practices of sympathetic magic. Jealousy can kill via a look.(Spooner 1976:77).*

In the South Asian contexts, mothers avoid exposing their babies to strangers completely: "A village mother would no more show off her baby to an admiring visitor than an American mother would deliberately expose an infant to a contagious disease" (Spooner 1976:77). He documents the use of lampblack marks on babies' foreheads to divert envious looks and the use of smudges on their cheeks to make them look imperfect. The imperfect child does not attract the evil eye (Maloney 1976:128). During the Fulbe nomination ceremony, when the seven-day-old baby becomes exposed to many people's gazes at once, she/he is "made up" with kohl around the eyes and a black smudge down the forehead. I was told that this protected the child from *gite*. Spooner comments on the existence of a "cognate conception of an evil tongue" (Spooner 1976:78). This mirrors the parallels in the Fulbe discourse between "tongues" and "eyes." He interprets the danger of the "doting glance of the mother . . . as an extension of the concept of the evil eye. An outsider envies, an insider dotes. Both attitudes are forms of undue attention" (Spooner 1976:79). He cites a Persian saying that "the loving eye is more dangerous than the evil eye" (Spooner:78). Maloney quotes South Asian villagers who avoid praising their children in the belief that this will spoil them: "If we praise, the child will think we love him too much, and then he will not be under our control" (Maloney:135). Margaret Trawick discusses a similar formulation in a Tamil context: "For a mother to gaze with love at her own child is the most dangerous gaze of all" (Trawick 1990:93).

The Fulbe categories of *garsa*, *demde* (tongues), *haala* (talk), and *gite* (eyes) form a cluster of syndromes caused by excessive admiration or envy directed at an infant. Of these, *garsa* is the most salient, since it is usually caused by the excessive love in a mother's gaze. As discussed in chapter two, the Fulbe view of emotionality emphasizes the need for control of emotions, even feelings of love and affection. Excessive emotion is frowned upon and even labeled as madness. In the same way as hunger, pain, jealousy, anger and grief, love is to be moderated by *hakkilo*, or sense. One who is dominated by emotion has lost her or his sense and is therefore "mad." Although the discourse of "madness" focuses on the negative effects of excessive feeling on the part of the one who feels love or jealousy, the beliefs discussed here focus on the effect of strong admiration/love on the object of affection. Who loves a child more than her/his mother? The mother is, therefore, the focus of prophylactic medicine protecting a child from excessive admiration.

The most common protective medicine for *garsa* is a string of white beads tied on the child's ankle or wrist. The whiteness of the beads is said to deflect the injurious gaze. Some beads work to prevent people's tongues (*demde*) from injuring an infant with their talk (*haala*). Symptoms of *haala*, or *demde*, are distinct from *garsa* symptoms. *Haala* causes a child's whole body to hurt ('*bandu pat nawan*), whereas *garsa* illness is characteristically asymmetrical. As Hawwa explained, it affects one eye, one arm, one leg. "It twists the body (*garsa kam wuraago*). It strikes the joints—it fissures the bone (*garsa kam haa jokkude—seeka i'al*)."

Did You Go to France to Get Such a Pretty Child?

Tongues (*demde*) can cause dramatic weight loss and fevers in the afflicted infant. According to Nenne, her son Adama (now fully grown and a father of two children) nearly died from the sickness caused by *demde*.

> When he was three months old, he was fat and pretty. Everyone held him and spoke about him: "A yehi France na? A danyi nasaara! Did you go to France [to get such a pretty child]? You have given birth to a nasaara [European]." Tongues (demde)! He became very sick. I brought him home, and he nearly dropped stiff. I sprinkled drops of water on him, blessing him three times (juraago). I took him to mallums. I took him to the hospital. They gave him shots, over a hundred of them! The doctor came from Kaele three times. This continued until he was ten years old. Even now he still has no body. He's very skinny. All my children are like this.

Nenne's last phrase suggests that her children's victimization by *demde* says something about her. She allows this fact to be emphasized by using it to end her narrative. "All my children are like this." It tells us first of all that she produces children worthy of praise. Only beautiful, healthy children will fall victim to *demde*. It also puts the mother beyond blame for the deterioration in their health, which follows from a case of *demde*. Finally, it suggests that the people around her, in their admiration of Adama (and later of her other children), were in effect causing him harm, whether they intended to or not. She is telling me that they hurt her child, almost killing him through admiration. If this dynamic is common knowledge (admiration causing harm), why didn't they avoid praising the child? Others resort to playful insult to detour harmful effects praising can have on a child. Why didn't they? A Fulbe person might argue that they are overwhelmed by feelings of admiration/desire/jealousy for such a beautiful child. Their *hakkilo* ("sense") is displaced by excessive emotion, and they act unthinkingly in ways that will harm their neighbor's child. The alternative is that they intentionally speak praises to harm the child out of jealousy and spite for the mother.

SEASHELLS, WHITE CHALK, AND UMBILICAL CORD: RABIYATU'S MEDICINE CHEST

The utter secrecy surrounding women's distinctive curing techniques was demonstrated to me by Rabiyatu one day in 1991, when she unpacked for me her "medicine chest" containing an umbilical cord, a large seashell, a cowrie, and a chunk of chalk. All of these items, pulled out in turn, represent medical technologies belonging to the world of women:

> *Rabiyatu and I are sitting together in her house one day when she decides to take me into her confidence. She opens her enameled tin dishes, the Fulbe woman's equivalent to a chest of drawers. There are small ones tucked inside larger ones, stacked under many other, plates containing more prosaic items, like cloth or makeup.* "Here, do you know what this is, Helen? This is the umbilical cord (jaaburu) of Goggo Peetel. If I give it to someone who has not had children, she will give birth. As for me, if I give it to her, it is so that I will never again have children. When it returns to me, I will give birth again. Theirs (the other girls' umbilical cords) I buried on the other side of the house. You eat it with nyiiri (millet). If someone did not eat of it, they will not give birth.
> *She pulls out a seashell, large and clamlike.* "This is a wajawujo. They get this from a large river. If your breast hurts, you wear it on your breast on a string so it cups over your breast. Haa jamditi. Until it is well again. You know it swells? (Naa 'don buuto du?) It will be useful

for mambraw *[another severe childhood illness involving wasting] too*
(nafan). This sickness exists among the Hausa. If the child has it, he
will become thin, he will not breast-feed, he will not eat. If it swells (to
uppi do*) it is very bad, it will kill! (*mbaran!*) Others get* huutooru, *a*
*very ugly disease. This illness (*mambraw*) is ugly, worse than* huutooru. *(*Nyawu 'do kallu'dum, 'buran je huutooru*)."*

The next item pulled out of the tin is a cowrie shell (jeke). To prevent
garsa. *Also a white bead necklace can be used for* garsa. To a laari do a
laaran daneyjum do. Ngam daneyjum. *If you look [at the child], you*
will look at this white. It is because of the white [that it is effective].
The shell can also be used as medicine for tandaw *which is synonymous*
with mambraw. Nyawu bikkoy. *A sickness of small children.*

She pulls out a chunk of chalky white powder, do'de. *You break it,*
grind it smooth, and give it to the child to drink.

Mambraw. *Some babies are born with it, others get it after two*
months. The child swells and gets spots on his face and it "comes out
his butt." [His lower intestine begins to come out of his anus.] Once
you've recognized the illness, you go out and look for the following
medicines: kolkolwaaje, koyjooli, 'daleeja. *You combine them, you*
*soak the child's bottom in it (*lumba*), you make him drink it. For*
seven months, you soak the child in it ('bingel don lumbo*). Someone*
*else too will use cow urine (*cille nagge*), put it in a bucket, soak the*
child in that bucket. The child will vomit and vomit. The sickness will
*come out (*nyawu wurta kadi*).*

This personal medicine chest—a vessel of enameled tin—doesn't confine itself
to a single curing discipline or etiological paradigm. Rather, it reflects a woman's
personal history; it constitutes a record of episodes of sickness and cure, a reposi-
tory of intimate conversations in which particular technologies of cure and influence on healthy bodily processes (such as fertility) are exchanged and stored for future use. In another conversation between Rabiyatu and a visiting friend, I learned
of other items in this secret medicine chest: Arabic inscriptions and diagrams, carefully folded and stacked into small boxes and arranged inside one of the plates. She
pulled them out, one by one, talking to her friend about them and, asking me for a
pen and paper, copying one of hers to give to her friend. The manipulation of
Arabic writing for medicinal purposes is not restricted to the learned (and usually
male) *mallums*. Specific writings are passed from woman to woman, carefully
copied onto new pieces of paper, and taken home, where they will be shared with
another and another. The giver explains what the medicine is for and how it is to be
used. Often, both the giver and taker of medicinal script are illiterate, but they copy
the writing faithfully, while using the spoken word to communicate purpose and
instructions. The opacity of the writing for these women does not weaken its per-

formative power. It remains for them a powerful and accessible technology of cure. Like the average western consumer, who buys and uses antibiotics without possessing the scientific literacy required to understand its functioning, the Fulbe mother confidently manipulates the curing technology of Arabic writing.

In this chapter, we can see that women's distinctive medical practices regarding fertility, birthing and caring for infants involve some dissonance with Islamic "orthodoxy." This reveals interconnections between gender and Islam, since women repeatedly seem to embody the "pagan" side of the Muslim/Pagan dichotomies. The following healing ceremony further illustrates how this dichotomy is elaborated in ritual form.

THE SACRIFICE ON THE TERMITE MOUND

In the first part of this chapter, I discussed the effects on the unborn child of what the mother takes in through her eyes. Gazing on a wild animal by an expecting mother can cause a sickness in her unborn child. His eyes become wild, and he goes into fits or convulsions. A mother-to-be's gaze on an antelope can cause her unborn child's fingers to be beautifully long and slender. Looking upon a *huutooru* (lizard), however, can cause a severe wasting illness which makes the infant look like a lizard in that his skin will hang on his body in loose folds. Women are reluctant to make a *huutooru* diagnosis, as it is extremely serious and often fatal. No woman wants to be responsible for forecasting a child's imminent death. However, on several occasions, women told me that another woman's child was afflicted with "the sickness of the lizard." The cure for *huutooru* involves the afflicted child in a drama outside the social space of the village. Although I never witnessed this cure, it was described to me by several women I knew. Here is Rabiyatu's account:

> *Buulo's child is sick with the* huutooru *sickness. The child's body wastes away. [The cure features] the Goggo (father's sister) and the Yaapendo (mother's sister). The Yaapendo takes the child, and carries it to a termite mound. The Goggo arrives with a knife. She says "I will slay him. (Mi hirsan mo.) [using the verb used for Muslim sacrifice (hirsugo) rather than the ordinary verb meaning to kill (mbarugo)]" The Yaapendo says "Don't slay him. (Taa hirsu.)" Then the Yaapendo takes and lays the child down on the termite mound. The Goggo raises the knife to sacrifice him. She puts the knife to his neck, as if to cut it. When the knife touches the neck, the Yaapendo takes the baby and runs. They do this for three days, then the child is healed.*
>
> *Ya'uba [the child of the Lawan and Fadimatu] had this sickness. He was born with* huutooru. *Dija Suwaajo was the goggo and Adda Habiiba was the Yaapendo—they did it [performed the curing ritual].*

The particular deployment of kinship relations which save the child by sacrificing him may clarify the meaning of the ritual drama. What does it mean that the *goggo* is the one holding the knife? The one who wants to sacrifice him. Both of the actors are women, but the *goggo* is structurally closest to the father, and thus to Isaac's or Ishmael's father, Abraham. The *goggo* (father's sister) is to the *yaapendo* (mother's sister) as the Father is to the mother. The father is the one who can perform the sacrifice of his son in submission to God, just as he is the one who can sacrifice a ram at *Layha* (the feast of sacrifice). Only men can ritually slay an animal, and the duty to sacrifice rests on the head of household, also usually a man. The sacrilegious aspect of this drama becomes salient when we recall that only men can sacrifice in Islam, so that raising the knife into the air to slay the offering is itself a sacrilege, a transgression—a trespassing by women onto male territory. Small wonder that this curing drama is kept secret from men.

The kinship relations deployed in this ritual slaying further illuminate the meaning of the drama. A child respects his *goggo*, but is usually more at ease and intimate with his *yaapendo*. The *goggo* is feared, respected and can be tough with a child. In case of divorce, it is often the *goggo* who raises a child. Both are "lateral" relatives, but *goggo* is a member of the same lineage as the child, whereas the *yaapendo* is not. The father's sister and mother's sister also simply can be said to stand as father and mother. *Goggo*, because she represents the patrilineage of the child and stands for the father, can perform the sacrifice. But as *goggo* she is the one, too, who is tough with the child. She stands for the father. For any cure that involves a *mallum* specialist, a representative of the patrilineage must be present. The *goggo* here serves the role of authorizing the treatment, the radical cure. The *yaapendo*, being outside of the patriline, can permit herself to be more indulgent and to show feeling for the child. Here, she intercedes on the baby's behalf, confronting the tough father-figure of the *goggo*. "No! Don't slay him!" The drama requires the cooperation of the two kin groups represented by *goggo* and *yaapendo*.

The key actors in Ya'uba's cure reveal the workings of classificatory kinship in Domaayo. Ya'uba is the son of the *Lawan* (chief). Dija Suwaajo, who takes the role of *Goggo*, is the *Lawan's* father's brother's daughter, and thus the *Lawan's* classificatory sister. The children of brothers are themselves siblings and are referred to as such in everyday parlance, though when asked to specify, people will say, "She's my father's brother's daughter, so we are children of paternal uncles—siblings (*bi'be bappayibe—derdiraabe*)." Children of such "children of uncles" are also siblings (*bi'be wappitayi'be*). She is then Ya'uba's "father's sister" or *Goggo*. Adda Habiiba is Fadimatu's father's brother's daughter, and therefore Fadimatu's classificatory sister, once again by the *bi'be bappayibe* (children of uncles) relation. This makes Habiiba Ya'uba's maternal aunt, or *Yaapendo.*

Another aspect of the ritual cure is the parallel between the bush world of the termite mound (*wande*) on the edge of the bush (the remoteness of the location being necessitated in part by the secrecy) and the bush world of the *huutooru* (lizard) for which the sickness is named. What is the relation between the termite associated with the cure and the lizard said to cause the sickness? Dehydration, wasting away, marasmus (loss of flesh) are the symptoms of the sickness. Termites are insects that eat up structures of buildings, destabilizing them from the inside. And their homes too are dried out, hollow structures. They swarm during the rains, the season when they are most visible, flying into the students' kerosene lamps. The *huutooru* is said to dwell near watering holes and to survive the dry season by burying himself in the sand near a water source. Both animals can be said to have an ambivalent relation to rain. But the termite, in its predatory hunger, can be seen as an invisible agent of consumption of structures, whereas the lizard's body is a symbol for the result of consumption, a wasted body. In this sense they are opposites. In their relations to humans, termites are agents of consumption/destruction, lizards figures of the destroyed/consumed body.

The ritual is sacrilegious at a more general level. In its "poaching" on scriptural history, it involves a reappropriation of Islam "with a difference" by women who seek to save this child's life *with their own methods.* The ritual involves trespassing onto a territory that ought to be kept hallowed (de Certeau 1984). Reinterpreting scriptural stories in this way is simply blasphemous, and claiming to perform a cure without deferring to God's will is, again, blasphemous. God is the origin of all illness and all medicine, and only his will can cure a sickness. Any technology of cure that does not explicitly defer to Allah's will in healing the sick is illegitimate. The ritual cure for *huutooru* draws on the poetics of scriptural themes of sacrifice and the forces of bodily destruction/consumption in the immediate living environment of the Fulbe in attempting a drastic life-saving strategy for a child whose wasting body, seemingly consumed by invisible forces, seems doomed to die.

CONCLUSION

In this chapter, a wide array of mothering concepts and practices have been discussed, in the context of concerns about the well-being of the newborn child. The child is perceived as exceedingly vulnerable to the forces of sickness, particularly those caused by excessive admiration, desire, longing and jealousy. Preventive medicinal practices are numerous, and many of them are visible to those who would be harmful agents of a child's ill-health. Wild animals (*kuje ladde*) and spirits (*ginnaaji*) are associated with the world outside the village, whereas "tongues," "talk," "eyes," and *garsa* represent forces of harm emanating from the domestic world of the village, indeed from the child's very own mother. The cures and preventive medicines, significantly, are often drawn from the domestic resources of a woman's own (natal) family, as well as from her network of women friends created through dyadic relations of reciprocity forged through mutual visiting and gift giving at life-cycle ceremonies. Women's medicines often draw on the male-centered world of Islamic scripture, while using it for their own purposes, often in unauthorized cures, which men would view as unorthodox or even blasphemous. I could not test my hypotheses about men's reactions to the "sacrifice on the termite mound" or to women's fertility-regulating practices, because I learned about them in confidence, "as a woman," and this was a trust I could not violate.

I have explored the world of medical discourse and practice centering on Fulbe motherhood. In much of this material, we see women coming to terms with their experience of motherhood. They grapple with feelings of reproductive power, on the one hand, and on the other hand with a heightened sense of vulnerability in their own bodies and those of their children, especially their very young children. The fulfillment of motherhood is pitted against the ever-present possibility of loss. Many of the medicines employed in mother-child health are prophylactic, working to protect mother and child from many dangers. Many of the substances and practices surrounding mother-child health occur in a women's spaces and are considered "women's medicine." The experience of giving birth itself takes place in the woman's house within her husband's *saare* or in her mother's home, and many of the medicines relating to fertility and infant health are stored and controlled by women. Some of women's medical practices are kept secret from men because they contradict male plans and orthodoxies. White plates serving as a woman's medicine chest contain fertility medicines, which a mother might use to avoid or bring on a pregnancy, and the "bush" space of the termite mound serves as an altar on which women save their children by poaching androcentric Koranic stories for their own purposes.

Women's distinctive medical practices regarding their fertility involve some considerable dissonance with Islamic "orthodoxy." In the following discussion of Islam and paganism, we may elucidate why women repeatedly seem to embody the "pagan" side of Muslim/Pagan dichotomies.

6
Intimate Others:
Cannibal Witches and Spirits

MISTIRAAKU: VISCERAL IMAGES OF SCARCITY AND PREDATORY CONSUMPTION

For weeks prior to the Islamic feast of sacrifice (*juulde layha*), commemorating the prophet Abraham's obedience to God and his near-sacrifice of his son, conversations become to turn to the upcoming event. Many are planning for how they will accomplish their religious duty. Some are saving money to purchase a sacrificial animal, while others are feeding a special goat or sheep, watching it grow, as the date of the feast approaches. During the holiday, all heads of families will offer an animal in sacrifice, which their families will then consume in a rare feast. Meat is a very small part of the diet for most Fulbe people I knew. Yet it plays a central part in the Islamic feast of sacrifice (*layha*). The obvious delight that villagers take in this holiday, jokingly referred to as *juulde kusel* ("the holiday of meat"), suggested to me that many would prefer to eat meat more often than they ordinarily do. Children and adults fantasized about the upcoming holiday for weeks, conjuring up images of grilled meat, stewed meat, meat cooked in tomato-and-onion sauce. . . . These musings dramatized for me the fact that Fulbe people I knew thought of animal flesh as a scarce resource.

The Fulbe imagination about *mistiraaku* and the illicit consumption of human flesh emerges out of their quotidian relation to animal flesh. Some people eat more meat than others. Their ability to eat meat frequently is an index of their greater socioeconomic power. Moreover, their eating is directly linked to someone else's *not* eating. In the metaphor of *mistiiraaku*, the notion that one person's "wealth" erodes another's "health" demonstrates a conception of wealth as a zero-sum game (Foster 1965). "Eating" is a central metaphor for winning at someone else's expense. "*O nyaami!* (He ate!)" is the exclamation that describes the winner of a card game. "*O yaari luwal* (He drank the horn)" significantly is the metaphor for characterizing defeat. Thus, eating is the act of winners, of power, whereas drinking is the gesture of the defeated. The images of winning as eating suggests that winning destroys/consumes the opposition. This notion is carried over and intensified in the discourse of *mistiraaku*. The sense that the prosperity of one's neighbors is directly linked to one's own impoverishment (loss of flesh) is viscerally depicted in the image of the cannibal witch, who eats meat everyday. "Everyday a plate of intestines!" mused my friend in a half-joking display of admiration for the cannibal. "*Il est bien*. (He is doing well for himself)."

In the Fulbe imagination about *mistiraaku*, the figure of the witch condenses tendencies found in all humans. Mistirii'en are people who want what they do not have. This covetousness will sometimes attain such an amplitude that the person, on the point of desperation, becomes a cannibal. Uninhibited eating combines with aggression in the most antisocial act conceivable. In psychological terms, the believer in *mistiraaku* is aware of his/her own antisocial hunger for what another person has and projects that cannibalistic urge onto another, elusive figure—that of the *mistiriijo* (cannibal-witch). In light of the Fulbe concept of personhood, or *pulaaku*, discussed in Chapter two, the cannibalistic urge of the *mistiriijo* signifies bodily desires gone out of control. Pamela Schmoll (1991:283–312) finds a similar meaning for the Hausa discourse of soul-eating:

> *The images, symbols, and ideology surrounding soul-eating continue to provide a viable discourse, not only for ascribing meaning to crisis, but for contemplating the nature of humankind, his social relationships, and the place of a specific kind of evil in that social universe. [The ideology of soul-eating] provides a rich conceptual framework . . . for understanding and coping with certain destructive forces which, in Hausa eyes, have been exacerbated by colonialism and the far-reaching social economic changes which have come in its wake (1991:289).*

It has become increasingly difficult for people to maintain their sanity and self-control in the presence of the seemingly insatiable need and desire for money created by the postcolonial economy. The boundless hunger of an increasing number of individuals calls into question the predominance of social sense (*hakkilo*), which is the very basis of individual and social sanity.

One of the chief characteristics of the Fulbe cannibal-witch is that he/she is not easily recognized by ordinary people. He or she appears normal and engages in ordinary activities. No identifying marks single out the body of one who has become a witch. The *mistiriijo*'s slipperiness is evidenced in the belief that his condition, like measles, is contagious. Contagion is central to the meaning of *mistiraaku*. "People who eat together get the same illnesses," Fulbe villagers say. Any human is theoretically capable of contracting the condition by contagion. It is thus, a human trait and not at all supernatural. It also follows that the condition of being a cannibal witch is not willful. It afflicts one unknowingly—through intimate association with one who is affected.

Cannibal-witchcraft conquers one's being unwillingly. There is no exorcism for *mistiiraaku*. Affected persons appear to be normal but are "doubled" by an animal familiar: a bird creature (*sondu mistirii'en*), who does the pursuing and capturing of victims. *Mistiraaku* involves the doubling of personhood as the victim becomes the dwelling place of an agency other than the human self. The cannibal's double, however, moves independently of his human body. While the *mistiriijo*'s visible body sits talking and joking with friends, his bird counterpart flies about eating and killing its human prey. Yet the *mistiriijo* is still completely and irrevocably fused with the bird, which has become the detachable predatory dimension of his person. The *mistiriijo*, poignantly, is permanently colonized by *mistiraaku* witchcraft. It has become an elusive but integral dimension of his person.

A Foolproof Diagnostic Test

As an affliction, *mistiraaku* can be difficult for ordinary persons to diagnose. It has no consistent pattern of symptoms, although those affected are often said to exhibit high fevers, severe pain, and delirium, and may appear to be near death. I asked Mal Sanda, the healer of cannibal-witch attack (*kurgowo mistirii'en*), how he distinguishes between cases of *mistiraaku* and other sicknesses. He explained to me that he can only establish the presence or absence of *mistiraaku*. But when *mistiraaku* is not involved, he cannot distinguish between spirits and other illnesses. His method is limited in its applications but, he suggested, unfailingly precise. He enters the *saare* with the medicine in his pocket. Even as he enters, the afflicted may rise up or struggle. Then you know that it is the *mistirii'en*, who are "tying him." If he comes and places his medicine, and the patient does not move, if his condition does not change, Mal Sanda cannot say whether there are spirits or it is common illness (*nyawu non*). But it is certainly not *mistirii'en*.

The knowledge of the *mallum*s is more extensive. They can cure everything, for the Koran contains everything. "Nothing is left out. (*Walaa ko lutti*.)" But the *mallum*'s work is slow. "He can work for three or four days in order to cure the patient. Whereas Sanda, he puts the medicine on the sick and they are cured instantly. For the *mallum*, they are only prayers. He can pray, and God refuses. The mallums learn the Koran. Sanda inherited [his knowledge] from his father. He works with just *gaade bee ce'be* (succulents and barks)." Mal Juulde, a *mallum* himself, summarizes the different fields of expertise: "*Marabouts 'don huwa bee crayon. Sorciers 'don huwa bee le'd'de.* The *marabouts* [*mallums*] work with pens. Sorcerers work with plants." The French words *sorcier* and *marabout* are used by many villagers, whether or not they have a working knowledge of French. The distancing affected by the use of the French, for a Fulfulde speaker, works like an euphemism to suggest a sensibility of worldliness and discernment in the speaker. The French word *sorcier* is used to refer to the cannibal-witch and the curer of cannibal-witch attack, as well as encompassing the "sorcerer" of anthropological parlance—one who can affect things at a distance through the knowledgeable manipulation of words and substances. The use of the French blurs the distinctions commonly made in Fulfulde: cosmopolitan Koranic knowledge is to the local knowledge of Mal Sanda as literacy is to orality. The *mallums* have coopted the power of the written word, whereas Mal Sanda taps into the field of natural forces/elements. Both types of healers have an ambivalent identity since they manipulate knowledge, which can be used to heal or to kill. Knowledge is both powerful and dangerous. Mal Sanda, who is renowned as a curer of *mistiraaku* attacks, thus, bears the same name in French as the *mistiriijo* itself. And Mal Juulde himself, though identified with the Koran and Koranic practice, also works with plants. So the distinction works to differentiate technologies of cure but does not always serve to characterize practitioners.

In nearby Nigeria, where a similar phenomenon is known as *maita* among Hausa speakers, the possibility of purchasing the stones that turn one into a soul-eater is said to be a recent development, motivated by greed, envy, and the increasing societal pressure to earn money (Schmoll 1991:298). Monetarization of Hausa life, the increasing unreliability of income from agriculture, and the fragmentation of the extended family have all contributed to increasing villagers' anxiety about money and the accumulation of wealth in their lives and have heightened the salience of beliefs in soul-eating (*maita*). In this Fulbe community, however, the language of *mistiraaku*, with no overt references to economic change, speaks to a struggle over meaning between men and women and between Islamic orthodoxy and its "others." Belief in *mistiraaku* and the practices of diagnosis and cure are considered un-Islamic by most men I spoke with. For women, it seems to speak to the anxiety of the dispossessed, who find themselves entangled in affinal relations, which they do not trust.

Pious Ambivalence and Shifting Interpretive Frames

Fulbe discourse on these forces is far from uniform. Though some assertions and distinctions may be commonly heard, others vary both with the position of the speaker in the social structure of the community and with the immediate context of the conversation (Lambek 1992). Belief and disbelief rest on personal experience, as well as on the politics of gender and religion. A young man like Bakari who identifies with French as a marker of schooling is inclined to be skeptical about such phenomena, yet he sometimes spoke like one who believes:

> There is a nocturnal bird which we call sondu mistirii'en. It takes flight at night with a fire on its behind. It's real. They say it comes out of the anus of the mistiriijo. They say that it is with this bird that the witches eat men. If you see it, you must try to kill it. They say that if you kill it, the witch will die. If you kill it, you will hear that someone has died tomorrow. There is a family of mistirii'en in a nearby village, who inherited that from their mother. She came here with that, and gave it to the father. The mother eats a little, the father eats a little. Then the father gave that to the children—they are all living—each one now manages in his own way.
>
> They say that the human flesh is better than all other flesh. Those birds there cannot be stopped. If they want it, they just go. They say that sometimes, [eating] is an obligation for them. They say that they don't want to eat a person, but the birds force them. They force them like that.
>
> Now, the man has daughters who are too old. No one likes them. One is even twenty years old! If you marry one of these daughters, you are yourself a witch. Finally, you will eat. "You cannot refuse?" I ask "No. After a time, you feel yourself. . . well, I have never been a witch myself, but after a while there, you feel yourself to be a witch. You cannot refuse. What can you do?
>
> Once you have that, it's good. [laughing] It's even good. You are there with your wife, every night, a plate of intestines.

Bakari voices the fantasy of being a *mistiriijo*: never having to worry about food again. Eating without working. Having a partner who, though domineering, works for you to obtain food for you, while you sit with your friends or family and chat. To eat the very best meat, of a nature that most humans will never taste—these are the advantages of being a witch. There is, however, a price to pay: the enslavement to the will of the bird, who forces you to eat even when you want to refuse, who makes you kill against your will—a bird who cannot be stopped. This is the frightening aspect of the phenomenon for someone who might be within reach of the contagion. But what about its victims? How does the cannibal witch choose on whom to prey? I asked Bakari. Although he is not an expert on such matter, many of his assertions were corroborated by others. His answer is worth quoting at length:

> *I have never seen an honest man, one who does not lie, fall ill, have*
> *medicines placed on him, and he names the witch. That I have never*
> *seen. That is how I don't know if I believe in witches.*
>
> *It is always women who have this, they lie. Or the men who do not*
> *pray. What, not serious guys. They pray, but they are not . . . he is negli-*
> *gent. He sins. Maybe instead of praying five times a day, he prays twice or*
> *three times. There, he can be struck. He is not honest. He lies.*
>
> *Someone who fears God. A fearer of God, him a* mistiijo *will not eat.*
> *One must be sure that God exists. You see the sky, you see the earth. You*
> *know that everything which happens to you in life, it is God who has*
> *done it. One must know too that God made you so that you would*
> *obey. You do what he wills. Like that* mistirii'en *will not eat you at all!*
> *You look at the sky, you look at the earth, you look at the stars, you look*
> *at the moon, you look at the sun, don't you know God exists? Then a*
> mistiriijo *will not eat you.*
>
> *But you are negligent (*a don negligea*). Will you pray? Will you not*
> *pray? Don't know. Does God exist? Is there none? Is it truth or a lie?*
> *That one will not be spared. He cannot avoid the witches.*
>
> *"Can gendarmes fear spirits too?" I ask.*
>
> *Who has more fear than they do? They are very much afraid of the*
> *bush. With their big guns, they are the most fearful!*

There is a subtle shift in the discourse from saying that those afflicted are liars (implying that they are not really afflicted) to arguing that they are vulnerable to attack because they are not devout Muslims. The difference between the two arguments is the difference between saying that only the impious believe in witchcraft (which puts the narrator in the position of pious unbeliever in witchcraft) and saying that only the impious become victims of witchcraft (which assumes the narrator believes that the impious are being attacked). In the first stance witchcraft is not real. In the second, witchcraft is real. Significantly, both explanations blame the victim for his alleged attack by a *mistiriijo*. Both give men closely identified with Islamic orthodoxy a way of distancing themselves from victims and from the possibility that they themselves might one day be victimized.

"Women lie." From the perspective of the male speaker, women's victimization by witches does not need further explanation. All of the cases involving female victims are thus dismissed with a single phrase. From an androcentric perspective, one cannot believe what women say. It is also suggested that women are vulnerable because they lack faith and do not pray as consistently as they should. They are, therefore, without the protection that the more pious gain from their religious faith and practice. Cases involving men, however, require explaining. Of course some individual men may be lying, explaining some of the cases. Other men, lax in their Islamic faith and practice, may have actually become vulnerable

Fa'dimatu studying. Her marriage interrupted her formal Koranic education.

to attack (like women) due to their impiety. Orthodox faith and practice, like the drinking of bitter medicines, is a powerful prophylactic shield against attack.

The bird is an alter-ego that cannot be stopped. Yet it is a familiar that is deeply, organically linked to the person. It cannot be exorcised. If you kill the bird, its human host and partner will die. The link between the two is so intimate that the bird apparently dwells in the bowels of its host, flying out of its anus, and returning with food intended for the other pole of the digestive tract.

Thus the *mistiraaku* bird inverts the normal alimentary process, ingesting raw food through the anus, where waste is normally excreted. The anus is featured repeatedly as a central image, as the bird flies out of the witch's anus and into the night with a fire in its own anus, whereas the mouth goes unmentioned. This bird makes fellow humans into food, thus placing the *mistiriijo* outside the realm of humanity. In witchcraft, defecation precedes and makes possible feeding, inverting the ordinary human physiological sequence.

Ultimately, the ordinary person may not want to express too sure a view on these matters. Not knowing, in this case, is more desirable than knowing. This was observed by Last (1992) with respect to Hausa therapeutics and by Lambek (1992) in Mayotte. Lambek relates the story of an Islamic scholar (*fundi*) whose excessive knowledge leads to his near destruction by God. Knowing too much ultimately one may become morally suspect for two principal reasons. First, arrogantly approaching the omniscience of God amounts to sacrilege. Second, the same knowledge employed to cure the afflicted, can also be used to cause harm (Lambek 1992). The curer of a sorcery attack must know the technology of attack in order to cure and thus is always potentially suspected in an attack. In Bakari's narrative about *mistiraaku,* he humorously extolls the advantages of becoming one of them: "Everyday, a plate of intestines!" But then he catches himself, "I don't know, I am not a witch myself!" The thought occurs to him, in spite of the fact that he is talking to someone outside the system (i.e., the anthropologist), that knowing this much could make him suspect. He emphasizes that he is *merely imagining* what it must be like to be a *mistiriijo.*

SPIRIT TALK

Everyone is afraid of the bush—it is full of spirits.
Here the river is dangerous, especially at night.

In the preceding discussion, Fulbe discourse about *mistiraaku* was seen to be revealing of the conflicts pervasive in Fulbe society and of fissures and discontinuities inherent in Fulbe cultural pluralism. The discourse about spirits (*ginnaaji*) further reveals Fulbe awareness of "Otherness." In talking about spirits, people reveal the possibilities for constructive reciprocity with them, as well as the potential for serious aggression coming from them. People may become wealthy because of a constructive engagement with spirits. Or they may end up mad, infertile or paralyzed, due to the action of spirits. As with *mistiraaku,* Fulbe discourse about spirits is far from homogeneous. People are especially apt to differ in their understanding of how spirits ought to be dealt with. Those most closely identified with Islamic orthodoxy are likely to recommend avoiding dealings with spirits and meeting spirit attack with exorcism. But many others who are also Muslim believe in the possibilities for a more constructive relationship with spirits. I never heard a Fulbe person doubt the existence of spirits, though people certainly doubted particular stories and claims made about them. Fulbe people say their existence is supported by the Koran; therefore, it is beyond the criticism of Muslim clerics. In fact, clerics are believed to be the most powerful exorcists of spirits.

In everyday discourse, mention of spirits occurs in two kinds of stories. The first kind are generalized narratives about spirits' relations with humans. In these tales, the humans are usually unnamed and are presented as having lived in an indeterminate time and space. The second kind of stories are concerned with particular individuals whose names and villages are specified. They relate these individuals' particular interactions with spirits. These are usually stories dealing with spirit-caused afflictions, which relate the circumstances in which spirits were provoked. Often, humans unknowingly trespass on their territory, and healers who are renowned for their ability to work with spirits attempt to discipline or cajole them into leaving their victims alone.

Women, Work, and the River

Spirits dwell in ant hills, among rocks, in large old trees and in rivers. I was often told not to sit under the inviting shade of particular old trees that were known to be haunted. Not insignificantly, these trees tend to grow on the banks of rivers, where their roots can tap into the underground pools of water. As villages tend to be built near rivers, they provide the most frequent source of spirit attacks and stories about spirits. I was told that although *maayo* (river) spirits are always dangerous, they are more harmful to strangers, who are far from home.

Since residence is patrilocal, women who have married into other villages will be routinely exposed to the spirits of rivers other than their own (their native village's rivers). Although men go to the *maayo* to water their livestock, and both men and women go to the river to wash clothes, women's task of provisioning the household with water means that they, more than any other group, make frequent trips to the nearest *maayo*. Many women I knew made ten to twelve trips to the river daily. They are usually made in the early dawn or at night after the evening meal. During the dry season, when the water table was at its lowest, it was not uncommon for women I knew to work until 11 p.m. They had to wait for the water to seep up through the sand in the deepest wells before each pail of water could be filled.

The companionship among these groups of women who travel to the wells in the river together is developed and affirmed as they stop to exchange the latest news, tease each other, help one another to lift the heavy buckets onto their heads and march once again towards their respective *saares*. Some women may make ten or twelve such journeys every night. The work of fetching water forms a large portion of women's daily work, as well as representing a significant part of their social life. For the most secluded women, these trips may be their only occasion to leave their *saare* all day. The women who call each other in the evening to come to the well are close neighbors, usually wives of brothers. In this way, a community of women is formed around those who draw water from the same wells in the *maayo*. This social space is different in tone from the more intimate, usually dyadic, visits between friends which occur during the day, when one of them finds a moment of leisure, either because her husband is away, or because a co-wife is taking her turn to be on call that day. It also differs from the larger and more formal gathering of women on the occasion of a birth, circumcision, wedding or a death.

The gatherings at the watering holes are "work parties," and the relations between the women have a more casual, taken-for-granted character. They are together for the purpose of performing strenuous labor, rather than socializing, and their interaction correspondingly takes on a tough, aggressive quality. Emotional resilience and the ability to endure hardship (often felt to be caused by their husbands) serve as important aspects of the performance of womanhood, which takes place on these occasions. They display an autonomy from and a nonchalance toward the world of men, which can be loudly proclaimed in jokes and stories in that space because it lies outside of their husbands *saares* and outside of the village proper.

On one evening in which I participated in the water-fetching session, my friend Rabiyatu and her crew were being characteristically defiant of their husbands when her neighbor, Jeeba, asked her about the house her husband was building in the *saare*. Rabiyatu made some dismissive response, to which Jeeba parried, "Do you think they won't make you a co-wife?" implying that the extra house would be used to house a second wife. Rabiyatu answered, "Let them do it, what is it to me?" Rabiyatu has for eight years been her husband Bakari's only wife, and her neighbor's teasing reminds her that she is no different from them and warns her not to feel too secure in her cozy domesticity. She can be made a co-wife at any moment. Her response is a characteristic declaration of bravado and "toughness." Her self, her integrity, and her personhood are beyond the reach of such masculine manipulations. She is not vulnerable to "his" (for the man is never named) machinations. Let him take another wife. It is significant that women's most important context of conviviality, the *maayo*, is also the most common site of spirit attack. Fear of spirits reinforces the desire for companionship, encouraging women to work in groups rather than working alone. It also introduces into the heart of women's daily work parties the presence of dangerous and unpredictable agencies.

SPIRIT ATTACKS

One man told me his older sister was attacked by spirits at the *maayo*:

> *She went to the* maayo *Tilim to wash clothes. She tried to get up and couldn't. The spirits had got a hold of her and held her down. Her mother came, called her, then tried to pull her up but couldn't (dimbataako do nazgi mbang)." She could not be budged; they held her fast. The mother went to see a Marabout, who told her to throw* tabac noir *("indigene," or local tobacco), grains of rice, and white kola. Her mother threw these in the water, and she got up. Ever since that day, she was not in good health. She died of spirits* (ginnaaji) *like that. She was in chains for many years. I grew up with her in the* saare.

The offerings of white and black things thrown into the river are reminiscent of descriptions of spirit-offering throughout Africa (Gibbal 1994). For the child growing up with his older sister in chains, the existence of spirits is an incontestable reality. I was often told that "madness is a thing of spirits." Indeed, spirit attack is integral to Fulbe understanding of madness.

Although the daily trips to fetch water provide the most common occasion for spirit attack, some women spoke of their vulnerability on other journeys. Daada Manga, widow of the *Liman* (the religious leader of the community) and mother of many male children, including my friend *Bakari*, told me of her spirit attack many years ago. I paraphrased her account in my field notes:

> She had gone out with her neighbors, with her co-wives, to give condolences in the west of the village. She was walking last, behind the others. That is when she tread on the hearth of a devil. So the devil penetrated her like that. Ever since that day she is no longer in good health. Of course, she didn't know it at the time. This is what the mallum told her in Bindir. He treated her. He worked a lot. But he could only do his best. They made many mallums work on her case.
>
> When I asked her son about it he shook his head. "Who has not 'worked' on my mother's story?" he said.

As I told people of my interest in spirits, I discovered that those I spoke with displayed dramatically different attitudes. A young man spoke to me about spirits in a manner that revealed his self-image as knowledgeable but above fearing such things. Muusa, younger brother of the chief, my immediate neighbor in his *saare*, and my frequent companion in late-night conversations, told me the following spirit story:

> There is a man who works with spirits. He lives in [name of a nearby town]. His name is Umaru Mordidi. One girl was taken by spirits in the water hole over there [he points in the direction of the bridge across the maayo]. They saw her hand linger above the water; then it was gone. The water was deep, above her head. When they pulled her out of the water, they saw that her nasal septum was gone. It was cut! Umaru Moridi came. He scolded [the spirits]. He left. He had come upon hearing the news of the attack.
>
> We still bathe there. Because we go in numbers, five, seven or even ten of us. I too go there to bathe [boastfully]. I ask him, "why aren't you afraid to bathe there?" We have forgotten about that. Only the old people talk about it. Since the young are not afraid to die.

A young woman troubled by ginnaaji withdraws while Alhaadi (center) veils in a playful manner.

By expressing fearlessness, he detaches himself from the world of married women, domestic routine, and slippery afflictions. The vivid images of the hand lingering above the water and of her missing nasal septum gives his story the frightening feel of reality. Yet Muusa immediately distances himself from the story by saying, "We have forgotten about that." In the same moment, he tells the story and claims to have forgotten it. My neighbor Asatajam, married to the chief's brother Usumaanu, protested vehemently when I asked her about spirits. "I don't know anything about it! Go ask the old people. They know about such things." Most people I knew did not question the reality of spirit attack as a valid explanation for sickness, although they might withhold judgment about its applicability in a particular case. Typically, someone might say, "If it's *this* sort of sickness, then the *mallums* are the best people to treat it." Although preeminent expertise about spirits is attributed to *mallums*, there are unmistakable signs, which ordinary people discuss among themselves, unaided by the weighty and costly diagnosis of experts. Nonspecialists can detect that there is something at work inside someone's body other than *nyawu non* (simple sickness). Daada Manga's co-wife, I was told, had died of spirits. She was sick a long time in bed. Her whole body hurt. The proof that she had spirits was that she was sick a long time without eating or drinking, and she *did not lose weight* or appear to become thinner at all. The visible manifestation of an unnatural internal economy points to the interference by an invisible external force.

The Mallum's *Daughter*

The experts, *mallums,* known to work on spirit sickness develop an aura of authority and severity, which ordinary people respect through deference or avoidance. Their close association with spirits is also potentially dangerous to the *mallums* and their families, as the following story told to me by Bakari illustrates:

> *In Bindir there was a girl, a very beautiful girl like that. She is very beautiful. She is so beautiful. . . . The father of the girl is a Marabout. He treats spirits [i.e. sickness caused by spirits]. The girl is so beautiful. She has a man who wants to marry her. Good, the man married the girl. After one or two days of marriage, the man was dead. The girl returned. She got another, a second husband. Well, she got married again. After one or two days, the husband was dead again. Well, she returned to her father's once more. She waited for the third husband. She received a third husband. Well, the day of the "tying" of the marriage, the man fell gravely ill. [It was after the "tying" took place.] Well, after this, being sick, he said that no, he didn't want the girl any more. Afterwards, he became well again. He found himself. So, the girl is there [unmarried] until the present time.*
>
> *They say that she is the wife of a spirit. Her father is there. Because he is a great* mallum, *he treats those sick with spirits. They say that it is for this reason that the spirits came back onto his daughter. I have heard people talk. Bindir is near us. So, there is surely some truth in it. They say that she is the wife of a spirit. If you marry her, the spirit comes to kill you.*
>
> *Here, people say there are spirits who are men. There are spirits who are women. They have chiefs, animals. They have their chief, their* mallums, *their witches, they have their griots. They have everything.*

This narrative is reminiscent of the Mami Wata stories of West and Central Africa (see for example Amadi 1966; Nwapa 1966; Drewal 1988), in which beautiful women who experience difficulties in their marriages or in bearing children are revealed to have strong connections to water spirits. These spirits may bring them fortune, but they may also prevent them from having human families and children. The story of the *mallum's* daughter encourages men to inquire into their women's marital histories before "tying" the marriage. A woman who already belongs to a spirit can bring her suitor to a premature death. As in the Mami Wata stories of Nigeria, the girl in question is beautiful—extremely beautiful. Perhaps one should be suspicious of such unearthly beauty to begin with. Perhaps also one is better off without such beauty and the problems it may bring. Imperfection in a woman is perhaps something a man should be grateful for, if it decreases the likelihood that she already belongs to a water spirit.

Girls Fetching Water

The story also points to the limitations of *mallumku* (*mallum* practice). This man is a great *mallum*, we are told. He treats difficult cases with some success. But he is unable to prevent his own daughter from being tied in marriage to a spirit— thus, she can never successfully marry a normal human. Because marriage and motherhood are the only avenues for fulfillment available to Fulbe women, the *mallum*'s daughter is fated to be deprived of her own fulfillment because of her spirit marriage. The story amplifies the power of the spirits and underlines the breadth of their influence.

Whites and the Maayo

> *"I hear it said that there are some whites who build bridges, the spirits destroy them during the night. They bring out the* engineers . . . *the whites know how to catch spirits. They say that they capture the spirits. They say that they catch it. The spirit says "I leave you be." They release him then and can now go on with the construction.*
>
> *I learned that the spirits have captured a white man in Chad. Until now the man is there, if they come with their binoculars, they see him, captured. He is alive. He is in the water. It happened a long time ago, but he is alive. He is in chains. "Can Africans see him too?" I ask. Yes,*

*but the whites have gadgets, they have binoculars, they can look. And
see him. The Africans don't have these tools. It is far—one thousand
meters or so. A lot of water.*

As the *mallums* see things (through their book knowledge) that ordinary people
cannot see, so the engineers and other whites armed with their technology
(knowledge structures and practices) can see things Africans cannot. The story
articulates the equation which most Fulbe people employ: Europeans have technology (gadgets) whereas Africans have *mallumku* (ritual knowledge). Quotidian
observations—about such varied objects as watches, airplanes, cars, motorcycles
and quinine—express people's alienation from that technology at the same time
that they wish to make use of it. Africans who *do* possess these tools and those
who are practitioners of these power/knowledge disciplines are said to be "like
whites." They do not challenge the categories but switch positions from one category to the other.

Engineering and bridge-building are inextricably linked to *nasaaras*
(Europeans), even as they are employed and maintained by African people.
When pumps, grain mills, watches, and radios broke down, I often heard the
Fulbe people I knew blaming the African custodians of those things for their
breakdown (including themselves). They would sometimes say to me, "We don't
know about such things. These are the objects of the *nasaaras*." Thus these tools
and machines retain their mark of "otherness" even as they are appropriated for
local use. Kees Schilder (1994), in his work on Mundang ethnic identity in the
Kaele district argues that the Mundang interpreted the European modalities of
power according to their "precolonial" constructs derived from their experience
with Fulbe hegemony. I would argue similarly that Fulbe people I knew interpreted European deployments of technology in terms of their experiences with
the practical knowledge of the *mallums*. Engineers were seen as a new type of
mallum. Like *mallums*, therefore, they must be both willing and able to wrestle
with spirits. Characteristically willful, mischievous, and resistant to control,
spirits proved a formidable test to *nasaaras'* knowledge and practice. Spirits figured as personifications of entropy, destroying the bridges which were to stand
as monuments of European prowess.

The captured white man, like the mallum's daughter who is tied in marriage to
a spirit, serves to define the limits of the engineer's *mallumku* (medicinal practice). Their discipline may empower them to build bridges over the opposition of
water spirits, but they are not able to prevent the capture of one of their own by a
water spirit. Their binoculars give their sight the power to penetrate the depths to
see their captive "brother"—but not to liberate him. He is still alive, in chains, and
under a thousand meters of water. The Africans may be bested by whites in the
practical technologies of engineering and armament, but whites are also bested by
spirits—the spirits of those rivers who are never completely subjugated.

The Differing Within: Spirits as Generative Metaphors for Otherness

The discourse of spirits is not only applied outward in evaluating the techniques of colonialism, but it is also turned "inward" to characterize some aspects of domestic relations. Willful, mischievous, resistant, chaotic—the qualities attributed to spirits work surprisingly well for men seeking to describe women. It is a way of implicitly recognizing that women are powerful contrary to appearances. From a male perspective, women are like spirits in that they can (and do) toy with or oppose men's projects. The attribution of disorder to women is an attribution of the force to derail men's plans, such as plans of marriage. The following quote (which we first examined in chapter three) is useful here in elucidating Fulbe construction of power relations in the context of the landscape:

> *Women are spirits.* (debbo boo dum ginnaaji 'dum.) *If you want to make a shelter, you have to ask your wife whether to put it here or there. You build it the place of the spirits. [implied: that's O.K. because it won't last anyway.] A* danki, *no matter how well you build it, is a thing of the spirits. It won't last.* (Danki koo a wa'd'di fal ni na hu-unde ginnaji. Naa nebbata.)
>
> *But a house, you should put in the opposite place than what she chooses. That will tell you the right place to put it.* (Do wi'ete pelel gonga.)
>
> *They play with rocks [a reference to divination].*
>
> *If your wife tells you something, you must not repeat it, or they will laugh at you. They are lies. One who believes what a woman says is also a woman.* (Tokkidu haalo debbo boo debbo).

The work of the womanly spirits of entropy on the *danki* (shelter) mirrors the work of water spirits on the bridges of the *nasaaras* (Europeans). The strategic projects of Fulbe men in their *saares* and that of Europeans in their colonies are similarly thwarted in the efforts to erect enduring structures onto their landscape. Mitchell (1994:149) writes of the power of structures built in the colonizing of Egypt to "conjure" an order of meaning or truth that "seemed to stand apart as something conceptual and prior" to ordinary things. The Fulbe have to confront a prior order of spirits whose hearths and compounds preceded those of the Fulbe on the landscape. Similarly, the *nasaaras* have to confront a prior order of spirits in constructing bridges across rivers, which are already managed by an ordering force. Bridges are grand public works, which give the colonial project the prestige that only the demonstration of engineering prowess confers. They flex the muscles of the colonial structures of knowledge and practice in the construction of an edifice, which gives bold and ongoing testimony to the potency of the colonial project. Specifically, it makes possible passage over rivers that are seasonally impassable, thus guaranteeing communication between otherwise isolated territories and in so doing expands the country's penetration by the colonial state. De Certeau (1984:128) writes, "the bridge is ambiguous everywhere . . . it liberates from enclosure and destroys autonomy." When such a construction project fails, it puts the supremacy of the colonizer's technology into question and fuels doubts concerning the permanence and "naturalness" of their hegemony. Though the construction is sabotaged, not by defiant Fulbe but by river spirits, the Fulbe may nonetheless take great delight in it. In these stories of spirits undermining the power of the *nasaaras*, spirits are sympathetic to the Fulbe position as reluctant colonial subjects.

In narrating stories about spirits who sabotage the projects of the colonial state, Fulbe people I knew expressed their ongoing defiance of the postcolonial state. The spirits in these stories represent the prior inhabitants of the land who resist European hegemony, and, by extension, they represent the contemporary Fulbe who resist the ongoing colonizing of "development" projects of the postcolonial state. The collapsing of a bridge, which the European builders might interpret as the result of faulty workmanship or inferior raw materials or as being due to a design error, is interpreted by a Fulbe narrator as the result of the actions of a disgruntled river spirit. Like the spirit described above who possessed the young woman who trampled on its hearth, this river spirit seemingly resented the European engineers' usurping of its terrain. The bridge would enable travelers (Europeans and others) to cross the river without risking its rain-engorged waters—avoiding contact with the doyen of the river and bypassing its authority over that space. Significantly, I was told that a child of a village need not fear its river, but those traveling from elsewhere should be afraid of its spirits. The bridge thus specifically favors foreigners by permitting them to avoid negotiation/confrontation with a water spirit and enables them to move freely across a landscape which is not their natal land. In this vein, all Fulbe people (to the extent that their ancestry is Fulbe, and thus from elsewhere) are vulnerable to these water spirits in the same way that all Europeans are vulnerable to its indigenous resistance.

When the construction projects undermined are those of the Fulbe themselves, the mischievous spirits become antagonists. For the man building a shelter in his *saare*, spirits become the cause of impermanence and unpredictable collapse of apparently solid structures. Spirits, like women, introduce chaos and disorder in an otherwise peaceful androcentric world. Like women, they challenge the givenness, priority, and stability of the order/truth of men's projects.

The Fulbe are not unwilling to consider death and deterioration as "natural." They are familiar with the weathering-and-aging processes of sun, rain, rot, and termites (Evans-Pritchard 1937; Lambek 1992). But deterioration sometimes happens so quickly, and collapse is so sudden as to seem unnatural.

In the crumbling and collapse of *danki* (outdoor shelters), as well as in sudden illness and death of seemingly healthy persons, other agencies are sometimes sought for explanation.

Conclusion

The idioms *mistiraaku* and spirits all give voice to Fulbe experiences of conflict, alienation, anxiety, insecurity, jealousy, and competition. Cannibal-witchcraft underlines the combative character of social relations, through the language of scarcity and predatory consumption (*mistiraaku*). The discourse about spirits speaks to a historical and geographic consciousness about people, land, conquest, and resistance to domination. Specifically, it addresses temporal changes in the relations of people to the land through the large-scale historical processes of conquest and colonialism, as well as the intimate historical process of marriage.

7

Domaayo
and the World Bank

Long ago, they used to build hospitals, build schools, hold vaccinations. They used to pay people. They would beg from wealthy countries and share the money among the people in the form of loans, which were paid off in reasonable time. They would call us, call someone honest, and give him a loan. They were useful (don nafa).

Mal Oumarou

Now, if you are ill, what will you do? Sey alla hoynu tan! *You can only hope that God will have mercy on you.*

Daada Abba

This chapter examines how neoliberalism is experienced by ordinary villagers, as well as by civil servants, doctors, nurses, and administrators of the public health system. Domaayo residents, such as Oumarou and Daada Abba who are quoted above, express their distress about the way in which medicine is currently distributed in Cameroon. They feel neglected and mistreated by a state that continues to take but no longer gives as it once did. Taking a close look at medicine in Domaayo, it is possible to see how a rural community in a seemingly remote part of Africa is intimately connected with global economic forces, the Cameroonian state, and powerful international institutions, such as the World Bank. One could discover similar dynamics by examining any other domain of public life, be it education, agriculture, religion, transportation, or the media. It so happens that medicine is what got me to Cameroon in the first place.

This chapter therefore begins with an ethnographic account of Domaayo's medical system in the 1990s, and includes a brief overview of medical pluralism and how the Fulbe people approach medicine based on their own understandings of disease. The economic crisis, multiparty politics, and the financial institutions that became the architects of structural adjustment are then examined in turn. The final section examines the neoliberal health policies, in theory and practice, as viewed by public health workers.

THE EMBODIMENT OF THE STATE

At the local level, in Cameroon's far north, the local health center/dispensary constitutes, along with the local grade school, the preeminent local embodiment of the state. The nurse (along with the schoolteacher) is the civil servant that locals are most likely to seek out. The doctors, nurses, and lab technicians who work in these clinics do not, perhaps, wish to play a political role; yet they and their actions are often politically interpreted by their clients. The ruling *Rassemblement Démocratique du Peuple Camerounais* (RDPC) is now one among many parties. But the ruling party has weathered several multiparty elections, maintaining firm control of all levels of the civil service and territorial administration. The fact that local health workers, including nurses and doctors, have continued to be actively involved with RDPC politics, including election campaigning, strongly suggests that their role as health workers is going to be affected by local perceptions of the RDPC party itself. One high-ranking health official I interviewed felt strongly that public health centers should be dissociated from the dominant political party. "People should not come to health events in uniform. Now that there are numerous political parties, vaccination should not be identified with a specific one." Clearly, though, the ruling party seeks to take credit for the few "free" services it continues to provide and vaccinations are among them. But if the RDPC continues to be seen as a "provider" of jobs and services, it has nonetheless lost much of its former standing since the development of multiparty politics. Thus, the loss of legitimacy of the RDPC party has eroded the legitimacy of the local health center itself, and of its personnel as well.

The empty health center has become a potent symbol of a state that has lost its efficacy. As a result of budget cuts and privatization, the state is no longer perceived as benevolent purveyor of desirable goods and services. This is particularly true in Domaayo, which overwhelmingly voted for the UNDP in the 1997 elections but where the head nurse had not reported to work in months. He had essentially abandoned this insubordinate village. The chief, as well as members of the local health committee—a group which is theoretically the focus of "local empowerment" initiatives—felt helpless before this abandonment of their health center by its chief medical officer. They had no idea how to file a complaint or to whom. They begged me to help them, to *do something* about their health center. The chief in particular asked me to intervene. Clearly, he like the other villagers, felt alienated from the same state infrastructure, which might offer a solution to their dysfunctional dispensary.

Oumarou's perspective illustrates how the new policies are perceived in Domaayo. A farmer and market vendor with a large family to support, Oumarou was among those most sorely disappointed with recent political and economic developments. Full of anger, wry humor, and frustration, his statement reveals how medicines and state power are linked in a complex narrative about indifference, greed, and cruelty.

> *Long ago, they used to build hospitals, build schools, hold vaccinations, they used to pay people. They would beg from wealthy countries and share the money among the people in the form of loans, which were paid off in reasonable time frame. They would call us, call someone honest, and give him a loan. They were useful* (don nafa). *If they wanted money from me, they would ask me to buy a license. It was small small money.*
>
> *Right now, it is not like this. They want a license, they grab my arm. I have 20,000 francs, they want 30,000. My house has collapsed, they won't give me anything. My child goes to school, they say [snaps his fingers] "Money!"* (ceede). *I go to the hospital, they ask for money. I am sick and you want money? My wall has collapsed—it's my problem! My field is ruined—you won't give me any. Even a tiny bit of money you won't give to people? You won't give any. I have none, and you want money from me. If I steal—encore! [He holds out his arms, wrists held together, to indicate they are being bound in handcuffs]. Until the day of the vote, when they come and say, "Please, please, won't you help us?"*

Another Domaayo resident, a traditional bone setter, expressed his view of the neoliberal policies, as part of a historical process that began with the introduction of western medicines in Cameroon:

> *They [the government] have made us want their "quinine" [pharmaceuticals] and then they have taken it away. Now, they give us nothing [in the public clinics] and yet we no longer know what our parents and grandparents knew about plants, to go into the bush and get the medicines we need to treat our ailments and those of our families.*

Thus a desire for western medicines (*quinine*) was intentionally created by public clinics giving away free medicines. Then, the need created, and traditional medical knowledge eroded, they took it away. Now, one can only acquire those medicines for cash, but the prices are beyond the reach of many. Far from being isolated from global economic processes, residents of Domaayo are profoundly connected to globalized flows of medicinal commodities, such as antibiotics, anti-malarial drugs, and vaccines. Yet they are profoundly aware they don't control the terms of trade. Many, like Mal Goni, feel tricked into depending on goods they can no longer afford.

MEDICAL PLURALISM

For ordinary people in Cameroon, the medical system *is* the social system. They draw on networks of kin, neighbors, friends, and relations of reciprocity and trust in their quest for health. This sometimes leads them to seek out a specialist, but more commonly, medicine is obtained from relatives and close friends. Indeed, throughout Africa, people are making use of old and new types of medicines at the same time. The situation is one which anthropologists call medical pluralism (Crandon-Malamud 1991; Janzen 1978; Kleinman 1980; Lambek 1992; Sharp 1993), meaning that many different therapeutic traditions and orders of medical knowledge coexist and that most people use a wide variety of medical options in seeking therapy, even for the same illness. In Cameroon, people use home remedies, medicines from family, neighbors, and friends, pharmaceuticals sold at roadside stands, public and mission-run dispensaries, herbalists, Koranic healers who work with scripture, and Fulbe surgeons and bone setters as well as hospitals. For a high fever, someone may go to the dispensary for medical treatment while at the same time drawing on herbal, or Koranic medicines. People learn from experience and are willing to use whatever works. It is an empirical process, and information about medicinal efficacy circulates widely.

Fulbe people understand disease to have a variety of causes. There are "common-sense" illnesses, such as back pain caused by heavy labor in the fields. Seasonal, or "hot and cold" illnesses are caused by an imbalance of heat and cold in the air, water, food, and the body. Malaria, arthritis, and schistosomiasis, for instance, are believed to be caused by an excess of damp cold (*peewol*). Fulbe people also believe that sickness can be caused by exogenous parasites, such as worms and germs. As discussed in chapters five and six, several types of sicknesses are thought to be caused by mischievous spirits, and admiring or jealous people, as well as witches. Domaayo residents have an assortment of local therapeutic traditions, and biomedicine (often called Western medicine) is incorporated into that pluralism. Rather than completely displacing other medical traditions, western medicine has become one of many options people have for seeking treatment.

Western pharmaceuticals are extremely popular in Domaayo to treat malaria, intestinal infections, headaches, eye infections, and fevers. Domaayo residents use government clinics, hospitals, and mission-run health centers for their preventive health programs, such as well-baby clinics and vaccinations, as well as for their diagnosis and treatment facilities. For all these reasons, the opening of the local health center in Domaayo had been widely anticipated.

Biography of a Clinic

The Domaayo dispensary opened only a few weeks after my arrival in the Spring of 1990, and, because of their prior experiences with white women as medical missionaries, many villagers assumed that I had come to open it for them. The imposing building, which was rumored to have cost the Cameroonian state several million CFA Francs, had created quite a stir in the community when it was built in the late 1980s. After it stood empty for several years, the villagers had begun to ignore it and walk by it as they would an old ruin. My arrival, however, revived interest in the health center, and in my first weeks, I was asked about it constantly, often being addressed with the unnerving title "*Madame Dobtor*".

Construction of the clinic completed in the late 1980s, the administration was slow to staff it with health personnel, since freezes on new hires in the civil service meant that staff members would have to be transferred in from elsewhere. When the long awaited *dobtor* actually arrived (he turned out to be a certified nurse), the regional hospital in Guidiguis had supplied him with only a few of the basic necessities for opening a health center, and so he went to the chief to ask for help. He implored the chief to provide the center with its most urgent needs: paper for writing prescriptions (and for folding into convenient containers for tablets), a blue pen and a red pen, a ruler, a *cachet* (an official rubber stamp with the nurse's name, title, and the name of the health center printed on it), a pad of ink for the stamp, a kerosene stove for boiling water and sterilizing instruments, kerosene, and a broom. In response, the chief called a meeting of the village elders and heads of households, from whom he raised enough money for the supplies. I donated pens and paper and the doors were opened the next day.

In the first few weeks, the nurse successfully treated a number of minor illnesses, as well as several cases of malaria, giving out his medicines sparingly and writing prescriptions for the less common drugs he did not have in his small pharmacy. He organized several vaccination campaigns, arranging to have the vaccines driven in from Kaele and to have the event announced widely in the village. He drew large enthusiastic crowds of mothers (and some fathers) with their infants and young children to have their arms and legs "scarred" (*yaarugo*), as they put it. The flow of men, women and children to the dispensary satisfied the nurse, and the villagers took pride in finally having a functioning health center. When an illness recognized to be within the diagnostic purview of the *dobtor* struck a family member, they would set off in the direction of the clinic in search of treatment.

About two months after the nurse's arrival, however, the dispensary's supplies of medicine ran out. The flow of villagers to and from the dispensary was reduced to a trickle, and the nurse spent long hours every day thinking about his situation and his prospects for the future. I asked my friends with sick children why they didn't take them to the dispensary. "What's the use? All they will do is write a prescription for me to buy in Kaele." The health center did, from time to time, get new supplies of medicine, but they soon ran out, and after a while most residents learned not to rely on the dispensary.

"SYSTÈME D"

The nurse was one of thousands of civil servants throughout Cameroon whose salary was paid only intermittently (if at all) in the early 1990s. Like many others, he suffered from the frustration of having to figure out how to get by on inadequate means, in his workplace and in his family life. Cameroonians from all walks of life talk about this struggle to get by using the French term *débrouillardise*, also known as the "*système D*," which implies a creative, and often unorthodox way of operating in difficult circumstances, fending for oneself when institutional support systems fail (MacGaffey 1987:137; 2000). Posted by the government far from his natal village, the nurse could not easily rely on family support to get by. It is likely that his family was hugely disappointed in his economic hardship, which belied their own expectations that an educated relative would be able to help them after years of schooling and upon finally landing a good government job. Once again, as when he first opened the health center, the nurse went to the chief for help. This time, he asked for use of a field, with which he could grow millet to feed his family, and perhaps some cash crops, with which he would be able to pay for a few basic commodities, clothes and school fees for his children. When the rains began to fall in earnest in May, the nurse was out in the field with his assistant and several village children planting his millet.

I learned later that the health workers in Domaayo and elsewhere were resorting to selling medicines both in the public clinics and out of their homes. The crisis in pharmaceutical supplies and the difficulties of being paid one's salaries were proving to be chronic problems and not temporary lapses, as some of us had hoped. The Domaayo nurse told me he was more than 8 months behind in salary payments and doubted that he would ever be paid in full. For this reason, when new health policies were finally announced, they occasioned rather less protest than they might have otherwise. It had become clear that the old system was completely dysfunctional and one could only hope the new policies would restore the functioning of a health system which had seemingly been abandoned by the government itself. But the crisis in the public health system was only part of a larger malaise striking the nation, indeed most of Africa.

ECONOMIC CRISIS

The deepening economic crisis in the 1990s and International Monetary Fund (IMF) and World Bank–imposed structural adjustment policies had wrought profound changes in public institutions in Cameroon. In addition, the move toward democratization and multiparty politics in the early 1990s revived popular hopes for a more responsive and equitable type of government. By the end of the decade, these hopes were largely frustrated and citizens increasingly resented the state institutions they had once looked to for support.

Structural adjustment policies imposed by the IMF and World Bank involved severe belt-tightening measures across the public sector. Freezes were placed on new hires, budgets were slashed, and salaries were paid intermittently. Public servants at all levels increasingly sought opportunities in the black market to supplement inadequate and unreliable paychecks. Since 1991, civil servants' salaries have undergone de facto 75-percent cuts, when actual pay cuts and devaluation are taken into account. The vast majority of people in the far north province, who receive no government checks, have seen the prices of most commodities skyrocket while they have come under increasing pressure from "freelance" gendarmes, police, inspectors, and civil servants across public sector to provide bribes in order to obtain basic services or avoid harassment.

After six years of absence, I returned to Domaayo in the summer of 1997 to find dramatic changes in the living standards of people I knew. The village chief, who had been driving a Peugeot was now reduced to driving a leased motorcycle. Others, who I had known to drive motorcycles, were riding bicycles or walking on foot. Women, who had only worn fancy Holland or Java wax cloth wrappers, were now wearing humble Cameroonian prints. Hospitals and health centers now universally charged for medicines. The state was increasingly being privatized, and charging for basic services. Phones, which were formerly located inside a government office, were now answered by the private phone and fax company next door, which took messages for those working at the government office. This is how neoliberal economic policies are experienced on the ground.

I asked Daada Abba, Rabiyatu's neighbor, how life in Domaayo had changed in the last six years. Her answer reveals that women are just as concerned about "*la crise*"—the crushing economic crisis—as men.

> "*How have things changed, Daada Abba?*" *I asked.*
> "*Only in difficulty, Elen!*" *She exclaimed, laughing.*
> "*People go to the market all day so that they can come back with one or two coins. They are unable to make any money. Women also, who are secluded, and who sit in their compounds with their trade goods, they don't sell. Don't you see, it has changed? In the past, if you had a trade, and you set it up in your compound, you could make sales. Right now,*

there is none of that, Elen. People are just here with their suffering
(Himbe don bee bone non!).
   Now, if you are ill, what will you do? Sey alla hoynu tan! You can only hope that God will have mercy on you."

The above descriptions show economic crisis to be part of people's everyday experience, in their efforts to make a living, to feed their families, and to provide them with clothing, medicines and other basic commodities. It also places increasing strains on family relations, between husbands and wives, parents and children, and also between neighbors, as relations of reciprocity are more and more difficult to maintain. Before examining the global economic and medical policies directly, we must briefly explore the dramatic changes taking place in Cameroon's political landscape as the new public health policies were being planned.

MULTIPARTY POLITICS, STERILIZING VACCINES

A major factor affecting the public health centers is the "failed transition" to genuine multiparty democracy. In Cameroon as in many other parts of Africa, the "democratic transition" was marked by dramatic conflicts between a diverse opposition movement and powerful incumbents maneuvering to stay in office. It was in this context of political ferment that the new health policies began to be implemented. Opposition political parties were legalized at the end of 1990, and laws that guaranteed the liberalization of the press began to take effect. Between 1990 and 1991, I witnessed dramatic change in the conversations among people I knew in the region. People began discussing politics, openly criticizing the government and expressing hope for political change. People dreamed out loud of the possibility that the Fulbe would once again become important political actors in a newly revitalized political system (Regis 1997).

At independence, northern Cameroonians had found themselves in a privileged position when Ahmadou Ahidjo was elected president of the new state. During Ahidjo's presidency, one-fourth of all cabinet members were northerners, many of them Fulbe, and the north was systematically favored in the allocation of financial resources (Azarya 1978: 156). In 1982, Ahidjo resigned from office and his hand-picked successor, Paul Biya, took office. Two years later, an unsuccessful *coup* attempt led to a broad sweep of Fulbe and their allies from leadership positions. Many of those implicated in the *coup* attempt were executed or imprisoned (Burnham 1996: 40). The Biya era that followed is spoken of as a period of tremendous loss by Fulbe people: loss of access to political power, loss of resources, loss of development initiatives in their region.

The vicissitudes of the "democratic transition" in Cameroon have had dramatic consequences for public perceptions of the public health campaigns. In

1991, when a national vaccination campaign designed to vaccinate women and children for tetanus was initiated, rumors began circulating that this "vaccination" was in fact a sterilizing procedure. The public health strategy for tetanus vaccines was to focus on young women of childbearing age, in an effort to prevent neonatal tetanus. The rumors highlighted the gender and age targets of the vaccination teams, which found schoolchildren fleeing from the windows as they approached area public schools. A WHO vaccination specialist I interviewed told me of similar interpretations of vaccination in Guinea, Madagascar, and the former USSR during 1991 and 1992. In each case, the rumors of genocide which circulated around national vaccination campaigns coincided with dramatic political changes, and in particular, the end of single party monopolies.

The long-term effects of such rumors of genocide are difficult to gauge. But they are significant as a way for citizens to express their skepticism about the benevolence of the state and its "medicines." The rumors have given form to widespread feelings of insecurity, apprehension, and angst in connection with the "democratizing" state in such a way that it could be examined and discussed publicly by members of concerned communities.

This heightened anxiety about the state would only strengthen people's tendency to go outside the government health centers to acquire pharmaceuticals. Certainly, those drugs are of uneven quality and are often sold after they have expired or have been damaged in sunlit market booths—people I spoke with are aware of those risks. But can one be sure that the medicines purchased at state-run health centers are any better? In Domaayo, I was told the head nurse purchased medicines in the market to resell in the clinic. Villagers were not fooled. They recognized the packaging from their own market purchases. Small surprise that they preferred to go to the market directly. The profound alienation of many Cameroonians from state institutions was expressed in these rumors and in the increasing reliance on market vendors as providers of medical commodities. In this way, the social space of the market became a refuge for those seeking medicine in a civil society distinguished from the single-party state and its agents.

THE IMF AND THE WORLD BANK

The IMF and World Bank were created at the end of the Second World War by the Bretton Woods Agreements. The IMF was founded to increase stability in international financial institutions, whereas the World Bank was designed to promote international investment, initially for the reconstruction of post-war Europe, and to promote economic growth in developing countries. Currently the World Bank states that its principal mission is "to fight poverty with passion and professionalism for lasting results" (World Bank 2000). Robert McNamara instituted structural adjustment programs (SAPs) at the World Bank in 1979, which aimed to transform the economies of developing countries by *adjusting* them to the realities of the global economy. The understanding of this global economy employed by the World Bank's leading policymakers reflects current neoliberal perspectives of the world's most powerful economies. SAPs typically attempt to decrease governmental management of the economy. The latter is accomplished primarily by easing restrictions on wages, agricultural product prices, interest rates, and foreign investment; privatizing public corporations; and reducing bureaucracy and public expenditures in the areas of health, education, housing, and environment.

The IMF and World Bank have also become the leading force in setting international public health policy, overtaking the role of the World Health Organization (WHO). Two decades earlier, the WHO had set the standard for public health incentives in developing countries with "primary health care." In the developing world, most deaths are due to infectious disease and parasites, diseases (such as diarrhea, measles, and malaria) which are either preventable or easily treatable, if people have access to health education and basic health services. However, health professionals have a tendency to build, staff, and operate hospitals in urban areas, neglecting the rural majority of the population. The 1978 WHO directives aimed to provide basic medical care for all people, and thereby prevent the majority of preventable deaths.

As Bretton Woods institutions replaced the WHO in setting global public-health priorities, the 1978 directives were being abandoned. According to Turshen, the World Bank and the IMF "counseled governments to look to the private sector to provide basic goods and services that formerly were a public charge" (1999:5). Health was included in these reforms and, like other state-run enterprises, it was recommended that the health-care sector be privatized. "The arguments [for privatization] embody the view that health is a commodity and health care is a privilege" writes Turshen (1999:3).

Furthermore, structural adjustment policies favor routing international development monies away from top-heavy and corrupt governments. Nongovernmental organizations (NGOs), therefore, became the principal agents of change as public health reforms privatized training of personnel, distribution of drugs, and local implementation of policy and oversight to a variety of groups. NGOs were considered fundamentally as grassroots organizations independent of centralized governments, and so channeling development funds through them was meant to contribute to the democratization of society. However, the reality on the ground was considerably more ambiguous. The interaction between simultaneous changes in the economy, public policy, and the political system were complex and seemingly unpredictable.

THE REORIENTATION OF PRIMARY HEALTH CARE: PERSPECTIVES FROM YAOUNDE

By the time I returned to Yaounde, Cameroon's capital, in May 1997 to talk with public officials, major administrative reforms were already being implemented. In addition to those changes that affected all public administrators and civil servants, such as salary reductions and monetary devaluation, there were changes specific to the public health sector. Cameroon had adopted policies that would drastically change the organization and financing of the public health system. The reforms in Cameroon were commonly known as the Reorientation of Primary Health Care, or "Reo" for short. In response to the chronic drug shortages of the early 1990s, "cost-recovery" (requiring clients to pay for both consultations and pharmaceuticals) would now generate funds in local health centers that could be used to purchase basic drugs. Under the new system, health centers would be semiautonomous, with only the salaries of professional staff coming from the central government, the rest being financed through cost-recovery.

Prior to the Reo, doctors, nurses, and technical assistants all saw themselves as purveyors of public resources, agents of distribution of public goods, givers of medicine. In these roles, they had a certain amount of prestige in the communities where they worked, and they benefited from the local networks of reciprocity. The Reo—by making health workers into salesmen—deprived them of their ability to be generous and to benefit from the goodwill and indirect material rewards they had long enjoyed. Indeed doctors and nurses were now seen as local embodiments of the stinginess of the neoliberal state. These workers were doubly hit, because they had already undergone salary reductions and experienced a loss of buying power due to the devaluation of the currency (the CFA).

Numerous NGOs, such as Save the Children and Care, each working in discrete zones of influence, have been instrumental in implementing the Reo policy. That most of these are international organizations with non-Cameroonian leadership is a point that is not missed by local observers. In spite of NGOs' attempts to develop a grassroots character, the initiative for projects typically originates abroad. As one Yaounde-based Ministry of Health official told me, "*On mange des projets ici*" (literally, "we eat projects here"). This bodily metaphor vividly illustrates his experience as a consumer rather than an initiator of public health initiatives. A Domaayo resident also showed his keen sensitivity to the foreign agency in reorientation efforts. Discussing the reform of a local health center, he specified: "When they opened this new pharmacy, it was the whites (*nasaara*) who did that." In this way, the implementation of Reo policies is locally perceived as an external effort coming not only from outside his community and from outside of Cameroon, but from outside of Africa—from the whites. The head nurse of one health center I visited in June 1997 told me that the center was completely left out of the new programs and that it had been abandoned by the NGOs, which had previously been involved in the area. "We have no cofinancing. The Belgians never came. Save [Save the Children] has closed shop." His statement reveals that local health workers refer to NGOs by national-ity—"Americans," "Germans," "Belgians," "Swiss," and so forth.—suggesting that their efforts to include local partners in development efforts are transparent. It is the *bailleurs de fonds* (international donors) who make policy here. Though not all Cameroonians are conversant with the specific reforms initiated by the IMF and World Bank, many people I spoke with are not convinced by the rhetoric of local empowerment and democratization, which has filtered down to them from afar and from above.

In an interview with Rene Owona, then director of Primary Health Care at the Ministry of Health in Yaounde, I asked him what challenges were being faced "on the ground" as the Reo was implemented throughout the country. His answer was a blunt and devastating indictment of governmental paralysis.

> *We have no idea. The old system is gone. There is no follow-through to see how the new system is being put in place. We have no budget for site visits. Zero. Our last Minister of Health had no background in public health. He has quit to run for the presidency. Our new Minister is a for-mer school principal.*

In summary, the director concluded, "*On est completement bloqué*. (We are completely stuck.)" Another high-level administrator, a Provincial *Délégué* for Health (one of the top-ten public health officials in Cameroon) told me that each province is creating its own plan for applying the new policy. The responsibility falls on each *Délégué* to invent a plan for his province. Another high-level public health professional, who has a long involvement with public health in Cameroon, told me that each NGO has its own plan to train health workers in its area. The problem is that the health workers are often transferred to jobs outside the NGOs' area, so that the resources invested in training them are lost to another region (and another NGO), where they will have to be retrained. In his province, the *Délégué* informed me, the turnover rate of personnel is nearly 80 percent. They may be posted to an area where cost-recovery has not yet been implemented or to an area with a different system. The new policies place more responsibility than ever on health-care professionals, and they have less pay than ever. There is a lack of super-vision and a lack of incentives for good job performance due to the absence of a system of rewards and penalties linked to performance.

The public health system suffers from a highly cumbersome administrative structure for rewarding or penalizing personnel. Each employee's *dossier*, or file, must be discussed by three ministries: the Ministry of Health, the Ministry of Finance, and the Ministry of Public Service. Furthermore, those with the authority to make any decisions on an individual's file are in Yaounde, many administrative levels away from the local clinic, where a worker's performance might be observed and documented. For example, if a health worker did not report to work for a year, the supervising medical officer at the local level would have to relay a request to Yaounde via the district and provincial administrators, and the file would have to be discussed there with representatives from all three ministries before the worker's salary could be suspended. "This almost never happens," he concluded. There is a lack of fit between the decentralization of resources and decision-making implied in the Reo and the centralization of salaried professionals in the civil service in general. NGOs can be somewhat more responsive by giving rewards for good work through training programs, conferences, and supplies. Health workers I spoke with during my visits to clinics confirmed this view, commenting on how contacts with NGO staff, and participation in training seminars and conferences helped to boost their morale and to maintain their commitment to providing high-quality medical care for very little pay.

CONCLUSION

The globalized state in Cameroon, as in many parts of Africa, is losing its ability to act as a benevolent purveyor of public goods. With its revenues flattened by economic crisis and its institutions reformed by World Bank and IMF directives, the neoliberal state is increasingly viewed with ambivalence, anxiety, and even disgust. As embodied in the local medical clinic, the state in Domaayo is perceived as "refusing to be generous." A close examination of recent medical reforms reveals how the Cameroonian state is powerfully shaped by international forces and policy directives imposed by global financial institutions. Four decades after the formal ending of the colonial era, Cameroon is "postcolonial" but by no means independent.

Conclusion

Right now, if you want to gain control of your accounts, you must go to a mallum. Everybody is competing against you.

Rabiyatu

Bakari and I have maintained an intermittent correspondence since I first left Cameroon in 1991. Through his letters, I received news of Dija and Adda Habiiba, of Fa'dimatu and the chief, of the millet harvest, and of the many births, deaths, and marriages taking place in my absence. At times, Bakari used these letters to reflect on his marriage, as he had often done during our many long walks together in Domaayo and elsewhere. In our early conversations, he had always maintained the position of the youthful skeptic vis-à-vis his cultural traditions. He spoke French and identified with the critical discourse of "schoolboys" toward the tradition received from his community. "I would never be polygamous," he told me once, musing. "I have plenty to worry about as it is! Besides, when you have co-wives, there is never peace in the household. You have to constantly be caught up in managing the domestic chaos. No, one wife is enough. Those who marry more than one do so out of pride—they are trying to be bigger than they really are." He emphasized his contempt for the big men of the community, pretentious, claiming to be important, weighty, and influential. Bakari's identity as a "simple man" contrasted with those who are "complicated" and "difficult" characters.

But his marriage with his wife, Rabiyatu, was far from simple. Several times, during my field stays, she left her marital home for prolonged visits to her natal family. Though I was rarely privy to the specific arguments that led to her departures, both Rabiyatu and Bakari spoke of the material strains of poverty on their marriage. Rabi dreamed of another life, a sweeter and more generous world, in which she would feel cherished and well-treated. Although I believe she cared deeply for this man, she displayed the characteristic detachment and ironic distance of Fulbe wives toward their husbands. She had her own identity, her own dreams, her own destiny, which may or may not merge with his. As the economic crisis in Cameroon deepened and SAPs shaped increasing material scarcity among families, their marriage was not spared from the increasing strain on all relationships. During our conversations in 1997, she often spoke to me about the growth of occult practices (*siiri* and *mistiraaku*) and the erosion of kinship and friendship ties that resulted from the economic hardship. Hard times have distorted the ordinary give and take of kinship, not only affecting the traditionally fraught relations between husbands and wives, but even the sacred bond between mothers and their sons. She glanced at her own son who slept by her side as she talked.

> There is a man who sold his mother in Maroua. He was caught. I know the mother, and I know her son. He sold his mother so that he could get some money. He told his mother he had bought a wonderful house in Nigeria, and that they should go there. With his children and his wives in Maroua, they all went together. When they arrived, he told his mother that they should enter through a doorway. They entered the saare. And as they went through a doorway, it would close behind them, and they would reach another doorway, and that one also closed behind them. And so on until they reached a woman, a puldebbo. [He left his mother with the puldebbo and returned home with his family.] When they arrived in Maroua, he said they had been traveling and that his mother had fallen on the road and died. They sat in mourning for her.
>
> Meanwhile, inside the saare the puldebbo, an old woman, said to the mother: "What brings you here?" She said, "My son brought me." "Your child, that you gave birth to?" She said "Yes.." The old woman said, "Well, he has sold you to nyaamoori'en." She showed her the parts of people: heads, hands, torso, intestines! All of these she showed to her. She said "Do you see to what kind of place you son has brought you?" And the mother said, "I see." The puldebbo said "Come here. If this man that you gave birth to did this to you, go. Do what you can to leave this place." The old woman took some money and put it in the mother's bag. She opened the door for her and the woman ran and ran and ran until she got to the paved road (goudron). She got out the money to pay for the car. She returned to Maroua and found that her funeral had already taken place seven days earlier. She found the people all sitting there in mourning.
>
> "This is happening in Maroua," Rabiyatu concluded. "It happens a lot!" "What happened to the son?" I asked. "The boy is in prison." "Don't kill him," the mother had said to them.

Some sons have become so desperate, so crazed by their economic woes that they are driven to sell their mothers' bodies for cash to a race of people eaters. But a mother's compassion somehow survives the crisis, at least in this story, as she asks the authorities to spare her son's life. I struggled with the '*nyaamori*' term, which sounds like the Fulbe word *nyaama* (to eat). "What does it mean to say these people are *nyaamori*?" I asked.

> *They are all Nigerians. If you hear about* nyaamori, *they are all from Nigeria. Because if you go to Nigeria, here is a boutique of* nyaamori, *and her is a boutique of a Hawsaajo. If you say you are looking to buy something and then you tell them it is too expensive, they'll tell you, "Go ahead and buy it in the* nyaamori *boutique." And that is how they are. Because, their boutiques are open, and you, seeing beautiful things, go in to look at all the great things they have for sale. You walk in and they close the door behind you. You are looking, you keep going, and they close another door, and you are lost. 'Be don nyaama kam. Indeed they do eat.*

Thus Rabiyatu's story joins the desires of the market for things one cannot afford, with a violent and shocking inversion of kinship relations. In Fulbe tradition a son must care for his mother, as he owes her his life. She risked her own life in giving birth to him, and he is eternally tied to this sacred debt. If the globalized economy has seen the increasing commodification of all spheres of life, including relations between bride and groom, husband and wife. Never before, the story suggests, has the desire for wealth and worldly goods corrupted the mother-son relation as it has now. "Your own son, that you gave birth to?" the old woman had asked. And the mother affirmed, "My own son." Even the old *nyaamoori* woman, long familiar with the occult trade in human flesh for profit, was shocked at this development. And Rabiyatu hummed to her son as he slept, while I thought : A mother must protect herself. Never has there been more demand for the work of *mallums*, who practice the secret art of *siiri*.

I often read in Bakari's letters about the vicissitudes of their marriage, through several separations and reconciliations. Then, shortly before I returned to the field in 1997, Bakari announced that he was planning to remarry. He was, he confided, looking for a girl. After my arrival in Domaayo, I learned that it was his mother who had advised him to take another wife. "You see, each time Rabi left, I was stranded here, with all of the children, crying, dirty, and hungry. I had to ask [my brother's wives, and my neighbors] to help me with cooking. And each time I was accumulating another debt to them. After a while, they began to complain." Bakari's mother, the doyenne of this large patrilineal family, was highly aware of her son's marital instability and the strain it placed on Bakari's children and his kin. She lived in his *saare* and received her daily meal from Rabiyatu. So if a meal was missed, she was among the first to know, and to feel the gnawing hunger in her belly while Bakari struggled to make other arrangements. "You see, we sons go into her house every morning for tea, and we sit on the floor of her house, chatting as we sip our tea." It was at one of these morning gatherings that she told me to "Marry." I could not oppose her.

Preparations for the wedding were in full swing in June and July of 1997, but the wedding date came and the marriage was suddenly cancelled. The girl (*bingel*) to whom he was betrothed mysteriously changed her mind at the last minute and married another man. Village rumors accused Rabiyatu of using sorcery to call off the wedding. She laughed when we talked about it early one morning in the privacy of her gravel-floored house.

> *"Everyone knew the wedding was going to be called off," she explained, "except for the groom himself. I wanted to tell him, but in the end I couldn't bring myself to do it. I didn't want to hurt his feelings. It was shameful. And there are those who accuse me of* siiri. *Those who ask me to my face, I tell them 'I did it!' So there. And if I denied it, would they believe me anyway?"*

But Bakari was undeterred. He immediately began receiving letters of sympathy from friends and acquaintances, men offering him their daughters in marriage. Though still in shock from his dramatically failed attempt at re-marriage, he resolved to marry within the year. We parted with sadness, but determined to stay in touch. Since Rabiyatu does not write in roman script, I was going to have to rely on Bakari for news of her as well, at least until I could learn to read and write Arabic. Two months later, I received a letter from Bakari, dated August 7, 1997.

> *Finally here is my wedding day. It is for me a great pleasure, a great joy, a historical day in my life. My sister, I have really missed you. God did not accept that you should see my wedding. But in any case, I will explain it to you a little.*
>
>   *Here is what I paid for my marriage: 8 pieces of cloth, 4 pairs of shoes, 4 bottles of perfume, 3 bottles of lotion, 15 pieces of laundry soap, and 15 cosmetic soaps. . . .*
>
>   *My gifts (*njaayo*) from the village are : Daada Manga, 1 piece of cloth; Gogga Fanto, 4,000 CFA, Umaru, Usumaanu, and Garga (his brothers) each one piece of cloth. I have two sisters who each gave me 2,000 CFA. Ubbo gave me a large enameled plate and 500 CLFA, her brother, one plate and 500 CFA, Jebba Hawwa, a plate and 200CFA, Maaji, her sister, one plate. Umarou, another brother of Ubbo, gave me 15,000 and my older brother in Maroua gave me 60,000. The Lamido*

of X asks me to salute you, he gave me also 15,000. He is also against [the previous bride's father].

My sister, it is difficult to explain, but almost the entire village loves me and participated in my wedding. For me, it is difficult to host so many people at my place. I want you to know that I killed four sheep and used four sacs of millet, just so that those in attendance could eat.

The suitcase of my 'bingel is composed of: three lengths of cloth, two pairs of shoes, soap, kola, perfume, lotion, earrings, one slip, one brassiere, and other things. For Rabiyatu, I gave two lengths of cloth, which cost a lot, one pair of shoes, perfume, and lotion, which were expensive. She is also happy with her family. For the mother of the girl, three lengths of cloth, one pair of shoes, perfume and lotion. For the father of the girl, one gandura (a large elaborately embroidered gown), one pair of shoes, and some perfume. For the maternal grandmother of the girl, one length of cloth. The sisters and maternal aunts and paternal aunts all are dress [all received a length of cloth]. It is my two sisters who brought these things over to my in-laws. As a reward, to let my family know that they are happy [with the marriage and the gifts] they gave each one money, about 5,000 for kola, etc.

After that, my in-laws came here with many plates, something like 20 plates. The plates belonged to my mother, so my mother gave them 500F to let them know she is very happy, but she is old . . . [so she could not give more].

I will summarize. The women who accompanied the bride spent the evening here eating the sheep I had slaughtered for them. The next day, I slaughtered a goat for myself and my friends. That evening, instead of inviting people to my house, I did something a little different. I preferred to distribute the food to all the homes in the village. Each household got a plate of prepared food and some gateaux (fried cakes).

. . . After that, I must say goodbye to my in-laws and with 10,000 and four lengths of cloth and some soap. They all went home. There remained only the Kamo [the bride's age mate and companion, who traditionally escorts a girl to her first marital home] who will also go home with a length of cloth.

Here is something amusing. When the marriage party was coming here, there were girls who were singing, the ending of the song was "wandoufoul" I think this is an English phrase. It means something surprising perhaps. After that, we brought the girl to Rabiyatu, so that she could give her a name. Her proper name is Asma'u, but Rabiyatu called her "Bouri Weltougo," which signifies " this one surpasses the other one" or literally, "sweeter" than the other.

Everyone likes me and speaks of my marriage. . . . Helen, you have wiped the tears from my eyes. There is a Fulbe proverb, "A wostaniyam

Bakari with puldebbo *matchmakers.*

gondi." *Without you I would have cried a lot. I wish you good luck, a
long life, and courage in your research. I am a feeling more at peace
now. Only the marriage cost me a lot, like you would not believe. It is
my first time and my last time to have such a marriage.*
    Give my greetings to your mother, your father . . .

Your friend,
Bakari

Glossary

FULBE GLOSSARY

akawo—a government official or bureaucrat; one who works for whites (*nasaara*).

asungal (pl. *asli*)—lineage; sometimes refers to race.

azabaajo—a free woman, divorcée; any previously married woman of reproductive age.

basura'u—songs about the life of Mohammed that are sung on Mohammed's birthday.

diina—the faith; Islam.

dunya—the secular world; often in opposition to the world of faith.

en'dam—mother's milk; generosity, benevolence, trust of those breastfed by the same mother or who have gone through circumcision together.

entaado—a prematurely weaned baby whose thinning body inspires pity.

ginnaaji—spirits, or djinn; sometimes translated into French as *diables*, or devils.

gomna—government; used to refer to the (post)colonial state, as opposed to Fulbe rulers.

haabe (sing. *kaado*)—pagan; black African; anyone who is of non-Fulbe ethnicity or of a non-Islamic faith; equivalent to the French term *kirdi*; it is applied to African Christians but not to European Christians; historically, *haabe* were potential slaves.

huutooru—a wasting illness afflicting infants; a large scaly lizard whose appearance resembles that of afflicted infants; *huutooru* (translated as "caiman" by Fulbe-French speakers).

kuugal—work; ritual or ceremonial work (such as a wedding or healing ritual); efficacy.

maayo—seasonal river; during the dry season, a sandy riverbed into which shallow wells are dug for drawing naturally filtered water; gathering place for youth; also one of the principal dwelling places of spirits.

mallum—a Fulbe term of respect for an adult male, especially a learned one; title given to one (male or female) who has read the Koran.

mistiraaku—soul eating; cannibal witchcraft; a contested belief that Koranic scholars denounce as un-Islamic.

Mundang—main local non-Fulbe ethnic group; many residents of Domaayo are descended from Fulbe and Mundang unions.

munyal—patience, tolerance, and acceptance for the things one cannot control. *Munyal* joins in one word the strengths a person needs to face a life that simply does not offer what one desires. In this way, it resembles the Brazilian expression, *se conformar*, which is central to how Nordestino women face death and life (Scheper-Hughes 1992).

nasaara—literally Christian; also European, white person; one who is perceived as European in education, occupation, life-style, or appearance.

njaayo—gifts offered at key life-cycle ceremonies: baby namings, circumcisions, marriages; may be composed of money, grain, cloth, plates, perfume, decorated calabashes, or hand-woven basketry; they represent a type of generalized reciprocity, a complex rotating-credit system that is especially important for Fulbe women.

pulaaku—Fulbeness; a code of behavior that distinguishes Fulbe from *haabe*.

Pullo (pl. Fulbe)—someone of Fulbe ethnicity, or one who behaves or looks like a "true Fulbe"; also known as Fulani, Fula, Peul, Woodabe, Mbororo (pej.), Halpulaar.

puldebbo—postmenopausal woman; an "old" woman who is no longer concerned with men; also, a woman who has gained respect and authority from experience.

saare—family compound; usually a large courtyard enclosed with an earthen wall, dotted with individual round or square houses, and intersected with internal privacy walls; also refers to the extended family living inside this space and sharing resources.

sembe—strength; wealth; ability to make things happen; also '*bawde*.

semteende—shame, modesty, self-restraint; a key component of *pulaaku*.

siiri—secret knowledge; spells based on Koranic know-how; medicine.

wure—wrapper; cloth; differentiated according to quality (wax vs. print, or *abada*) as well as to country of origin (Cameroon vs. England, the Netherlands, or Java); a prestige item, it constitutes the quintessential gift of courtship and marriage.

CONCEPTUAL GLOSSARY
(WITH REFERENCES FOR FURTHER READING)

agency—the ability of individual subjects to act within, and often against, the constraints of a social structure that restricts freedom of action (*see* Giddens 1984, Comaroffs; Drewal 1991).

"belly politics"—*la politique du ventre*, a phrase coined by Jean François Bayart (1993) in reference to the political culture of Cameroon but a similar discourse operates in other parts of Africa (*see also* Geschiere 1997); the language of witchcraft is a way for ordinary people to criticize the powerful on ethical grounds; and eating is a way of consuming the power of others; those who display excessive bodily resources are implicated in illicit "eating" of others.

collective memory—a social phenomenon in which people "remember" things they may not have experienced directly, because they have been exposed to stories about events which affected their community (for example, colonization, Fulbe jihads, slavery); a community's view of their past.

commodification—a process in which an increasing number of things (such as objects, processes, relationships, services, knowledge and cultural heritage) are sold, rather than being exchanged according to social rules of reciprocity. This concept is involved in larger debates about economic change; exchange systems; globalization (*see* Hutchinson 1996; Appadurai 1986 ; Friedman 1994); also commoditization.

devolution—political economic theory that emerged during the Reagan/Thatcher era and which has influenced the shape of World Bank and IMF policy; characterized by the criticism of 'big government,' centralization and bureaucracy. Devolution is often spoken of in terms of privatization, decentralization, and local empowerment.

discourse—ways of speaking, communicating, and interacting, which are imbued with relations of power; often attuned to the micropolitics of social life (*see* Foucault 1972; 1980), "discourse" is defined by Abu-Lughod as "the actions and words of everyday life as shaped by the dominant ideology" (1986:275) and "a set of statements, both verbal and nonverbal, bound by rules and characterized by regularities, that both constructs and is patterned by social and personal reality" (1986:186). *See also* Said (1978) and Urban (1991).

discursive practices—ways of talking, structured by cultural norms and power relations, but employed by individuals in creative and subversive ways.

"dis-ease"—the absence of well-being; the hyphenated dis-ease includes a broad range of sicknesses, malaise, and ill health caused by all manner of social and political ills as well as the more narrow biomedical categories of disease.

essentialist—considering something (such as race, ethnicity, or gender) to be immutable, when it is in fact the product of historical and cultural (social, economic, political) forces, and thus subject to change (*see* Amselle 1998).

hegemony—the process though which consent is generated, and by which working classes "agree" to a particular social order; ideas, values, and beliefs are negotiated, rather than being simply imposed from above; what binds society together without the use of force; concept developed by Antonio Gramsci (1971).

monetarization—increasing reliance on money. *See also* commodification.

performance—social actors enact traditions while simultaneously improvising on received knowledge, or scripts. An approach which entered cultural anthropology from sociolinguistics and the study of speech acts; Performance also refers to embodied, ritualized enactments of social values, history, identity, community. According to Bauman, "they are cultural forms about culture, social forms about society, in which the central meanings and values of a group are embodied, acted out, and laid open to examination and interpretation in symbolic form, both by members of that group and by the ethnographer" (Bauman 1986:133; Bauman and Sherzer 1974; *see also* Turner 1986).

postcolonial—the historical social and cultural moment that followed the end of colonialism, yet which was continuous with it in some significant ways. Years after most nations have gained their independence from colonial rule in Africa, societies still struggle with true political, economic, and intellectual independence; (*see* Desai 2001; Fanon 1967; Appiah 1992; Lionnet 1995; Mbembe 2001; Stoler 1995; Trinh 1989; Vergès 1999).

polysemic—having more than one meaning, capable of simultaneously having multiple, and even contradictory meanings.

practice—theories of social life which seek to emphasize social processes (including transformation, negotiation, and "play") over deterministic structures; *see also* **agency**.

reciprocity—a pattern of gift exchange between two or more persons, which creates a relationship between those giving and receiving (*see* Mauss 1967 for the classic account and Strathern 1988 and Piot 1999 for a reinterpretation).

reifying—to make something seem more real (fixed, permanent) than they actually are. In social science writing, this often happens with social institutions which are culturally and historically constructed, but which can appear to be necessary, natural, universal and beyond critique.

structural adjustment—World Bank and IMF–imposed structural adjustment programs (SAPs) tie requirements of stringent internal reforms with the refinancing of debt for developing countries; SAPs typically include policies aiming to reduce inflation through a restrictive monetary policy, encourage exports to redress balance of payments and debt repayment, and generally decrease governmental management of the economy. The latter is accomplished primarily by easing restrictions on wages, agricultural product prices, interest rates, and foreign investment; privatizing public corporations; and reducing bureaucracy and public expenditures in the areas of health, education, housing, and environment. Often criticized for its heavy cuts in social programs, including health, education; for other critics, SAPs involve the erosion of the sovereignty of developing countries in determining internal policy (*see* Turshen 1999).

"writing against culture"—Lila Abu-Lughod has written of the power of narrative in "writing against culture" and constructing ethnographies that "showcase the texture of thought, and intimacy of life as lived" (Abu-Lughod 1993:14). Within limited discourses (that may be contradictory and certainly are historically changing), people can be shown to strategize, feel pain, contest interpretations of what is happening—in short, live their lives (1993:14). For writers in a contemporary global context where reifying and essentializing notions of culture seem to be increasing in popularity, the focus on narratives holds out the possibility of subverting "the most problematic connotations of 'culture': homogeneity, coherence, and timelessness" (1993:14).

References

Aardener, Shirley. 1975. *Perceiving women.* New York: Wiley.

Abbenyi, Juliana Makuchi Nfah. 1997. *Gender in African Women's Writing: Identity, Sexuality, and Difference.* Bloomington: Indiana University Press.

Abu-Lughod, Lila.1993a. Islam and the gendered discourses of death. *International Journal of Middle East Studies* 25:187–205.

_____. 1993b. *Writing women's worlds: Bedouin stories.* Berkeley: University of California Press.

_____. 1986. *Veiled sentiments: Honor and poetry in a Bedouin society.* Berkeley: University of California Press.

Amadi, Elechi. 1966. *The Concubine.* London: Heinemann.

Amselle, Jean-Loup. 1998 [1990]. *Mestizo logics: Anthropology of identity in Africa and elsewhere.* Trans. Claudia Royal. Stanford, Calif.: Stanford University.

Appadurai, Arjun. 1996. *Modernity at large: Cultural dimensions of globalization.* Minneapolis: University of Minnesota.

Appiah, Kwame Anthony. 1992. *In my father's house: Africa in the philosophy of culture.* New York: Oxford University Press.

Arnold, David. 1993. *Colonizing the body: State medicine and epidemic disease in nineteenth-century India.* Berkeley: University of California Press.

Azarya, V. 1978. *Aristocrats facing change.* Chicago: University of Chicago Press.

Bâ, Amadou Hampaté. 1991. *Amkoullel, l'enfant Peul: Memoires.* Arles: Actes Sud.

_____. 1994. *Oui Mon Commandant! Memoires II.* Arles: Actes Sud.

_____. 1999. *The fortunes of Wangrin.* Trans. Aina Pavolini Taylor, with an introduction by Abiola Irele. Bloomington: Indiana University Press.

Bauman, Richard. 1986. *Story, performance, and event: Contextual studies of oral narrative.* New York: Cambridge University Press.

Bauman, Richard, and Joel Sherzer. 1974. *Explorations in the ethnography of speaking.* New York: Cambridge University Press.

Bayart, Jean-François. 1993. *The state in Africa: The politics of the belly.* New York: Longman.

———. 1992. L'afropessimisme par le bas: Réponse à Achille Mbembe, Jean Copans et quelques autres. In *Le politique par le bas en Afrique noire: Contributions à une problématique de la démocratie,* Bayart et al., eds. pp. 257–265. Paris: Karthala.

———. 1989. *L'état en Afrique: La politique du ventre.* Paris: Fayart.

Bayart, Jean-François, Achille Mbembe, and Comi Toulabor 1992. *Le politique par le bas en Afrique noire: Contributions à une problématique de la démocratie.* Paris: Karthala.

Behar, Ruth. 1995. Introduction: Out of exile. In *Women writing culture,* edited by R. Behar and D. Gordon, pp. 1–29. Berkeley: University of California Press.

Behar, Ruth, and Deborah A. Gordon. 1995. *Women writing culture.* Berkeley: University of California Press.

Bledsoe, Carolyn, and M. Goubaud. 1985. The reinterpretation of Western pharmaceuticals among the Mende of Sierra Leone. *Social Science and Medicine* 21:275–282.

Boddy, Janice. 1989. *Wombs and alien spirits: Women, men, and the Zar cult in northern Sudan.* Madison: University of Wisconsin Press.

Bourdieu, Pierre. 1977. *Outline of a theory of practice.* Cambridge, U.K.: Cambridge University Press.

Boutrais, Jean. 1994. Pour une nouvelle cartographie des Peuls. *Cahiers d'Études Africaines,* XXXIV (1–3):137–146.

Breedveld, Anneke, and Miriam De Bruijn. 1996. L'image des Fulbe: Analyse critique de la construction du concept du *puḷaaku. Cahiers d'Études Africaines,* XXXVI (1–4):791–821.

Briggs, Charles. 1986. *Learning how to ask: A sociolinguistic appraisal of the role of the interview in social science research.* Cambridge, U.K.: Cambridge University Press.

Burnham, Philip. 1996. *The politics of cultural difference in northern Cameroon.* Washington, D.C.: The Smithsonian Institution.

Clifford, James. 1997. *Routes: Travel and translation in the late twentieth century.* Cambridge, Mass.: Harvard University Press.

Cohen, William B. 1971. *Rulers of empire: The French colonial service in Africa.* Stanford, Calif.: Hoover Institution Press.

Cohn, Bernard S. 1996. *Colonialism and its forms of knowledge.* Princeton, N.J.: Princeton University Press.

Cole, Sally. 1991. *Women of the Praia: Works and lives in a Portuguese coastal community.* Princeton, N.J.: Princeton University Press.

Comaroff, Jean. 1993. The diseased heart of Africa: Medicine, colonialism, and the black body. In *Knowledge, power and practice,* edited by L. Lindenbaum and B. Lock, pp. 305–329. Berkeley: University of California Press.

Comaroff, Jean, and John Comaroff, eds. 1993. *Modernity and its malcontents: Ritual and power in post-colonial Africa.* Chicago: University of Chicago Press.

Crandon-Malamud, Libbett. 1991. *From the fat of our souls: Social change, political process and medical pluralism in Bolivia.* Berkeley: University of California Press.

Crapanzano, Vincent. 1973. *The Hamadsha: A study in Moroccan ethnopsychiatry.* Berkeley: University of California Press.

De Bruijn, Miriam, and Heinrich Van Dyk. 1995. *Arid ways, cultural understandings of insecurity in Fulbe society, central Mali.* Amsterdam: Thela.

De Certeau, Michel. 1984. *The practice of everyday life.* Berkeley: University of California Press.

Delaney, Carol. 1991. *The seed and the soil: Gender and cosmology in Turkish village society.* Berkeley: University of California Press.

Desai, Gaurav. 2001. *Subject to colonialism: African self-fashioning in the colonial library.* Durham, N.C.: Duke University Press.

Diawara, Manthia. 1995. Malcolm X and the black public sphere: Conversionists versus culturalists. *The Black Public Sphere.* Ed. by The Black Public Sphere Collective. Pp. 39–52. Chicago: University of Chicago Press.

Dols, Michael. 1992. *Majnun: The madman in medieval Islamic society.* New York: Oxford University Press.

Drewal, Henry. 1988. *Performing the other: Mami Wata worship in West Africa. The Drama Review: Performance Studies* 32 (2):T118:160–180.

Drewal, Margaret. 1991. The state of research on performance in Africa. *African Studies Review* 34 (3): 1

_____. 1992. *Yoruba ritual: Performers, play, agency.* Bloomington: Indiana University Press.

Dupire, Marguerite. 1962. *Peuls nomades.* Paris: Institut d'Ethnologie.

Evans-Pritchard, E.-E. 1937. *Witchcraft, oracles and magic among the Azande.* London: Clarendon.

Fanon, Frantz. 1967 [1952]. *Black skin, white masks.* Trans. Charles Lam Markmann. New York: Grove Press.

Feierman, Steven, and John Janzen, eds. 1992. *The social basis of health and healing in Africa.* Berkeley: University of California Press.

Fisher, Humphrey. 1978. *The western and central Sudan.* In *The Cambridge history of Islam* (Vol 2a). London: Cambridge University Press. Pp 345–405.

Foster, George M. 1965. Peasant society and the image of the limited good. *American Anthropologist* 67:293–315.

Foucault, Michel. 1980. *Power/knowledge,* edited by Colin Gordon. New York: Pantheon.

_____. 1973. *The birth of the clinic.* New York: Random House.

_____. 1972. *The archaeology of knowledge.* New York: Pantheon.

_____. 1965. *Madness and civilization.* New York: Random House.

Friedman, Jonathan. 1994. *Cultural identity and global process.* Thousand Oaks, Calif.: Sage.

Geschiere, Peter. 1997. *Modernity of witchcraft: Politics and the occult in postcolonial Africa.* Trans. Janet Roitman. Charlotte: University Press of Virginia.

_____. 1995. *Sorcellerie et politique en Afrique: La viande des autres.* Paris: Karthala.

_____. 1989. Sorcery and the state: Popular modes of action among the Maka of southeast Cameroon. *Critique of Anthropology* 8(1):35–63.

Gibbal, Jean-Marie. 1994. *Genii of the River Niger.* Chicago: University of Chicago Press.

Giddens, Anthony. 1984. *The constitution of society: Outline of the theory of structuration.* Berkeley: University of California Press.

Goody, Jack. 1968. *Literacy in traditional societies.* Cambridge, U.K.: Cambridge University Press.

Gramsci, Antonio. 1971. *Selections from the prison notebooks.* New York: International Publishers.

Greenwood, Bernard. 1992. Cold or spirits? Ambiguity and syncretism in Moroccan therapeutics. In *The social basis of health and healing in Africa,* edited by S. Feierman and J. Janzen. Berkeley: University of California Press.

Grima, Benedicte. 1992. *The performance of emotion among Paxtun women: The misfortunes which have befallen me.* Austin: University of Texas Press.

Gupta, Akhil, and James Ferguson. 1997. Culture, power, place: Ethnography at the end of an era. In *Culture, power, place: Explorations in critical anthropology,* edited by A. Gupta and J. Ferguson. Durham, N.C.: Duke University Press.

Hayes, Rose Oldfield. 1975. Female genital mutilation, fertility control, women's roles, and the patrilineage in modern Sudan: A functional analysis. *American Ethnologist* 2:617–633.

Herdt, Gilbert. 1999. *Sambia sexual culture: Essays from the field.* Chicago: University of Chicago Press.

———. 1997. *Same sex, different cultures: Perspectives on gay and lesbian lives.* Boulder, Colo.: Westview Press.

———. 1981. *Guardians of the flutes: Idioms of masculinity.* New York: McGraw-Hill.

Holy, Ladislav. 1990. *The Berti of Sudan.* Cambridge, U.K.: Cambridge University Press.

Hopen, C. 1958. *The pastoral Fulbe family in Gwandu.* London: Oxford University Press (for IAI).

Hunt, Nancy Rose. 1999. *A colonial lexicon: Of birth ritual, medicalization, and mobility in the Congo.* Durham, N.C.: Duke University Press.

Hutchinson, Sharon. 1996. *Nuer dilemmas: Coping with money, war, and the state.* Berkeley: University of California.

Ingstad, Benedicte, and Susan Reynolds Whyte. 1995. *Disability and culture.* Berkeley: University of California Press.

Jackson, Michael. 1989. *Paths toward a clearing: Radical empiricism and ethnographic inquiry.* Bloomington: Indiana University Press.

Jackson, Michael, and Ivan Karp, eds. 1990. *Personhood and agency: The experience of self and other in African cultures.* Washington, D.C.: The Smithsonian Institution Press (Uppsala Studies in Cultural Anthropology 14).

Jankowiak, William R. 1993. *Sex, death, and hierarchy in a Chinese city: An anthropological account.* New York: Columbia University Press.

Jankowiak, William R., ed. 1995. *Romantic passion: A universal experience?* New York: Columbia University Press.

Janzen, John. 1978. *The quest for therapy in lower Zaire.* Berkeley: University of California Press.

Kintz, Daniele. 1989. Formal men, informal women: How the Fulani support their anthropologists. *Anthropology Today* 5 (No.6):12–14.

Kleinman, Arthur. 1980. *Patients and healers in the context of culture: An exploration of the borderland between anthropology, medicine, and psychiatry.* Berkeley: University of California Press.

The Lancet. 1993. Editorial. *The Lancet* vol. 342, No. 8863, July 10, 1993 (North American Edition).

Lambek, Michael. 1992. *Knowledge and practice in Mayotte: Local discourses of Islam, sorcery, and spirit possession.* Toronto: University of Toronto Press.

Last, Murray. 1992. The importance of knowing about not knowing: Observations from Hausaland. In *The social basis of health and healing in Africa*, edited by Steven Feierman and John M. Janzen, pp. 393–408. Berkeley: University of California Press.

Lewis, I. M. 1971. *Ecstatic religion.* Harmondsworth, U.K.: Penguin.

Lionnet, Francoise. 1995. *Postcolonial representations: Women, literature, identity.* Ithaca, N.Y.: Cornell University Press.

Lindenbaum, Shirley, and Margaret Lock, eds. 1993. *Knowledge, power & practice: The anthropology of medicine and everyday life.* Berkeley: University of California Press.

Lock, Margaret, and Deborah Gordon, eds. 1988. *Biomedicine examined.* Dordrecht, Netherlands: Kluwer Academic Publishers.

MacGaffey, Janet. 1987. *Entrepreneurs and parasites: The struggle for indigenous capitalism in Zaire.* New York: Cambridge University Press.

Maloney, Clarence. 1976. Don't say "pretty baby" lest you zap it with your eye: The evil eye in South Asia. In *The Evil Eye*, edited by C. Maloney. New York: Columbia University Press.

Marcus, George E. 1998. *Ethnography through thick and thin.* Princeton, N.J.: Princeton University Press.

Masquelier, Adeline. 2001. *Prayer has spoiled everything: Possession, power, and identity in an Islamic town of Niger.* Durham, N.C.: Duke University Press.

———. 1995. Consumption, prostitution, and reproduction: The poetics of sweetness in Bori. *American Ethnologist* 22(4):883–906.

Mauss, Marcel. 1967. *The gift: Forms and functions of exchange in archaic societies.* Trans. Ian Cunnison. New York: Norton.

Mbembe, Achille. 2001. *On the postcolony.* Berkeley: University of California.

———. 1992a. Provisional notes on the postcolony. *Africa* 62(1):3–37.

———. 1992b. Pouvoir, violence et accumulation. In *Le politique par le bas en Afrique noire: contributions à une problématique de la démocratie*, edited by Bayart et al., pp. 233–256. Paris: Karthala.

Merleau Ponty, M. 1962. *Phenomenology of perception.* London: Routledge and Kegan Paul.

Mernissi, Fatima. 1987. *Beyond the veil: Male-female dynamics in a modern Muslim society.* Bloomington: Indiana University Press.

Messick, Brinkley. 1993. *The calligraphic state: Textual domination and history in a Muslim society.* Berkeley: University of California Press.

Mitchell, W. J. T. 1994. "Introduction" and "Imperial Landscape." In *Landscape and power*, edited by W. J. T. Mitchell. pp. 1-4; 5-34. Chicago: University of Chicago Press.

Mudimbe, V. Y. 1988. *The invention of Africa.* Bloomington: Indiana University.

Murray, Stephen O., and Will Roscoe. 1998. *Boy-wives and female husbands: Studies of African homosexualities.* New York: St. Martin's Press.

Nanda, Serena. 1999. *The hijras of India: Neither man nor woman.* Second edition. Boston: Wadsworth.

Noye, Dominique. 1989. *Dictionnaire Foulfouldé-Français: Dialecte: Peul du Diamare Nord-Cameroun* Paris: Librairie Orientaliste Paul Geuthner.

———. 1974. *Cours de Foulfoulde: Dialecte Peul du Diamare Nord-Cameroun.* Paris: Librairie Orientaliste Paul Geuthner.

Nwapa, Flora. 1966. *Efuru.* London: Heinemann.

Ong, Aihwa. 1987. *The spirits of resistance and capitalist discipline: Factory women in Malaysia.* Albany: State University of New York Press.

Piot, Charles. 1999. *Remotely global: Village modernity in West Africa.* Chicago: University of Chicago Press.

Pitt-Rivers, Julian. 1971. *The people of the Sierra.* Chicago: University of Chicago Press.

Popenoe, Rebecca. 1997. *"Girls' work is stomach work": Female fatness, sexuality, and society among the Azawagh Arabs (Moors) of Niger.* Ph.D. dissertation. Department of Anthropology. University of Chicago.

Prakash, Gyan, ed. 1995. *After colonialism: Imperial histories and postcolonial displacements.* Princeton, N.J.: Princeton University Press.

Raheja, Gloria Goodwin, and Ann Grodzins Gold. 1994. *Listen to the heron's words: Reimagining gender and kinship in north India.* Berkeley: University of California Press.

Rebhun, Linda. 1993. "Nerves and emotional play in northeast Brazil," *Medical Anthropology. Quarterly* 7(2): 131–151.

Regis, Helen A. 1998. A race of people eaters? Fulbe tales of marriage, structural adjustment and disappearing flesh. Paper presented at the African Studies Association Meetings, Chicago.

———. 1997. Bad sauce and the withholding of the rains: Medicine and cultural pluralism among the Fulbe of Northern Cameroon.

———. 1995a. Immodest knowledge: Fulbe women's laments and the discourse of impiety in north Cameroon. Paper delivered at the American Anthropological Association meetings, Washington, D.C.

———. 1995b. The madness of excess: Love among the Fulbe of north Cameroon. In *Romantic passion: a universal experience?*, edited by W. Jankowiak. New York: Columbia University Press.

———. 1993. Prostitutes, bakers, and the fear of Allah: Status and performance of free womanhood in Fulbe discourse. Paper delivered at the American Anthropological Association meetings, Washington, D.C.

Reminick, Ronald A. 1976. *Ethiopia: The evil eye belief among the amhara.* In *The evil eye.* ed. Clarence Maloney. p. 87. New York: Columbia University Press.

Riesman, Paul. 1992. *First find your child a good mother: The construction of self in two African communities.* New Brunswick, N.J.: Rutgers University Press.

_____. 1990. Living poor while being rich: The pastoral folk economy. In *The creative communion: African folk models of fertility and the regeneration of life*, edited by A. Jacobson-Widding and W. Van Beek. Sweden: Uppsala Studies in Cultural Anthropology.

_____. 1986. The person and the life cycle in African social life and thought. *African Studies Review* 29:71–138.

_____. 1981. Aristocrats as subjects in a multi-ethnic state. In *Image and reality in African interethnic relations*, edited by Emily Schultz. Williamsburg, V.A.: Studies in Third World Societies No. 11. Pp. 21–30

_____. 1977. *Freedom in Fulani social life: An introspective ethnography*. Chicago: University of Chicago Press.

_____. 1975. The art of life in a West African community: Formality and spontaneity in Fulani interpersonal relationships. *Journal of African Studies* 2(1):39–63.

_____. 1974. Defying official morality: The example of man's quest for woman among the Fulani. *Cahiers d'études Africaines* 44:602–613.

Riviere, Claude. 1974. Dynamique de la stratification sociale chez les peuls de Guinee. *Anthropos* 69(3–4):361–400.

Rosaldo, Renato. 1989. *Culture and truth: the remaking of social analysis*. Boston: Beacon Press.

Sahlins, Marshall. 1972. *Stone age economics*. Chicago: Aldine.

Said, Edward W. 1978. *Orientalism*. New York: Vintage Books.

Scheper-Hughes, Nancy. 1994. Embodied knowledge: Thinking with the body in critical medical anthropology. In *Assessing cultural anthropology*, edited by R. Borofsky. New York: McGraw-Hill.

_____. 1992a. *Death without weeping: The violence of everyday life in Brazil*. Berkeley: University of California Press.

_____. 1992b. Hungry bodies, medicine, and the state: Toward a critical psychological anthropology. In *New directions in psychological anthropology*, edited by Theodore Schwartz, Geoffrey White, and Catherine Lutz. Cambridge, U.K.: Cambridge University Press.

Schilder, Kees. 1994. *Quest for self-esteem: State, Islam, and Mundang ethnicity in northern Cameroon*. Leiden: African Studies Centre.

Schmoll, Pamela. 1991. Searching for health in a world of dis-ease: Affliction management among rural Hausa of the Maradi Valley (Republic of Niger). Ph.D. dissertation, the University of Chicago.

Schultz, Emily. 1984. From pagan to pullo: Ethnic identity change in northern Cameroon. *Africa* 54(1):46–64.

_____. 1981. *Image and reality in African interethnic relations: The Fulbe and their neighbors*. Williamsburg, Va.: Studies in Third World Societies No. 11.

Scott, James. 1985. *Weapons of the weak: Everyday forms of peasant resistance*. New Haven, Conn.: Yale University Press.

Selassie, Bereket H. 1974. *The executive in African governments*. London: Heinemann.

Sharp, Leslie. 1993. *The possessed and the dispossessed: Spirits, identity, and power in a Madagascar migrant town.* Berkeley: University of California Press.

Sherzer, Joel. 1987. *Explorations in the ethnography of speaking.* New York: Cambridge University Press.

Spooner, Brian. 1976. The evil eye in the Middle East. In *The evil eye,* edited by Clarence Maloney. New York: Columbia University Press.

Stenning, D. 1959. *Savannah nomads.* London: Oxford University Press (for IAI).

Stoler, Laura Ann. 1995. *Race and the education of desire: Foucault's history of sexuality and the colonial order of things.* Durham, N.C.: Duke University Press.

Stoller, Paul. 1995. *Embodying colonial memories: Spirit possession, power, and the Hauka in West Africa.* New York: Routledge.

Stoller, Paul, and Cheryl Olkes. 1986. Bad sauce, good ethnography. *Cultural Anthropology* 1:336–353.

Strathern, Marilyn. 1988. *The gender of the gift.* Berkeley: University of California Press.

Tall, Emmanuelle Kadya. 1985. Le contre-sorcier Haalpulaar, un justicier hors-la-loi: Étude de la dynamique du systeme thérapeutique des Haalpulaaren (Senegal). *Sciences Sociales et Santé* 3(3–4):129–150.

Taussig, Michael. 1980. *The devil and commodity fetishism in South America.* Chapel Hill: University of North Carolina Press.

Thomas, Nicholas, ed. 1994. *Colonialism's culture.* Princeton, N.J.: Princeton University Press.

Toulabor, Comi. 1992. Jeu de mots, Jeu de vilains: Lexique de la dérision politique au Togo. In *Le politique par le bas en Afrique noire: Contributions à une problématique de la démocratie,* edited by Bayart et al., pp. 109–130. Paris: Karthala.

Trawick, Margaret. 1990. *Notes on love in a Tamil family.* Berkeley: University of California Press.

Trinh, T. M. 1989. *Woman native, other: Writing postcoloniality and feminism.* Bloomington: Indiana University.

Tsing, Anna Lowenhaupt. 1993. *In the realm of the diamond queen: Marginality in an out-of-the-way place.* Princeton, N.J.: Princeton University Press.

Turner, Victor. 1986. *The anthropology of performance.* New York: PAJ Publications.

Turshen, Meredith. 1999. *Privatizing health services in Africa.* New Brunswick, N.J.: Rutgers University Press.

Urban, Greg. 1991. *A discourse-centered approach to culture: Native South American myths and rituals.* Austin: University of Texas Press.

Van der Geest, Sjaak. 1982. The efficiency of inefficiency: Medicine distribution in South Cameroon. *Social Science and Medicine* 16:2145–2153.

Van Der Veer, Peter, ed. 1996. *Conversion to modernities: The globalization of Christianity.* New York: Routledge.

Vaughan, Megan. 1991. *Curing their ills: Colonial power and African illness.* Stanford, Calif.: Stanford University Press.

Vergès, Françoise. 1999. *Monsters and revolutionaries: Colonial family romance and métissage.* Durham, N.C.: Duke University Press.

Wall, Lewis. 1988. *Hausa medicine: Illness and well-being in a West African culture.* Durham, N.C.: Duke University Press.

Wallerstein, I. 1974. *The modern world system.* New York: Academic Press.

Werbner, Richard, ed. 1998. *Memory in the postcolony: African anthropology and the critique of power.* New York: Zed Books.

Whyte, Susan Reynolds. 1998. *Questioning misfortune: The pragmatics of uncertainty in eastern Uganda.* Cambridge, U.K.: Cambridge University Press.

———. 1992. Pharmaceuticals as folk medicine: Transformations in the social relations of health care in Uganda. *Culture, Medicine, and Psychiatry* 16:163–186.

Wilce, James M. 1995. I can't tell you all my troubles: Conflict, resistance, and metacommunication in Bangladeshi illness interactions. *American Ethnologist* 22:927–952.

Willis, John Ralph. 1979. *Studies in West African Islamic history.* London: F. Cass.

Wolf, Margery. 1992. *A thrice-told tale: Feminism, postmodernism, and ethnographic responsibility.* Stanford, Calif.: Stanford University Press.

World Bank. 2000. The World Bank Group Mission. http://www.worldbank.org/html/extdr/about/mission.htm (August 8, 2000).

———. 1993. World development report 1993, *Investing in health.* Washington, D.C.: The World Bank.

Worley, Barbara. 1992. Where all the women are strong: Wrestling caps a desert tribe's infant-naming ceremony. *Natural History* 11/92: 55–63.

X, Malcolm and Alex Haley. 1965. The autobiography of Malcolm X. New York: Grove Press.

Index